ACKNOWLEDGEMENTS

Laurence Van Elegem. Thank you. I could not have done this without you. Your amazing talent with words is an inspiration to me. This book is as much yours as it is mine. Thank you, and I hope that we can make much more wonderful content together.

Ilse De Bondt. Thank you for helping me sort out my life, and work, and for providing a better work/life balance. You're the most wonderful person to work with. I hope you will continue to manage my world for a long time to come.

Marianne Vermeulen. Thank you for all the help in the background, not just in this book, but in all the others. Much appreciated.

I would like to thank all the people who were absolutely vital in making this book a reality (in alphabetical order): Andrew Beavis, Kim Bratanata, Peer De Maeyer, Felix Garriau, Griet Hemeryck, Niels Janssens, Marc Lerouge, Mitchell Pontzeele, Vera Ponnet, Nancy Rademaker, Chris Tournicourt, Hans Vandenberghe, Chantal Van De Ginste, Maxime Van Steen.

www.peterhinssen.com
www.nexxworks.com

I DEDICATE THIS BOOK TO:

My partners in crime, over the years.
Everyone I've worked with, had the pleasure to collaborate with, to think, to laugh, to work, to be amazed, to dream.

Patrick, who gave me my first period of work experience.

Luc, who taught me how to pitch.

All the e-COM coworkers, the craziest bunch of people I have ever worked with. I miss you guys.

All the StreamCase collaborators, for being the most awesome pioneers.

All the Porthus employees, the most professional group of engineers and professionals I have ever worked with.

All the Across consultants and staff, for providing a warm haven and for creating some wonderful experiences for our customers.

All the crazy, awesome nexxworkers, for sharing the dream, and rowing against the stream.

All the amazing people at the London Business School that I've had the pleasure to work with over the years, and the amazing sessions we've created together.

All my colleagues at MIT-Sloan, and MIT-CISR, for the inspiration that you gave me, and the chance to work with some of the smartest people I've ever met.

Rik, Annick, Steven and Nancy, for being the best partners anyone could ever dream of.

nexxworks NV
MeetDistrict - Ghelamco Arena
Ottergemsesteenweg Zuid 808 bus 331, 9000 Ghent, Belgium
hello@nexxworks.com
 +32 477 349 384

D/2017/45/479 - ISBN 978 94 014 4649 5 – NUR 801

Author: Peter Hinssen
Creation: Peer De Maeyer
Infographics: Saflot, Vera Ponnet
Portrait back cover: © Rob Clayton
Project managers: Ilse De Bondt, Laurence Van Elegem and Marianne Vermeulen

THE DAY

HOW TO SURVIVE IN TIMES OF RADICAL INNOVATION

AFTER
TOMORROW

PETER HINSSEN

nexxworks

CONTENTS

1

INTRODUCTION: WHY I WROTE THIS BOOK

My grandfather was an entrepreneur. During the Second World War, he raised a family in the Netherlands, where he endured five long years of German occupation. Especially the final winter, known as the 'Hunger Winter', was incredibly tough on the young family, as blockades cut off food and fuel shipments from farm areas, and millions of Dutch people had to survive on food kitchens.

After the war, my grandfather – who was mechanically extremely gifted – started a firm repairing failing equipment for farmers who had been unable to invest in their tractors and harvesters during the war. Soon he realized that Belgian farmers had suffered less than the Dutch ones and he moved his entire family to the neighboring country to start his business.

In true entrepreneurial spirit, he expanded into a wide variety of endeavors. He started a garage, sold tractors, built sheds and storage facilities, and launched a bus company that organized tours around Europe. One of his killer ideas was organizing inspiration tours to the holy city of Lourdes, taking busloads of Catholics on a journey to a remote village in the Pyrenean mountains, where the holy mother had apparently once materialized in front of Bernadette Soubirous. It was a goldmine.

His son, my father, was the brainy kid in a family of five children. The designated 'nerd', he was put in charge of father's business accounting when he was only 14, because he had a real knack for mathematics. That's when my father started to realize that my grandfather was constantly on the brink of bankruptcy. He noticed the serious cash flow issues, and knew that the repo-man could seize the family house and its assets any day. It never happened, the business of my grandfather pulled through in the end, but it left an emotional scar on my father. He swore he would never do anything that would put his family in financial danger, and vowed he would never take such foolish entrepreneurial risks. When he graduated as an engineer, he started a safe corporate career at Exxon where he worked his entire life.

Growing up, I remember my father coming home exhausted from meetings. As the years ticked by, I saw him become increasingly frustrated by bureaucracy and corporate politics. I listened as he told discouraging tales about an insane amount of incompetence and inefficiency in such a large, red-tape organization.

That's when I swore I would never, ever, work in a large corporation.

"We all turn into our parents someday." That's what they say (although I've never quite figured out who the 'they' are). Well I, for one, didn't. I turned into my grandparent and became an entrepreneur. My entire career has been centered on the startup life. Ever since I was a little boy, growing up in a world where technology was rapidly becoming commonplace, I knew I wanted to start things up myself. I dreamt of creating my own companies, and of building new exciting opportunities.

So. A life of startups it has been. I've had the extreme pleasure to be the founder of three technology startups early on in my career. And they were nothing like the hip, exciting and glamorous tales of entrepreneurship some will have you believe. Oh, there was excitement, and lots of it, but not the 'safe' kind that is offered by a rollercoaster ride or bungee jumping.

It was more the ominous kind, like when a 6,000 kg African bush elephant charges at you at 40 km per hour and there's no way of telling if he will crush you or just scare you off. Startups are hard. And scary. Very scary.

But I loved every minute of building them. These three pure adrenaline experiences made me into what I am today. They also left me with four big questions that I have been chasing ever since, and which eventually led to me to writing this book, trying to answer them.

KNOCK IT OFF, KID

The first big question was triggered by my 'drug addiction' and the almost simultaneous birth of the web and my first startup. Bear with me, it's (probably) not what you think.

Before I became an entrepreneur, I worked at Alcatel[1], because I realized that I did not yet have the maturity and practical experience to start up on my own when I just graduated. I liked my job very much. I learned a lot about ADSL and bandwidth and we were one of the first to work on Video On Demand, about 15 years before the concept was popularized by Netflix.

One day, I received a call from a university friend. He told me they had the first web browser up and running at my alma mater and that I just had to *see* it. So I did. But I did not see it. I did not understand the magic of the Web. My friend

was completely ecstatic about using the new browser to connect to a web server somewhere in Chicago to check out the weather report there. Yet I recall driving home late that night thinking: "Why the hell would I want to know about the weather tomorrow in Chicago?".

But somehow, commuting to work over the next couple of weeks and trying to get my head around the concept of a potential global communications platform, I got hooked. The virus had spread from my overly excited university friend to me and I started dabbling with browsers, servers and building my own websites. At first, to comprehend the ins and outs of the technology, which was clearly still in its infancy. But then I started to build websites for friends and then for organizations. What started as a hobby became a small business, and soon I was building websites several hours per day in addition to my day job. I became exhausted, but I couldn't stop.

And then, one morning, my boss called me into his office to ask me if I "was on drugs", thinking that might be the explanation why I looked so scruffy and tired. When I passionately tried to explain him about the World Wide Web and how I had started building websites, he told me this: "You know this World Wide Web thing is kid's stuff right? It's foolish, and it will never amount to anything. Knock it off, kid." I was so flabbergasted that I quit my job that same afternoon after my girlfriend (now my wife) told me "If you think you're right, then you should quit, and follow your dreams."

And I just did that. I took a chance on the foolish 'kid's stuff', and I never looked back. But my boss's reaction at Alcatel is also how I got to Big Question #1. I became fascinated by the fact that this large organization was biased towards making bets on the old, rather than making big bets on the new.

Big Question #1:

"Why is it almost impossible for large organizations to spot new and radical technologies quickly, and develop their potential? What explains this organizational blindness to new opportunities?"

My first startup was a company that built large-scale intranets. We developed a platform that allowed companies to use web technology inside their organizations to communicate, share documents and collaborate. We contrived a version of Microsoft SharePoint years before Microsoft did. And it was fantastic.

In the space of just four years, the company grew to about 200 people: working in perfect harmony, building amazing products, and serving customers around the world who were doing stunning things with our products. The startup had no structure at all and very little hierarchy, but this beautiful, fertile chaos worked perfectly. It was bliss.

And then we sold the company. To Alcatel, my first and only employer, where my boss thought that the World Wide Web was pure foolishness. Oh, the irony. In hindsight, it was a disaster. I should have known this would not work but, at the time, it made perfect sense in my mind. They had the global sales and distribution channels and access to the Fortune 1000, and we had a great team and a great product. But somehow, the combination did not work. At all. And the reason was organizational culture.

I was amazed at how hungry Alcatel had been to acquire us, how they had spared no expense to woo and obtain us. Yet the moment our 'honeymoon' was over, I was even more bewildered at how quickly the corporate reflexes and bureaucratic DNA had made our fertile, anarchistic startup life a living hell.

The sad pinnacle of this dissonant acquisition tale was me being fired over a tiff that had gotten completely out of hand: I threw a corporate controller from the Paris branch out of my office over a fight over the car policy. Not my proudest moment, but for me it was the final straw of six months of continual pointless discussions and frustrations over rules, procedures, policies and governance. I had been driven insane and had started to act like it.

After four years of working day and night developing my company, selling it, and for a full year trying my hardest to make it work inside a global corporation like Alcatel, shit had finally hit the fan. It was one of the strangest moments of my life. Having cleared out my desk, and carrying what was left of my dignity in a cardboard box, I was escorted out of the building by two security guards. And out I marched of the company that I had started myself, watched by scores of my employees, my friends in fact, as I left the building. Strange, eerie, bizarre and unnatural.

I will remember how I felt that moment for the rest of my life, but it also made me wonder about Big Question #2:

Big Question #2:

"Why are large corporations so eager to acquire new startups, and why are they capable of messing them up so profoundly in such a record time?"

When they fired me, the good people at Alcatel seemed terrified that I would just walk across the street and start over, 'stealing' away their best people in the process. So Alcatel had me sign a non-compete agreement that stipulated I would not be active in the IT, online, digital or telecom sector for an entire year. A year. That's a long time.

Faced with the prospect of spending an entire year in my backyard mowing the lawn, or learning how to grow petunias, I was rescued by a ringing telephone. McKinsey – the most iconic consultancy firm in the world – invited me to become an 'Entrepreneur in Residence': "You might learn something from us, we might learn something from you. Just spend the year with us as a guest. We'll put you in front of some of our toughest problems with our biggest customers in the field of digital, and you will be our special guest." It sounded like heaven to me after the previous match made in hell that my company's acquisition had turned out to be. I said "yes".

This was the almost magical period of the dot-com boom, when companies such as Yahoo, Amazon and Netscape were propelled into huge players overnight. McKinsey was flooded with questions from large global corporations to help them in their 'digital strategies'. But in March of 2000, the NASDAQ imploded, the dot-com bubble burst, and the whole fragile, nascent online industry collapsed.

Ironically, McKinsey never suffered. It was now being swamped with questions from large corporations about how to divest, in the quickest way possible, of their now toxic and dangerous online, digital and dot-com acquisitions, partnerships and developments.

I truly enjoyed my residency at McKinsey, where I had the pleasure to meet some of the smartest people on the planet, who were absolute virtuosos at the long-term strategy game. I also learned how difficult entrepreneurship and innovative thinking was for their large corporation customers. How hard it was for them to understand what the strategic end-games were, and how to move their organizations accordingly.

I saw how companies could easily get 'hooked' on McKinsey, and become completely dependent on their outside guidance, like a crack cocaine addict continuously craving his next shot, unable to escape his isolated nightmare of an existence. OK, possibly less dark, but just as obsessed. This insight gave rise to my Big Question #3:

Big Question #3:

"How is it possible that large corporations – even when they understand their own challenges and the directions they need to take – are incapable of moving on their own, without external help and guidance?"

We've finally arrived at the most important reason why I wrote this book. For the past few years, I've had the pleasure to talk to audiences around the world about the fundamental changes in society that (will) occur as a result of technology. My corporate audiences tend to stare at me like reindeer into the headlights of an oncoming car. They seem unable to move, unable to adapt, act, or respond swiftly. It's tragic.

Even the people who *are* performing 'radical' innovation in large corporates tell me how relieved they are that I talk about the need to fundamentally address these challenges. I really feel for them, because they often are the most frustrated individuals who are constantly banging their heads against corporate inertia. Being a 'Day After Tomorrow' thinker in a large corporation is one of the loneliest jobs to have these days.

This deadly inability to move brings me to the final Big Question that I want to address in this book:

Big Question #4:

"How can corporates accelerate their 'Day After Tomorrow' thinking? Why do large organizations – that understand the fundamental challenges coming at them, because of disruptive technologies, business models or concepts – seem to be too paralyzed to move fast enough to respond? How can companies become agile in their 'Day After Tomorrow' thinking, and be successful in developing an approach that works?"

For me this is probably the Biggest Question. One that I hope to clarify and even help solve. I believe that companies *can* change. That they can learn how to spot the potential of new technologies, integrate startups without killing them, kick their addiction to consulting and learn how to accelerate their 'Day After Tomorrow' thinking. Because others did it before them. And, in the following pages, I will share how you can too.

Thanks for sticking with me so far. I sincerely hope you will enjoy reading this book as much as I enjoyed writing it.

Written on a KLM Flight from Amsterdam to San Francisco on a Boeing 787, listening to Brian Eno.

Endnote: You can find the extended version of this introduction - with (among other things) a brutally honest recount of the failure of my second startup - on www.peterhinssen.com.

THE BIG QUESTIONS

Big Question #1
"Why is it almost impossible for large organizations to spot new and radical technologies quickly, and develop their potential? What explains this organizational blindness to new opportunities?"

Big Question #2
"Why are large corporations so eager to acquire new startups, and why are they capable of messing them up so profoundly in such a record time?"

Big Question #3
"How is it possible that large corporations – even when they understand their own challenges and the directions they need to take – are incapable of moving on their own, without external help and guidance?"

Big Question #4
"How can corporates accelerate their 'Day After Tomorrow' thinking? Why do large organizations – that understand the fundamental challenges coming at them, because of disruptive technologies, business models or concepts – seem to be too paralyzed to move fast enough to respond? How can companies become agile in their 'Day After Tomorrow' thinking, and be successful in developing an approach that works?"

2

SURVIVING SPEED BY BEING RADICAL

The 'Day After Tomorrow' Model

> *"I'm sort of a pessimist about tomorrow and an optimist about the day after tomorrow."*
>
> **ERIC SEVAREID**

NO LIMITS

This chapter explains the *model* behind the 'Day After Tomorrow'. In my humble opinion it's the simplest, easiest model in the business world today. Some might even call it naive. Those who have read my previous books might be surprised. They know that I like to use everything from Calculus Limits or thermodynamics to Algebraic Numeric Series just to prove a point.

Not this model. No Limits here. No Calculus, no Algebra. No scientific laws. This model is so simple, so 'common sense', that I can almost guarantee it will stick in your mind.

What is it about? Simply put, it will help you discover if you are prepared for a future that is coming sooner than ever before, and it will help you identify if you are spending enough time preparing for the advent of your 'Day After Tomorrow'.

For those of you disappointed by the fact that I'm not starting out with some extremely complex Daedalian set of mathematical equations (What? You might be out there!), I hope to comfort you with the prospect of learning how to draw killer diagrams that will help you shine bright in any boardroom discussion.

ARE WE GOING FASTER YET?

I absolutely love the rich and wonderful German language. I adore its capacity to make simple concepts sound thunderous and intense when you articulate them. Germans have a unique way of describing things: they combine words into super-long constructs that seem grotesque yet strangely enticing. One of my favorite words of this type is 'EisenBahnScheinBewegung'.

'EisenBahn' means 'railway'. 'ScheinBewegung' are false moves, typically performed by soccer players trying to trick other players into thinking they will head in a certain direction while they engage in a completely opposite maneuver. They literally put the others on the 'wrong' foot.

When you glue both words together you get 'EisenBahnScheinBewegung' which describes the false feeling of movement that catches you when you sit in a stationary train at a station and see the train next to you start moving. Your brain is tricked into thinking that *you* are moving, and that the actual moving train is standing still in the station. Why the Germans would find a need for such a word is beyond me.[1]

I love how 'EisenBahnScheinBewegung' conjures up the dilemma of how companies are trying to understand how the world is moving, how their competitors are advancing, and how sometimes they are tricked into believing that they are moving fast enough.

I believe that our 'Day After Tomorrow' is accelerating, hurtling towards us at ever greater speed. I believe we need to advance, become agile and speed up our innovation processes in order to be sufficiently swift and responsive to cope with this. When it comes to innovation, 'EisenBahnScheinBewegung' might the most dangerous word in the world.

THE GREAT ACCELERATION OR THE FALSE PERCEPTION OF SPEED?

But are we really going faster? Is innovation speeding up in society? There are plenty of people out there who will tell you that the world is *not* moving faster now than it has been throughout the course of history. Not Klaus Schwab though.

Klaus Schwab is one very smart man. Since 1971, he has been founder and Chairman of the World Economic Forum, an international not-for-profit foundation for public-private cooperation that is "committed to improving the state of the world". Its yearly meeting of great minds in the Swiss Alps, in Davos, has become the absolute must-attend winter event of the year. Above all, it has developed into a sizeable and influential organization that tracks the 'big' themes in society, and alerts business and government leaders on fundamental changes.[2]

At the World Economic Forum of 2016, an elite group of no less than 2,500 world-leaders descended on the tiny mountain village of Davos. This time, Klaus Schwab opened the meeting with a very serious message and warned all the attendants of the coming of the 'Fourth Industrial Revolution'. He introduced it as follows: "From social media to the Internet of Things, digital fabrication to robotics, virtual reality to synthetic biology, new technologies are racing forward across the board. Together they are ripping up the rule book for people, firms and governments alike."[2]

"Ripping up the rule book". As an opening statement, that was quite impressive. He went on to say that "We stand on the brink of a technological revolution that will fundamentally alter the way we live, work and relate to one another. In its scale, scope and complexity, the transformation will be unlike anything humankind has experienced before. We do not yet know just how it will unfold, but one thing is clear: the response to it must be integrated and comprehensive, involving all stakeholders of the global polity, from the public and private sectors to academia and civil society. The speed of current breakthroughs has no historical precedent. When compared with previous industrial revolutions, the Fourth is evolving at an exponential rather than a linear pace. Moreover, it is disrupting almost every industry in every country." According to him, we have to think, work and evolve together – from individuals to corporations to countries – to solve this huge challenge that lies before us. And we'll have to do it now. Klaus Schwab is a firm believer that the world is changing faster than ever before.

FASTER? NOT.

Not Robert J. Gordon though. Robert Gordon is a renowned economist and researcher at Northwestern University who wrote an intriguing piece of work in 2016: *The Rise and Fall of American Growth*[3]. In it he argues that we have too many 'techno-optimists' who are claiming that the rise of the new (digital) innovations is going to redefine our global economy, reshape society and transform humanity.

Gordon clearly despises these techno-optimists with a vengeance.

In his view the real impact of technology on society, since the 1970s, has actually been quite dismal and disappointing, albeit dazzling at times. He claims that we are all too goo-goo-eyed with the advent of transistors, the PC, the internet and Facebook. That we are constantly amazed at silly, shiny new things like PokemonGo or the selfie revolution. Instead, he argues, we miss the point by ignoring the huge impact we've seen with the dramatic decline in infant mortality in our world. This was the result of our increased understanding of healthcare and hygiene: like the dramatic effect that simple things like indoor plumbing have had on our living conditions.

In his book, Gordon states that the 'special century' between 1870 and 1970 was the 'grand' period of true, unprecedented economic growth and dramatic improvements in health and living standards for most (American) citizens. He vividly tells the story of the amazing and awe-inspiring three-month period in 1879, when US citizen Thomas Edison was able to get the first practical light bulb working, German Karl Benz created the first workable internal combustion engine, and UK-based David Hughes transmitted a wireless radio signal for the very first time. Those were the days, according to Gordon. Nothing compared to the present day where we frivolously think that Angry Birds, PokemonGo and SnapChat are going to change the world.

Gordon was educated as a macro-economist. He looks at the numbers... and is convinced that they are not great. At least not in the US. According to this King of the Skeptics, the average growth of output per US worker was, on average, a massive 2.3% per year between 1891 and 1972. While in the period between 2004 and 2012, it was only 1.3%. Eat that PokemonGo.

You can't argue with his observation over the importance of indoor plumbing. I am as thankful as anybody out there for it. Perhaps more. But it would be great to put Schwab and Gordon in a room together to battle it out on what the future will bring.

ACCELERATION

Over the past few years, we have seen some pretty impressive technologies change our landscape. Many industry analysts have coined stupendous narratives to describe the coming together of technologies that reinforce each other's outcome and effect. I've had the pleasure to give many keynotes over the past few years for Gartner, one of the largest technology research firms globally, which conceived (somewhere in 2012) the magnificent concept of the 'Nexus of Forces' which is composed of 'Social. Mobile. Cloud. Big Data.' This 'Nexus of Forces' has changed how information plays a crucial role in today's society.

Scary to think how quickly these 'new' technologies have become 'normal', stale and uninspiring. Social, Mobile, Cloud, Big Data: Boooooring.

Social networks have rapidly become the most common way to reach customers, understand social sentiment, and reach out to individuals on a one-to-one basis. But, let's face it, talks on social media tend to be about as exciting as the proverbial paint drying process. Mobile is now the dominant platform if we want to stay relevant for consumers. And yes, we have all become slaves of our smartphones and cannot possibly live without them. Our addiction to mobile technologies has only increased, but we consider them as 'normal'. Data science has invaded our organizations. We now run marketing departments based on information, rather than gut feeling, and entire companies have become 'data driven'. And true, there are still some companies who still run computer servers and infrastructure on their own premises, but the majority of corporations have realized that if they want true technological agility, the cloud has a convenience and efficiency that is almost impossible to beat.

I can almost hear you thinking: "well, duh", while you're reading this. Social, Mobile, Big Data and Cloud went from 'hot' to 'mainstream' to 'tedious' in record time. They have become the 'Nexus of Meh'. To think that, a few years ago, data scientists were called 'the new rock stars'. Poor guys. Back to being nerds. Oh well.

Now we have a new set of forces. A new 'Nexus' of technologies, models, concepts and ideas. We will describe these technologies in great detail in the next chapter, but the advent of novel enablers like Deep Machine Learning, Artificial Intelligence, blockchain technologies, the Internet of Things and advanced robotics make the old 'Nexus of Forces' look like a bunch of retired accountants in big, high-waisted, beige pants. Anything but rock stars.

ACHIEVING 'IMPOSSIBLE CHALLENGES'

At the complete other end of the spectrum – far, far ... far away from plumbing aficionado Robert Gordon – stands the Singularity University. This fellowship was established by Ray Kurzweil and Peter Diamandis based on their mutual admiration for 'exponential' growth. Created in 2009, today they describe themselves as "a global community using exponential technologies to tackle the world's biggest challenges".[4]

Kurzweil made the concept of the 'Singularity' big. He did not invent it. That honor goes to John von Neumann who launched it in 1958 and to Vernor Vinge, who made it popular in the nineties. But Kurzweil made it Big, with a capital B. He is larger than life and a truly amazing character. He is a visionary thinker who has taken the concept of serial entrepreneur to the level of 'frequent-flyer-emerald-status'. He has received 21 honorary doctorates, has authored seven books and is the principal inventor of many technologies ranging from the first CCD flatbed scanner to the first print-to-speech reading machine for the blind. He now has a post as long-term thinker at Google.

But his claim to fame is his prediction that somewhere around 2045 we will be able to upload our brains into a computer. More accurately "we will multiply our intelligence a billionfold by linking wirelessly from our neocortex to a synthetic neocortex in the cloud".[4] Kurzweil has been tracking the 'exponential growth' of computing power, and his research shows that today's purchase of USD 1,000 worth of computing power is about the equivalent of the brain power of a field mouse. By 2045, he predicts that for USD 1,000 we will be able to buy the equivalent of *all* the human brains of the planet combined. We'll have a computer a billion times more intelligent than every human combined. That's the Singularity. Mark that in your calendar.

Kurzweil's partner in crime is Peter Diamandis. From an early age, he wanted to explore space. And that is exactly what he spent his entire career doing: building companies and organizations that are tackling the great expansion beyond our planet. Some of his ventures were successful, some were not. But the XPRIZE foundation is by far the most impressive one.

Diamandis was instrumental in getting a group of high-net worth Silicon Valley entrepreneurs to pony up enough money to reward yearly XPRIZEs for achieving 'impossible challenges'. The founders were inspired by the story of Charles Lindbergh, who crossed the Atlantic in the 'Spirit of St. Louis'. Lindbergh did not harbor an obsession to be heroic when he risked his life crossing the Atlantic in an airplane. He just wanted to win a prize of a USD 25,000 – set by wealthy French hotel owner Raymond Orteig – which was an absolute fortune in those days. As a result, we now take a plane like we take a bus.

The XPRIZE foundation believes that if you give a government subsidy to a research field, all you get is a sloppy conference, a spiritless academic book and a white-paper that no one will read (except maybe those retired accountants in big, high-waisted, beige pants I mentioned earlier). But if you set the bar high enough and create a real challenge, you can spark an entirely new industry.

The first effort of the XPRIZE foundation was the Ansari XPRIZE for Suborbital Spaceflight (1996-2004). The USD 10 million reward sparked the creation of pioneers like Tier One, which – together with giants like SpaceX and Virgin Galactic – have now forged a multi-billion dollar commercial space industry. It must make Diamandis really proud that he has triggered that evolution, a childhood dream, with the creation of the XPRIZE foundation.

THE SECOND HALF

Singularity is not a university as we know it, but its faculty members are awe-in-spiring. Paul Saffo, previously with the 'Institute for the Future', board member at the 'The Long Now Foundation', teaching and researching long-range social and technological forecasting at Stanford University, is the chair of the 'Future Studies and Forecasting' track at Singularity University. Then there's Craig Venter, regarded as one of the leading scientists of the 21st century for his invaluable contributions to genomic research. He was instrumental in the very first mapping of the human genome in 2000. He is the faculty member at Singularity University who focusses on Biotech, Genomics and Synthetic Biology. There are some more controversial faculty members as well, like Aubrey de Grey, a biomedical gerontologist from Cambridge University, who studies the ageing process and how we can slow it down. He is also the founder of the Methuselah Foundation that aims to extend the healthy human life span by advancing tissue engineering and regenerative medicine therapies. Professor de Grey teaches Longevity and Ageing at Singularity University.

If you have Craig Venter teaching Synthetic Biology, Paul Saffo lecturing on Future Thinking and Aubrey de Grey tutoring you on Ageing, you probably have the 'best of the best' faculty in the world.

It is indeed quite a wild and multifarious bunch, the Singularity Faculty. But there is one thing they all have in common: a fundamental belief, an unshakeable conviction, or some would say a blind-faith in 'exponential' evolution.

They have a brilliant story to explain this: the 'second half of the chessboard'. The concept was created by Singularity Founder Ray Kurzweil. It is based on a parable about the inventor of chess who shows his creation to his country's ruler. The emperor loves the game, plays it day and night, and wants to thank the inventor with a reward of his choosing. So, he summons the inventor to his palace.

The inventor, who's a mathematician, refuses the reward. But the emperor insists. So, he asks for rice, and in a very specific fashion: that one grain of rice be placed on the first square of the board and that this is doubled on each subsequent square. The emperor protests, believing that the reward is too small – but the mathematician persists that this is all he requires.

When the payout of the reward is executed, the emperor is truly amused. The second square has two grains of rice, the third one four, the fourth eight. By the time they reach the 32nd square, halfway around the chessboard, the reward amounts to the production from a few acres of rice paddies – significant, but not unreasonable. By then, the Emperor's entourage had started to go really quiet. No more laughing, now.

By the 64th square, the total pile of rice should have amounted to about the size of Mount Everest. But the poor mathematician did not live to see that. The story goes that the Emperor became furious long before that, and beheaded him in a rage of fury.

It's a wonderful story. The Singularists claim they have proof that this is materializing in the real world, right in front of our very eyes. And they have Gordon Moore to thank for that.

In 1965, Gordon Moore, co-founder of Intel, observed that the number of transistors per square inch on integrated circuits had doubled every year since the integrated circuit was invented. Moore predicted that this same rate of improvement would continue into the future.

He was right. It has. The law was modified slightly to a rate of doubling every 18 months, and this has shown to be true since 1965. It's probably coming to an end, though. Some – including Intel – suggest that silicon transistors can only keep shrinking (and therefore growing in numbers on circuits) for another five years. I'll explain this more clearly in chapter three when I write about quantum computing, the 'Day-After-Tomorrow-est' (it is a word because I say so) of all the technologies I'll describe.

But, so far, this growth of transistors has been truly incredible. In an ironic but unintentional reference to the second half of the chessboard, Intel announced, in its 2013 annual report, that they had produced more transistors that year… than the world's yearly production of grains of rice, and that they had done so at a much lower cost.

Wow.

THE CHURCH OF WOW

American bestselling author and entrepreneur Steven Kotler and Singularity co-founder Peter Diamandis wrote two books on exponentiality together. *Abundance: The Future is Better Than You Think*[5], explains their exponential thinking and philosophy, and, after that: *Bold: How to Go Big, Create Wealth and Impact the World*[6] is about using exponential technologies, moonshot thinking and crowd-powered tools to create extraordinary wealth and abundance.

According to Kotler "these exponential technologies have an impact that extends beyond the limited notion of commercial success, or even shared value. They allow us to do more, learn more, and earn more than ever before. They transform our usual ways of thinking, behaving and relating to one another. They empower and enrich the lives of many people, not just an elite few."

The people at Singularity truly believe that we are about to turn the corner in many different markets and scientific areas. They believe that the advances we see in Machine Learning, Network Sensors, Artificial Intelligence, Robotics, Nanotechnology, Synthetic Biology, 3D printing, etc. are all examples of emerging technologies that will follow the exact pattern of Moore's law. And when they reach their second half of the chessboard, they will have the potential to massively increase human intelligence over the next two decades, and fundamentally reshape the economy and society.

Wow.

And that is exactly the unfriendly nickname that Singularity University received from some Silicon Valley pundits: The Church of Wow.

They have plenty of critics, though.

Vivek Wadhwa is one of them. Wadhwa is a fellow at the Rock Center for Corporate Governance at Stanford Graduate School of Business. He is a regular writer for the *Washington Post*, on technology matters, and when the *Bold* came out, he wrote a scathing review. Not just about the book, but about the Singularity movement as a whole. Wadhwa states: "The Singularity University's futurists are overlooking some of the risks in exponential technologies, particularly the legal and ethical dilemmas they are creating. As well, automation and industry disruption will have many negative social consequences — such as the elimination of the vast majority of jobs. Humans may have their physical needs met and live healthier and longer lives, but what about their social and professional needs?"[7]

Wadhwa states what many critics of Singularity feel: that the Singularity movement looks only on the bright side. That the followers of Kurzweil and Diamandis are starry-eyed techno-optimists, who fully believe that exponential technologies will guide humanity into an amazing era of abundance. And that blind belief would drive Robert J. Gordon up the wall.

6 D'S TO SOLVE THEM ALL

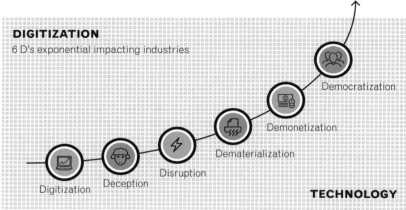

DIGITIZATION
6 D's exponential impacting industries

Democratization

Demonetization

Dematerialization

Disruption

Deception

Digitization

TECHNOLOGY

Source: Singularity University

The key framework of Singularity, as explained in *Bold*, is called the '6 D's of Exponentials': Digitization, Deception, Disruption, Dematerialization, Demonetization and Democratization. These six ingredients are the catalysts of a chain reaction of technological progress, the era of abundance.

Digitization, first. Everything is (becoming) digital which is why it is a normality. We've seen this happen in the past few years and I wrote about it in *The New Normal*[8] back in 2010. Anything that could be, has been digitized and became free to spread, reproduce and share over the network. This phenomenon has indeed created a consistent, exponential pattern of growth.

Deception. The interesting thing about exponential growth is that, at first, exponential growth seems to have less impact than linear growth. Before the 'bend' in the exponential curve, linear progress is more impressive. And this creates a period of 'deception' where people may doubt the real impact of exponential technologies before the curve skyrockets and leaves linear progress in the dust. We'll teach you how to draw a killer diagram on that in just a moment.

Disruption, then. 'Creative Destruction' was already coined in 1942 by the Austrian American economist Joseph Schumpeter who derived it from the work of Karl Marx. In his magnum opus *Capitalism, Socialism and Democracy*[9], Schumpeter described the creative-destructive forces unleashed by capitalism that will allow new players to topple old, static and conservative players. Today we see that technology is accelerating the disruption of entire industries with Uber and Airbnb as the poster children of this movement. And with technologies such as Artificial Intelligence, robotics, blockchain and 3D printing showing the potential, in the next ten years, to disrupt industries on a global scale.

Dematerialization. Technology makes 'things' disappear. A great example at the Singularity University was its flashlight app, which you downloaded for free on your phone, and turned your smartphone into a light when you needed it. And indeed, in our lifetime, we have seen all the functionalities of a camera, a GPS, a watch, a music player, a calculator, an encyclopedia, and even a VCR all dematerialize into apps on our smartphone.

Demonetization. The transition from bits to atoms makes things practically free. Digital cameras made film free in a way; it became digital, and the result is an explosion in the number of pictures being taken, because there is no more cost involved. Computers are becoming cheaper and cheaper, with our smartphones having more processing power than gigantic supercomputers once did. Many apps, websites, search engines and mail services are available for free. Though knowledge still has value, its worth keeps plummeting.

Democratization. The last D is a tricky one. More and more we are seeing technology move from the 'happy few' to the masses, thus allowing everyone access to progress. A third of the world's population still doesn't have access to a bank account. That's 2.5 billion people. And it has been proven that without access to financial services, this group will remain in poverty because it is impossible for them to save, grow, lend and develop. Technology can help. It can allow them to leap out of poverty, and show true democratization through digitization. That's why the Bill & Melinda Gates Foundation, for instance, helps people in the world's poorest regions improve their lives by connecting them with digitally-based financial tools and services. 'Banking the Unbanked' is a huge challenge.

When you list these 6 D's, and feel the enormous positive vibe when you visit Singularity, it's hard *not* to be a techno-optimist. But whether you are (too) confident about technological evolutions or indeed very cautious about them, possibly even scared (witless), one thing remains crystal clear: things *are* accelerating. Change *is* happening faster and faster.

Whichever the case, the 'Church of Wow' is a lean and mean money-making machine. Scores of executive students and corporate customers pay hefty sums to be wowed by the stories of the rise of exponential technologies, the second half of the chessboard, and the era of unbounded abundance. People are prepared to pay good money in order to understand how they can leverage the power of the exponential in their market, and organization.

Whenever Peter Diamandis gets criticized on his uber-positive view of the world, which is in stark contrast with some of the horrors, tragedies and catastrophes that we are continuously confronted with on the news, his response is simple: "The world is not getting worse, but the information is getting better." He *does* make a strong point. Over the past 30 years, the share of the global population living in absolute poverty has declined from 53% to under 17%. In the past 16 years, child labor has been reduced by more than 50%. In the past 25 years, under-five mortality rates have dropped by 50%. Over the past 50 years, the percentage of our disposable income spent on food has dropped by more than 50%, from 14% to less than 6%. Check out his June 2016 blog *Why the World Is Better Than You Think in 10 Powerful Charts* to see for yourself.[10]

DRAWING CURVES: CURVE #1: 'DECEPTION - ABUNDANCE'

If there is one thing you should memorize about this chapter, and even this book, it's how to draw killer diagrams that you will be able to utilize in plenty of meetings. If only to show off how incredibly profound you are, and how superb your grasp of current conceptual, cutting-edge theories is.

In fact, I've even created a graph to underline the impact of knowing how to draw graphs. Just to be sure, mind you.

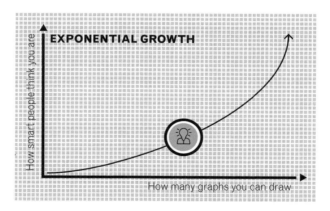

I'll start gently, with an example of the fundamental belief of the Singularists: first you draw a straight line, that shows 'linear thinking'. Then commencing from the original starting-point, you draw the 'exponential' curve, that intersects with the original linear line halfway, and then leaves it in the dust when it shoots up into the sky. There you go! You can now draw the very essence of exponential thinking.

A 'FALSE' SENSE OF SECURITY

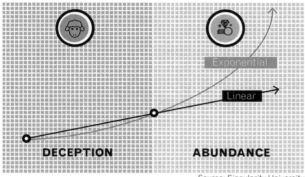

Source: Singularity University

This diagram uncouples into two parts. In the first part, the 'linear' movement actually outperforms the 'exponential' one. This is the area where exponential technologies are still gearing up, silently but ruthlessly preparing their explosive growth under the radar. The linear advance happens faster and more steadily while the exponential growth seems slow and negligible by comparison. This creates a false sense of insouciance, tricking your brain into 'first half of the chessboard' comfort. This is the part the Singularists call 'Deception'.

Then in the second part of the diagram, the full force of exponential growth matures, and pans out. The escalation of the exponential curve skyrockets, and the stunning full force of exponential leaves the 'linear' thinkers behind in the dust. Moore's law is the most popular example of exponential growth, but there are many more, like evolutions in bandwidth, Artificial Intelligence, mobile technology, internet availability, robotics, drones, self-driving cars, 3D-printing, biotechnology, the Internet of Things, nanotechnology or even solar power. All of which have or will disrupt entire unsuspecting industries.

I really love how waitbutwhy.com's Tim Urban explains this false sense of security in a brilliantly simple manner, with a little guy standing on a platform, just before the line becomes exponential. He starts by asking "What does it feel like to stand here?", showing the graph on the left. After which he states: "It seems like a pretty intense place to be standing - but then you have to remember something about what it's like to stand on a time graph: you can't see what's to your right. Here's how it actually feels to stand there", showing the graph on the right and adding "Which probably feels pretty normal...".[11]

That's where we are standing now, thinking that everything is pretty much same old, same old and linear, perhaps just a bit faster and steeper, but not by much. Well wise up, it's not.

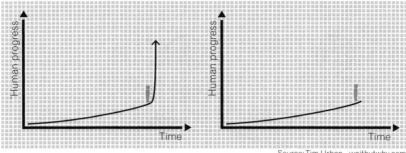

Source: Tim Urban - waitbutwhy.com

Tim Urban is on the very same page as Schwab and Diamandis when he claims: "The average rate of advancement between 1985 and 2005 was higher than the rate between 1955 and 1985 - because the former was a more advanced world - so much more change happened in the most recent 30 years than in the prior 30." He believes that human progress moves quicker and quicker because more advanced societies have the ability to progress at a faster rate than less advanced societies—*just because* they're more advanced.[11]

To put it in Kurzweil's words: "We won't experience 100 years of progress in the 21st century — it will be more like 20,000 years of progress (at today's rate)".[12]

QUIETLY INTO RETIREMENT

John Thomas Chambers is an impressive man. He was Cisco's CEO for more than 20 years, and instrumental in realizing its phenomenal growth as the undisputed leader in internet infrastructure equipment. Cisco ruled the dot.com waves, and became a global player of more than USD 46 billion when John Chambers handed over the reins of the company to his loyal lieutenant, Chuck Robbins.

After gaining his MBA, John Chambers worked for IBM as a salesman. When he was 34 he joined Wang Laboratories – one of the pioneers of word processing equipment and computers.

Wang Laboratories is a corporate roller-coaster-ride horror story in itself, with legendary founder Dr. An Wang. The latter was not only a brilliant scientist, he also craved to make his mark in the world of business. He sold his first startup to IBM in 1955, and with the proceeds he founded Wang Laboratories. The initial start of the company was rickety, but soon the company expanded from making calculators into making word processors and minicomputers. The company grew extremely fast, and when John Chambers joined Wang Laboratories in 1983, at the age of 34, he was caught in the maelstrom of a rapidly growing venture. Chambers became head of the U.S. Operations of Wang Laboratories in 1987.

And then it all fell apart. The meteoric rise and catastrophic decline of Wang Laboratories is splendidly described in the book by Charles Kenney: *Riding the Runaway Horse.*[13] Wang Laboratories grew like crazy to more than USD 3 billion in revenues, at its peak in the mid-1980s, employing more than 33,000 employees. But in the second half of the 1980s the glory years at Wang Laboratories gave way to a downward spiral of late product deliveries, massive debt and aggressive layoffs.

Chambers was caught right in the middle of this turbulent descent. In 1990, Wang Laboratories was coping with a USD 700 million loss. Not only was the organization burdened by nepotism issues and the uncompromising temperament of the founder, but Chambers also recognized how Wang Laboratories was incapable of making the switch to new technologies, new concepts and new ideas. This was the age that minicomputers, that had disrupted the mainframe world, were getting disrupted by the world of personal computers. Wang Laboratories was left behind by the new field of competitors, and the company was essentially a sitting duck. Chambers left the sinking ship in 1991 and, less than a year later, in August 1992, Wang Laboratories filed for bankruptcy.[14]

Chambers experienced first-hand what happens when disruption becomes material, and what it means to be incapable of making the jump towards the 'Day After Tomorrow'. He had had a narrow escape when he bounced across to Cisco in 1991.

Cisco had been founded seven years earlier by two formidable Stanford University computer scientists: Leonard Bosack and his wife Sandy Lerner. Together, they designed and built the first Cisco routers in their house, based on software that had been created earlier at Stanford by William Yeager and Andy Bechtolsheim. Initially, Bosack and Lerner went to Stanford with a proposal to start building and selling the routers, but the university refused. It was then that they founded their own company and named it 'Cisco'.

Its products started selling like hot cakes, and the founders stayed on at Stanford until 1986 when Bosack was forced to resign from Stanford and the university contemplated filing criminal complaints against Cisco and its founders for the theft of its software, hardware designs and intellectual properties. A year later, Stanford licensed the router software to Cisco, and the rest is history. Cisco started growing like crazy in the very young internet market.

Cisco Systems went public in February 1990 (with a market capitalization of more than USD 224 million) and was listed on the NASDAQ stock exchange. In August of that same year, however, Lerner was fired and, upon hearing the news, her husband Bosack resigned in protest. The couple walked away with USD 170 million.

That's the moment John Chambers entered the picture. He joined Cisco in 1991, and became CEO in 1995. His reign was spectacular and remarkable, growing the company from USD 70 million to more than USD 46 billion in revenue. His success story is one of the most spectacular in Silicon Valley's and that's saying a lot. Sadly, in his final years, Chambers also had to perform a massive restructuring of the corporation, laying off more than 25,000 employees. With the scars of the Wang Laboratories nightmare fresh in his mind, Chambers understood he had to act swiftly and brutally in order for the company to survive.

When Chambers left Cisco, he did so with a bang, not a whimper, channeling his inner T.S. Eliot. Clearly, he was not the kind for nostalgia and sentiment. Instead, he wanted to give his soon to be ex-colleagues and ex-customers a final speech at the Cisco Live Conference that would rattle their brains, and leave a mark. He made it very clear that the digital age was just getting started and they should not, by any means, get comfortable. "40% of businesses in this room, unfortunately, will not exist in a meaningful way in 10 years' time[15]," he told the stunned 25,000 attendees. He added that 70% of companies would 'attempt' to go digital, but only 30% of those would succeed.

"One-third of businesses today will not survive the next 10 years", Chambers continued, getting all fired up. "It will become a digital world that will change our lives, our health, our education, our business models at the pace like we've never seen before. Your choice in life is simple: Either you disrupt or you get disrupted". He went on to quote JPMorgan Chase CEO Jamie Dimon's annual letter to shareholders, in which Dimon warned that "Silicon Valley is coming", referring to the disruptive startups that were out to get, well, ... basically anyone. [15]

RUMBLING IN THE DISTANCE

When you listen to Chambers haranguing his customers in his farewell speech, or Schwab alerting his attendees at the World Economic Forum to the imminent Fourth Industrial Revolution, or Diamandis extolling the virtues of exponential thinking at Singularity University, they all have the same message: brace yourselves.

As Diamandis wrote: "The first technological steps — sharp edges, fire, the wheel — took tens of thousands of years. For people living in this era, there was little noticeable technological change in even a thousand years. By 1000 AD, progress was much faster and a paradigm shift required only a century or two. In the 19th century, we saw more technological change than in the nine centuries preceding it. Then, in the first 20 years of the 20th century, we saw more advancement than in all of the 19th century. Now, paradigm shifts occur in only a few years' time. The World Wide Web did not exist in anything like its present form just a decade ago, and didn't exist at all two decades before that. As these exponential developments continue, we will begin to unlock unfathomably productive capabilities and begin to understand how to solve the world's most challenging problems."[16]

You only have to look at these more recent adoption numbers, to actually see his point of accelerating change:

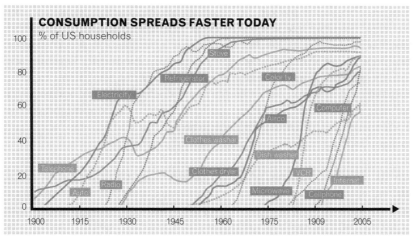

Source: Michael Felton, The New York Times. HBR.org

So yes, there is a rumbling in the distance, the suffocating humid silence before a tropical storm, an acceleration of technologies that could start a chain reaction at an unprecedented full-blown, global scale. Something is up. Except when you talk to Robert Gordon of course, who is still extremely enchanted with indoor plumbing.

In my previous books, I wrote about the concept of VUCA: Volatility, Uncertainty, Complexity and Ambiguity. I discovered this concept while conducting research for *The New Normal*, and I became quite intrigued by the subject. Since then I have had the chance to meet the founder of this concept, Bob

Johansen. Bob is one of the fellows of the Institute for the Future (IFTF) based in Palo Alto, a think-tank that was established to help organizations plan for the long-term future. I love Bob's view on the positive flip side of VUCA, which he sees as Vision, Understanding, Clarity and Agility. He says: "Leaders who make the future will transform Volatility into Vision, Uncertainty into Understanding, Complexity into Clarity, and Ambiguity into Agility."[17]

As he puts it: "Listening for the future is hard work. Leaders must learn how to listen through the noise of a VUCA (Volatile, Uncertain, Complex and Ambiguous) world. But leaders can make a better future. We need not and should not passively accept any future as a given. Disciplined use of foresight can help leaders make better decisions today. There is short-term value in long-term thinking."

In a world that is changing fast, Velocity is not an option anymore. It has become mandatory. Agility might be the single, biggest asset that any organization could possess. There's this popular saying in the South: "It's not the heat, it's the humidity". I believe that in a VUCA world "It's not the speed, it's the agility". Essential to this will be VACINE (yes, that *is* a disrupted version of the correctly spelt VACCINE): Velocity, Agility, Creativity, Innovation, Networks and Experimentation. It will come down to the capacity of organizations to foster Creativity and to let Innovation flow faster through the Network of employees, partners and customers. And perhaps most essential is the need to take the traditional corporate aversion to risk into an appetite for Experimentation, and to learn from our mistakes.

Whether it is Bob Johansen's Vision, Understanding, Clarity or Agility, or my VACINE of Velocity, Agility, Creativity, Innovation, Networks and Experimentation, we *will* need an approach to tackle the advent of acceleration, the arrival of fundamental changes and uncertainty, with seemingly less and less time to put our insights into action.

DISRUPTION

Most of us think about being violently destroyed or crushed by small but fast startups when we hear the word 'disruption'. But it is actually much more about the jeopardy of being left behind and becoming irrelevant.

I have done a lot of work for the telco sector over the years. It has profited tremendously with the advent of the internet and mobile communications: boatloads of cash thanks to more and more users wanting to consume more and more internet bandwidth and mobile minutes. For years in a row, Telcos grew large, political, and fat. And they were setting themselves up for a situation where they would lack the agility to respond quickly to disruption.

Despite all the growth, all the expansion and all the cash, the Telcos were getting increasingly worried about this one horrendous thing: becoming a 'Dumb Pipe'. The 'Dumb Pipe' syndrome is the fear of bringing connectivity to homes and users – providing the 'pipes' that connect the internet to the end-consumers – without really 'knowing' the customers they serve.

Telecom operators fear that the new set of platform players like Google and Facebook – the 'over-the-top' operators – are the ones capturing all the value. These platform players gather all the knowledge about the consumers. They are becoming more and more relevant to the end-user, while Telcos' Dumb Pipes are merely there to supply more and more bandwidth. Basically, you can switch from one Dumb Pipe to another without noticing any difference. Google and Facebook, on the other hand, 'own' our pictures, documents, emotions and friends. Switching them *will* be felt. Deeply.

Seems like the 'Dumb Pipe' syndrome wasn't just a nightmare for the Telco industry after all. It is rapidly becoming reality.

The graph that wonderfully illustrates this is the one portrayed in *The Economist* in March of 2015 in an article on the evolution of messaging called *The message is the medium*. The graph was ironically labelled: 'OMG, RIP txt'.[18]

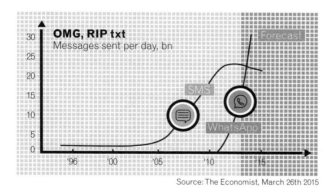

Source: The Economist, March 26th 2015

The trigger for this exponential explosion, was the purchase of WhatsApp by Mark Zuckerberg in February 2014. The young CEO of Facebook was prepared to buy WhatsApp – then a company of only 52 employees – for a whopping USD 19 billion. It had been founded four years earlier by Brian Acton and

Jan Koum. In 2007, Koum and Acton left their employer Yahoo and took a year off, traveling around South America and playing ultimate Frisbee. When they returned from South America, they both first applied for a job at Facebook. Both were rejected.

Lucky for them, they had the good fortune to start working on WhatsApp and four years later Zuckerberg shelled out USD 19 billion for their fledgling startup. WhatsApp had no revenue. None. It did not even have a revenue model. Acton and Koum basically had no idea how they were ever going to make any money. They built a free app that spread like wildfire, grew exponentially, and was starting to dwarf the traffic that traditional Telcos had with their SMS and Text Messaging services.

Yet, Zuckerberg had to have WhatsApp. No matter what. No matter the cost. But USD 19 billion was insane to most people in the industry. They thought Zuckerberg had gone mad, or at least high on crack cocaine when he signed that deal. There was a significant amount of smirking in many Telco board-rooms at the young Zuckerberg who'd made such a foolish move.

Two years later, the laughter died away. And that is when this amazing graph by Portio Research and Andreessen-Horowitz appeared in *The Economist*.

It showed that, by the end of 2015, the total daily number of WhatsApp messages was *twice* the volume of all the SMSs and Text Messages that were sent via *all* the mobile operators on the planet combined. That's *all* the messages on Vodafone, T-Mobile and all the others on this planet added up. And WhatsApp had twice as many as all of them.

Flashback to 2010. In 2010, the Telco industry was making a killing with messaging. Texting was quite expensive, and an absolute cash-cow for the mobile operators. They were constantly trying to convince consumers to switch to their platform by offering bundles of SMSs that were basically repackaged every month. End-users were continuously confused about the pricing and offering, as well as frustrated by the cost of messaging. But there was no alternative.

Until WhatsApp appeared. The technology was not groundbreaking. Not in the least. As a matter of fact, any group of telecom engineers at any of the big Telcos could have built it. Easily. But they didn't. It took a group of smart young people in Silicon Valley to build it. They were people with no prior knowledge of the Telco industry. People who were not 'corporately formatted'. And yet they made an easy, simple and user-friendly global messaging app ... for free.

The result is history. Users quickly saw the advantage that WhatsApp allowed them to use the Wi-Fi signals at home or at work to send free messages. And not just text. Pictures as well. And videos. And quickly after that, the possibility to make calls with the same quality as a normal mobile cellphone call.

Flashback to 2010. There was no WhatsApp. The guys who went on to build WhatsApp were still trying to apply for a job at Facebook. And the Telco guys were still like this little buddy below on the graph, standing comfortably on this platform, maybe eating a sandwich, chilling, possibly listening to 'Baby' by a Justin Bieber who – him too – was still innocent and uncorrupted. Just look at him, so cute, so unsuspecting, so trusting. Let's call him Lawrence Foster Lannister III, in case we need to refer to him again.

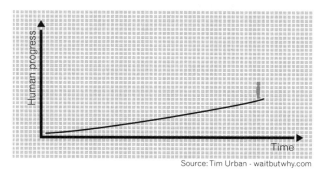

Source: Tim Urban - waitbutwhy.com

It's not Lawrence's fault, though. Imagine that *you* would have to present a strategy to the board of a large Telco in 2010 on the *future* of text messaging, and that this would be the only data you have:

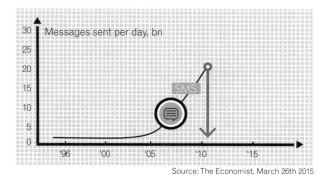

Source: The Economist, March 26th 2015

In my opinion, the below is the only logical future that the Telco industry saw back in 2010 for messaging. Year after year they had sent out a press release after every Christmas, New Year's Eve, Mother's Day or Thanksgiving about how many *more* text messages they had sent than the last time. Every industry analyst had rosy predictions, every consultant they hired talked them into predictions about incessant growth, and every model they had would extrapolate the past and come up with more, more and more.

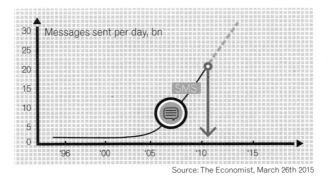

Source: The Economist, March 26th 2015

And then boom. WhatsApp suddenly ate their lunch. Not only is the sheer volume of messages that Facebook processes every day staggering – via the core Facebook platform as well as WhatsApp – but, on top of that, the Messenger and Instagram channels feed them ever more information about their users. Suddenly, by comparison, the 'Dumb Pipe' operators seem to have extremely little insight into the lives and behaviors of their customers.

THE FIVE STAGES OF GRIEF

Over the years, I have come to see a parallel with companies faced with disruption and people coping with loss and grief. When people become terminally ill, they often follow similar patterns of behavior to cope with their personal

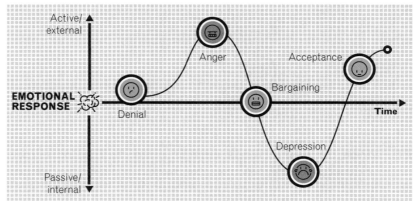

Source: Elisabeth Kübler-Ross, On Death and Dying, 1969

tragedy. Swiss psychiatrist scientist Elisabeth Kübler-Ross described this phe-nomenon for the first time in 1969 in her trailblazing book *On Death and Dying*, where she introduced her theory of the five stages of grief.[19] The various phases she described were Denial, Anger, Bargaining, Depression and Acceptance.

When patients find out that they have been diagnosed with an incurable or untreatable cancer, these phases play out in sequence. First comes Denial: "That can't be true. I don't believe it. I want a second opinion". When the verdict is confirmed, then comes Anger: "Why me? This is unfair. I've lived a healthy life, ate well, exercised, worked out and now this happens to me?". Realizing your finality, patients move on to Bargaining: "Doc, what can you do to prolong my remaining time as long as possible? I'd do anything for six more months. Anything". After the irrevocability of the outcome sinks in, a period of Depres-sion is, in many cases, followed by a final stage of Acceptance.

I have been a privileged observer over my career of many industries, many markets and many Fortune 500 companies. Thanks to my teaching at London Business School and MIT, I have had the pleasure of having intimate conversa-tions with many business leaders, and have often observed very similar patterns of behavior, when companies are confronted with disruption.

Denial is the most dangerous phase for corporations. If new ideas, new con-cepts, new business models or new technologies threaten to undermine a com-pany's core business, the problem of 'Deception' is bad enough. For a very long time, these new players can operate 'under the waterline' and give companies the false perception of (still) being in full control. But it is even worse when this period of 'Deception' is prolonged and stretched out by 'Denial'.

Corporate anger is often led by lawyers. When corporations finally see the fun-damental changes in a market, often way too late, they try to stop it with all the legal force they can muster. Media companies and Telco corporations around the world have used their legal and lobbying power to try and stop the rise of the likes of Google and Facebook in their markets.

Eventually, corporations realize that they might be better off understanding the dynamics of the new players, and might prolong their own relevance if they negotiate. The same Media companies and Telco players that battled the Giants of Silicon Valley at first, have moved on to create 'partnerships', 'strategic alli-ances' or 'privileged affiliations' with these very same disruptors.

One can only imagine the intense tragedy of corporations who realize their sit-uation is one of total collapse. How they must feel trapped in a sinking ship that is going down fast, like the sadness and depression of the scores of employees in companies such as Kodak, Nokia or RIM Blackberry: people who have given so much of their lives, their energy and their emotions to a company that they all believed in, just to see it wither away in front of their very eyes. I've never worked at Nokia, but even I had goosebumps when I read how ex-CEO of Nokia, Stephen Elop, choked up in tears when he said: "We didn't do anything wrong. But somehow we lost."[20]

REBELLION

I'm not the only one to have re-used Elisabeth Kübler-Ross' model in a different environment. One of its most popular forms of repurposing is to be found in change management, where it's called the Elisabeth Kübler-Ross change curve. What bothers me about all these models, though, is that they tend to end in a very passive mode: sometimes ending with acceptance, sometimes with 'integration', just dealing with something you cannot control. True, those who are terminally ill have no other choice. (Even though there are people out there who are genuinely trying to makes us immortal, or at least extend our lives in a very significant manner: Google Ventures' Bill Maris, Calico's Arthur Levinson and United Therapeutics' Martine Rothblatt to name but a few. But that's beside the point here.)

Though I believe Kübler-Ross' theory applies wonderfully to the world of disruptive technologies, I want to add something to her standard. Because acceptance of a disruptive environment is obviously not enough. Disruptors don't accept what everyone else holds to be true and normal. That's just the point of disruption. Elon Musk did not accept that humanity is an Earth-bound species, as did the rest of the world. Arthur Levinson does not want to put up with death. He wants to cure it. Brian Acton and Jan Koum did not accept that we have to pay for SMS. Augmented reality organizations like Blippar don't accept that reality is what can be perceived. These are rebels in the true sense of the word. They should scare us. But above all, inspire us.

To me, it only gets really interesting when you reach the end of the curve, ... and move beyond it. I call this next phase 'Rebellion'. It's nothing like denial, anger or bargaining. It's active. It's seeing a status quo you don't like and having the balls to change it and make it your own. It's turning something upside down, even if everyone around you is screaming "crazy". As we will see in the coming chapters, I *do* believe that large corporations are capable of this, not just the startups. And I have the practical business cases to prove it. So, stick with me for a while.

*"It ain't what you don't know that gets you in trou-
ble, it's what you know for sure that just ain't so."*
MARK TWAIN

TIME FOR A NEW CURVE

So far there is only one thing you need to remember: how to draw the 'Deception & Abundance' graph to show the difference between linear and exponential
evolution. If you're not sure how it was done, go back, and practice till perfect.
This has to become second nature if you want to impress. Just channel the consultant in you, who can whip out a two-by-two matrix faster than Dirty Harry
pulled out his Colt 45.

When the 'Deception-Abundance' graph glows up on your cortex when you
close your eyes, you're ready to move on to the second graph that you should
(also) know by heart.

Readers who are familiar with my previous books will recognize my fascination
with S-curves. I believe they are more common than 'exponential' evolutions
and that's where I don't see eye to eye with the Singularists who believe that
exponentiality is everywhere.

Even in the example we just gave, the disruption of the Telcos messaging market by the advent of WhatsApp, we can see a really nice S-curve appear:

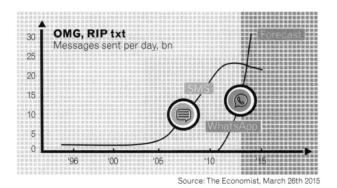

Source: The Economist, March 26th 2015

As stated, if you would have asked a Telco player, in 2010, to chart the future of
text messaging, well, it would rise forever. The most optimistic ones would even
chart an exponential growth. Instead of that, after the entrance of a disruptor,
growth becomes an S-curve and starts to slope down. Just like when the full
force of WhatsApp became clear.

I used the same S-curve in my book *The New Normal* to describe the transition that occurred when 'digital' evolved from being 'special' to being 'normal'. This forced companies to adopt a 'digital first' strategy in order to stay relevant to their customers.

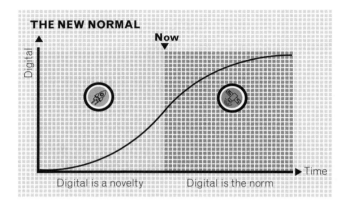

Since then, we have seen progressions of S-curves, all going faster than the previous ones, where new technologies reinforce each other. Ever since the 'digital' evolution from special to normal, we have observed similar patterns when 'mobile' went from being the exception to being mainstream, and companies had to adopt a 'mobile-first' strategy.

Practice on those S-curves. They should be flowing out of your hand like Picasso drawing a bull. Make sure your S-curves are fluid, graceful, elegant, uninterrupted and shapely. Then move on.

Ready for the next level? Here it goes:

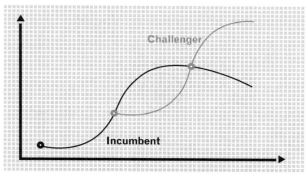

Source: Chris Bradley and Clayton O'Toole,
An Incumbent's Guide to Digital Disruption, McKinsey Quarterly, May 2016

I know this one is a little trickier. But it's important that you master it, if you want to make it as a Zen Master of Graph Drawing. Out of the emerging pattern arises an extremely interesting approach to disruption. It's similar in nature to the 'Deception-Abundance' philosophy of the Singularists, but much closer to reality in my opinion.

Chris Bradley is a partner of the consulting firm McKinsey & Company. Together with his colleague Clayton O'Toole, he wrote the thought-provoking article *An Incumbent's Guide to Digital Disruption*.[21] In it they describe four manifestations of (digital) Disruption: Detectable, Clear, Inevitable and New Normal. Undeniably, I was pleased that they referenced the final stage of acceptance of a new paradigm as the 'New Normal'. But what I really liked is their use of two S-curves to show the progress of the 'incumbent' and the 'disruptor' or challenger: these two curves overlap, and show the four symptoms of disruption, as well as what the reaction of the incumbents is.

The overlay of the two S-curves clearly shows the four phases. In the first part the disruptor has little impact on the traditional player. The disruption is 'detectable' and it requires a lot of attention and acuity on behalf of the incumbent. Most likely, the Elisabeth Kübler-Ross phase of Denial runs deep in many boardroom discussions at this point. McKinsey labels the inherent danger in this stage as 'Corporate Myopia'.[22]

When the disruptor starts to move and is picking up steam, the incumbents should move to 'Action', though they hardly ever do. The disruptor is causing some disturbance, but it doesn't hurt enough for the incumbents to really take

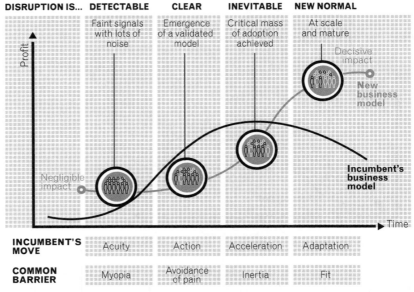

Source: Chris Bradley and Clayton O'Toole, An Incumbent's Guide to Digital Disruption, McKinsey Quarterly, May 2016

drastic action. Often, they will revert to a tactic of 'pain avoidance'. Perhaps the visibility of potential disruptive new business models will be 'clear', but 'corporate anger' will often think that the 'lawyers' can make the problem go away.

When the disruption breaks through the S-curve of the incumbent, the bubble bursts. Critical mass of the disruptive business model has been achieved. In other words, the disruption is 'Inevitable'. The incumbents should accelerate and put everything they have into changing their course. The right thing to do would be to direct their massive resources, talent and funding to preserving their position, strength and continuity. Unfortunately, at this point, many incumbents will suffer from paralysis. Their inertia will keep them from moving fast enough, and with ample agility.

Finally, when the disruption becomes the 'New Normal', the fate of the incumbents is sealed: they actually have no choice but to adapt (or exit the market). The real difficulty is trying to fit in this New Normal, in a way that is profitable to them. The disruptor has become the new ruler, and is ready to become the next incumbent. Basically, it's like the cycle of life. Only, it keeps on moving faster and faster and more ruthlessly. Yet so many of us are still living in Denial.

Let's recap. You should be able to draw the 'Linear-Exponential-Deception-Abundance' graph. And then you should practice on this one. Make sure to talk about 'Corporate Myopia' when you draw it; that always gets them. Probably because so many people *are* myopic and their number keeps growing: by 2050, 50% of the world's population, a total of nearly 5 billion, will be myopic, according to a study in the journal *Opthalmology*. Luckily, this is an excellent graph to observe up close.

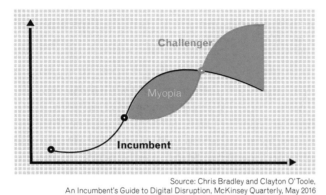

Source: Chris Bradley and Clayton O'Toole,
An Incumbent's Guide to Digital Disruption, McKinsey Quarterly, May 2016

RE-THINK. RE-BOOT. RE-SET.

Depressed yet? You probably got your hopes up about being a rebel and then I crushed it, talking about myopia and how most companies wouldn't recognize a new paradigm if it bit them in the face. Sorry.

But it is possible. There are companies that can reinvent themselves. I have seen them. They are the ones who are capable of re-thinking, re-booting, re-setting their course. They know how to survive the tsunami effect of disruptive technologies. They might be the 'rarest of beasts', but *they are* out there.

NETFLIX

Netflix is one of them. Originally a mail-order DVD platform, they have survived the onslaught of digital to become the world's leading video streaming business by far. Their founder and CEO Reed Hastings is quite right to point out that the most successful organizations fail to look for new things their customers want, because they want to protect their core businesses. This is what the Uber-Grandfather of disruptive theories, Clayton Christensen, calls 'The Innovator's Dilemma'. It's when companies choose sustaining innovation over radical innovation, because incorporating disruptive technologies is too difficult and will take their focus off their beloved price beast, the core, which is still what their largest and best customers want. Disruptive innovation often performs lower in many of the key features their top customers enjoy, so they disregard it.

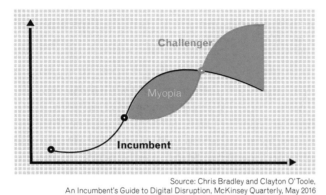

In the words of Reed Hastings: "Companies rarely die from moving too fast, but they frequently die from moving too slowly."[23] But Netflix has shown that you can, and you must. Reinvent yourself, I mean. I've had the chance to visit this pioneer on many occasions, and have found their story to be truly remarkable. Their company fighting spirit and culture is deeply reflected in their core values. You can find it in the way they hire, in the way they promote, and in the way they run their HR in general. It's a company where this fighting spirit and aggressive move towards change and innovation is palpable everywhere you look and in everyone you meet.

Many people I met at Netflix have recounted the moment when Netflix was both a mail-order-DVD company and a fledgling streaming video company at the same time. They vividly recall a now legendary management meeting where the charismatic CEO asked the 'old guard' people to stand up. They were the people who ran the mail-order DVD business: the incumbent business that was still going strong. After he'd asked these managers to stand up, he told the stunned crowd something along these lines: "Please give these people a warm hand of applause. They were the origins of our company and we would not have been able to survive without them. They were the heart and soul of our organization since its very beginning, but we now have to embark on a new chapter if we want to survive. Please give these people a really warm applause, because we will be saying goodbye to them'. The old unit was spun off, and everything was focused on the new business.

That was a bold move by Reed Hastings. At first the markets did not agree with him, as (financial) markets tend to show the same myopia, deception and extrapolation-bias of which many corporate boardrooms suffer.

But the gamble paid off big time for Netflix. It might be one of the most stirring, visible and perceptible sightings of those 'rarest of the beasts': companies who can successfully reinvent themselves in the face of disruption. Netflix is definitely one of them.

IBM

Another good example is that of IBM, one of the oldest technology companies out there together with the likes of GE and Hewlett-Packard. It was founded in 1911 with the extremely sexy name: the Computing Tabulating Recording Company (CTR), which was then changed to International Business Machines or IBM by 1924.

On its 100th birthday in 2011, IBM ran a rather cocky four-page ad in *The Wall Street Journal, Washington Post* and *New York Times*. It said: "Nearly all the companies our grandparents admired have disappeared. Of the top 25 companies on the Fortune 500 in 1961, only six remain today."[24] Slightly arrogant, but very telling. Only six survived. One in four. So, kudos to IBM for having made the cut.

True, the company has experienced rocky times since then. Very rocky times. We all remember the annus horribilis of 1993 when – having missed a number of key technology shifts – IBM lived through one of the biggest losses in the history of corporate America, in the form of a staggering amount of USD 8 billion. Yikes.

But the company succeeded in reinventing itself, by "exiting commoditizing markets and focusing on higher-value, more profitable markets".[25] In that awful period of 1993, it performed a massive transformation of its core business model in order to focus on providing IT expertise and computing services to businesses. Many thought it would crash and burn. And it almost did. As we will see later: waiting until you are almost dead, is not the best time to reinvent yourself as a company. That should come sooner. Much sooner.

But IBM succeeded in a business model pivot, even if it was all but annihilated. Simply put, it evolved from being a tech hardware pioneer – selling electric typewriters, punch card tabulators, and later, massive mainframe computers, personal computers and even printers – to providing mostly software and IT services.

True, IBM seems to be going through a difficult period again, having recently announced massive lay-offs, but it's still one of the leading pioneers in some of the hottest technologies of the moment. It has, for instance, been one of the most successful players in artificial intelligence since 1950. I'm really curious to see where it's heading, having recently announced that it's building a blockchain ecosystem.

GOOGLE

There are more of them, these rare beasts. One of the less obvious examples might be Google, because people tend to perceive it as quite a young company. Though its search engine business – initially called BackRub – is already 20 years old. As Wired co-founding editor John Battelle explains in his book *The Search*[26], Google used to be very unprofitable, unable to find a stable revenue source. After making marginally profitable forays into selling search appliances to businesses and its own search technology to other search engines, Google radically changed course. In 2000, it introduced AdWords, a self-service program for creating online ad campaigns and the rest is pretty much history. Almost overnight, Google took the leap from popular search tool to advertising juggernaut.

The beautiful thing about Google is that, apart from this 'old' and very profitable search engine and advertising business, it keeps investing in a very large range of (more) radical side-projects like smart home devices (Nest), healthcare (Verily), life expansion (Calico), Artificial Intelligence (Google DeepMind) and many more. But we'll come back to that later on.

OPTIONALITY

Mark Leslie is an observer of those 'rare beasts' in IT that are able to reinvent themselves; a zoo-keeper of sorts.

Mark Leslie is a lecturer at the Stanford Graduate School of Business where he teaches entrepreneurship and corporate innovation. He manages his own venture firm, sits on the boards of many startups and scale-ups, but he gained his insight into managing disruption when he ran technology companies such as Veritas Software. He was CEO of the latter from 1990 till 2001, growing the business from USD 4 million to USD 1.5 billion in revenue, after which the company was sold to Symantec.

His time at Veritas helped Leslie understand a fundamental principle in a world that is moving extremely fast: "The big lesson I learned is that whatever the business – no matter how great it is – it's not always going to be a great business. And you need to start thinking about that, and planning for the changes, when things are going well."[27]

Leslie has written many articles and blog posts on this subject, and has coined the concept of the 'Corporate Arc of Life': all successful startups (and corporate initiatives) go through an initial growth phase, with revenue and market share increasing each year. But, over time, this growth peaks, slows, and then plateaus as the companies and markets mature. This phase is followed by a gradual decline, plummeting into a negative trajectory as new (disruptive) players enter the market and the established companies fail to keep up.

The reason that Leslie likes examples from the technology world is that these companies have a cycle of life that is much shorter, since everything in the tech space is happening faster. Consider how quickly Blackberry was destroyed by the iPhone, or how Nokia was ruined by Google Android. But the rhythm of technology companies is rapidly becoming the rhythm of the corporate world, whatever industry or market you are in. Lessons learned from the rise and fall, and resurrection, of technology companies could become recipes for survival in the age of disruption.

Leslie wrote an influential blog post - *the Arc of Company Life, and How To Prolong It*[28] on this very subject. He begins with stating the inevitability of the 'Arc of Life': companies are born, grow fast, mature and die.

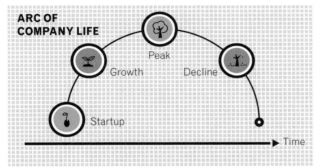

Source: www.linkedin.com/pulse/arc-life-mark-leslie

According to Leslie, the key to enduring growth is strategic transformation. Companies should not wait until they are in 'Decline' to start thinking of the 'Next Big Thing', so much is clear. What's surprising is his claim that starting to transform yourself as a company at your 'peak' moment – when you are still at the top of your game – is actually too late.

According to him, the only way that companies can re-invent themselves fast enough to have a chance of real transformative success, is that they start this process when things are going really, really well. When they are still growing like crazy. That is the ideal moment when strategic transformation can take root, and be carried out successfully.

This moment is what Leslie calls the 'sweet spot' of optionality: when the leaders of an organization focus their attention not only on the things they know very well – which are generating great success and revenue – but *also* on the radical transformation that is necessary to prepare organizations for the next 'Big Leap' forward.

It's only logical really, as this period of excellent revenue and growth offers the company the financial and human resources to invest in something that will not create revenue immediately, but will – more likely than not – cost money at

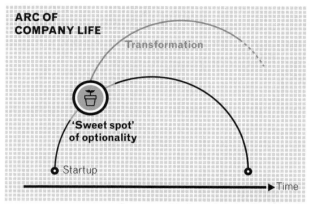

the beginning. If a company finds itself just before or at the decline of the core business, reinventing itself will become much harder and will meet with much more resistance from the top, who will probably want to do anything they can to protect and boost the existing business.

This is how Leslie describes the sweet spot, so you'll be sure to recognize it when it's there (or, let's hope this is not the case, when it's passed):

- You're finally out of the startup phase and no longer have to worry about scarce resources or traction.
- The organization has achieved a measure of stability — the future looks bright, revenue is climbing, and the business model has gelled.
- You just reached a point where you have the talent, money and market influence to do something new while maintaining and growing the core business.
- The wind is at your back! (Yes. Leslie did add this in his description, so I'm leaving it in.)

As Leslie says: "When a company forgoes the 'good life' of maturity, controlled growth and market leadership and is willing to take on the risk of transformation in the face of existential risks, it can achieve new levels of growth and extend its horizons." [27]

When companies are capable of doing this repeatedly, they will create some sort of a genetic code that will allow them to live forever. *That* is the holy grail of any organization in this world: finding the fountain of eternal corporate youth.

Netflix certainly has done so. Instead of milking the cash cow of the mail-order DVD business, Reed Hastings had the guts to invest in new ideas, new technologies and new business models. Streaming video was largely unproven when

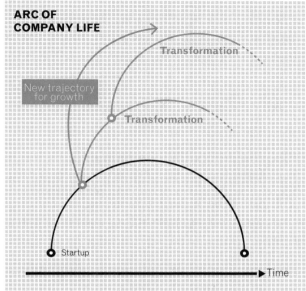

ARC OF
COMPANY LIFE

Transformation

New trajectory
for growth

Transformation

Startup

Time

Source: https://www.linkedin.com/pulse/arc-life-mark-leslie

Netflix engaged in it full blast. When Netflix started with this new business, there was not enough bandwidth, not enough security, no reliable browsers and no reliable technology to pull it off. But they engaged. Reed Hastings engaged. That is true leadership.

A similar example is what we see at Amazon. Amazon is known to most people on this planet as the absolute leader in e-commerce, a poster-child of the first dot-com era, a household brand and a clear ruler. But Amazon is also the undisputed leader in the new field of cloud-based computing, and is dwarfing other players like Microsoft, Google, IBM and Oracle in the field of web services.

Amazon did not wait until its core business (selling books and, later, other products online) started on a decline, or even a peak, to start its new cloud business. On the contrary, when Amazon was on all-cylinders building the greatest e-commerce platform in the world, when Amazon was doing really, really well in their traditional core business model, *that* was the moment when they transitioned into the new, unknown territory of the cloud, and became the 900-pound gorilla in that field.

Amazon launched the concept of zShops – a platform that enabled small businesses to set up their own virtual storefronts and sell products through the site. This, in itself, was not the game changer, but it ultimately led to the creation of Amazon Web Services (AWS), leveraging the company's internal software architecture to provide other businesses with affordable cloud services. This massively successful detour from the core business sprang from a smaller (failed) venture. AWS is now growing at a faster rate than Amazon's consumer-facing retail operations.

And that is virtually all down to the enormous drive and vision of their leader, Jeff Bezos.

And that is also the conclusion of Mark Leslie: "The ability to do this type of strategic transformation is largely dependent on the type of leader charting the course. Most leaders fall into one of two categories: Opportunity-Driven or Operationally-Driven." [27] Opportunity-Driven leaders like Reed Hastings and Jeff Bezos understand optionality, because that's the entrepreneurial unrest that flows through their veins.

If you have an Operationally-Driven leader, while excellent at driving efficiency and predictability for the short run, it could place the company at long-term risk as it will merely stay on track on the 'Arc of Life', leading inevitably to its demise.

According to Leslie, the key decision moment is the moment of maximum optionality: "At that point, the company can essentially milk its success — which it will do if its CEO is operationally-driven – or apply the capital and talent it has attracted to attack new market opportunities — the likely approach of an opportunity-driven CEO."

THE DAY AFTER TOMORROW MODEL

*"I'm so extremely busy doing my job,
I can't get any work done."* SETH GODIN

We're almost there. Just a little more time before I introduce the 'Day After Tomorrow' Model. But, first, I want to briefly recap. So far, we have established that the rate of change is undeniably accelerating, despite some stubborn nay-sayers out there. Things are changing and morphing faster than ever before. Yet, most long-lived companies are blinded into believing that they still have time before they can clean up their act, because they apply linear thinking in an exponential world. They suffer from corporate myopia and have no clue that some of the trends and evolutions in front of them are about to take off like rockets, leaving them far, far behind. Not good. Keeping the same course is definitely not an option these days.

After that we tackled the question of *when* we should start reinventing our companies. We've seen that there are two parameters to consider: one on the outside – which is logical, seeing that the 'outside change' is what forces us to keep evolving ourselves – and one on the inside.

Outside first: we have seen that the ideal time to start *acting* in case of a disruption is at the point when the disruption becomes clear: *before* it becomes inevitable, at the point when its impact on a company is deceivingly low.

Second, the best possible moment to start mutating, from an *inside point of view*, native to your own organization, is *before* its peak, at the moment when you are at full throttle and growing rapidly. It's the moment when, intuitively, you would focus every last ounce of your resources on making sure that everything that is going well will be going even better. Basically: when you feel peachy keen, on top of the world and are laughing at how you are crushing your competition, that's when you should start feeling fidgety about your next move. It's utterly and completely counterintuitive. It will probably sound insane to your board. But it is how you can become one of those rarest of beasts, that is fluid enough to change in par with the outside world.

Now we have arrived at my favorite part of the story: the 'how'. How will you be able to survive and even create your own 'Day After Tomorrow'?

Paradoxically, now that everything is changing so fast and yesterday sometimes seems like last year, I will be asking you to focus on the very long term: on ideas that are so radical that a lot of the things that will be needed to create them might not exist yet. I want you to think not about today, not about tomorrow, but about your 'Day After Tomorrow': a far off and radical future that has probably nothing to do with your current business model.

Why? Well, consider this. Now that technology has accelerated the pace of change, we could be disrupted in the blink of an eye. Business models change overnight, and safe havens and markets are preparing for fundamental disruptive changes. Companies feel like inhabitants of coastal towns preparing for an oncoming hurricane, boarding their windows, but knowing the hurricane could destroy their house if it happens to stand in the path of the eye of the storm. Our 'Day After Tomorrow' comes faster than ever before in history. It's scary. It's brutal. But we must face it. And we must take it into our own hands.

Just like the *when* I described earlier, I know that this *how* – this radical long-termism – might sound completely counterintuitive. That's because our species are hardwired to live in the 'here and now', because it's our reality and managing it takes a lot of energy. 'Now' is real. The future is not. Now is 'instant gratification', a concept that is very prominent in current society. 'Now' is safe. 'Now' is very present-day, while the future is a mere specter. 'Now' is our default setting. Especially in times that are rapidly changing, so complex and so unpredictable that we do not know what will be, or where we'll be, in a few years' time.

I beg to differ. If you are the one shaping that far future reality, then you can know what it will be.

But most of us are not. We are not shaping a faraway future, a long-term version of ourselves. Most of us pretty much spend our lives thinking about 'today'. There are a million reasons, every day again, why our attention is constantly drawn to this strange maelstrom of time that we have labelled 'Today'.

Today is messy, today is chaotic, but today is very real. Today is the 112 emails you received on Monday, which you did not even think you were going to get to the Friday evening before. Today is the 'dark matter' of our universe that we don't realize sucks up most of our energy and emotions.

We would like to spend more time on 'tomorrow', though. It's hard. But we know we must. That we have to think about the 'budget of next year', or the 'organizational restructuring of the next fiscal quarter', or the 'targets of our sales forecasts'. We would like to increase our attention to Tomorrow, because tomorrow is important. Tomorrow is where our pay check will be coming from, where our customers will decide to be loyal or not, where our shareholders will decide if we are worth our salt. Tomorrow is a shadow hanging over us, always present, always urging. We grieve the fact that we don't have enough time for tomorrow.

And then there is the 'Day After Tomorrow'. It's a mythical, almost magical place, distorted by its distance. It's where our dreams, hopes and ideals live. Where one can throw off the shackles of the past, and focus on the blue oceans, the unspoiled dreaming of the future. But the 'Day After Tomorrow' is far away. And just like New Year's Resolutions where we would love to lose weight, or spend more time with the family, the 'Day After Tomorrow' ambitions often wither away very quickly. The 'Day After Tomorrow' is usually too distant for us to really worry about, spend time in and/or plan.

THE SIMPLEST MODEL IN THE WORLD

I believe this 'Day After Tomorrow' model, is the simplest one in the world. It's naively simple, actually, but I have noticed that it helps people focus. It's about dividing your attention, budget, resources, talent, etc. into three simple buckets: Today, Tomorrow and the Day After Tomorrow.

I love to ask people how much time, attention, budget and talent they spend in those three buckets. As an individual, as a team and as an organization.

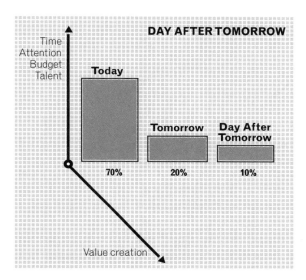

Many people tell me, just like the New Year's Resolutions, that the ideal proportion would be '70%, 20%, 10%'. Noble. And if that would be the case, there would have been no reason to create this model. You would be (and do) just fine if you spent 10% of your resources on the 'Day After Tomorrow'. Hunky dory. Fit as a fiddle.

But it rarely is the case. Most people realize, when they measure their real activities, that it's more a '93%, 7%, 0%' scenario. Despite the great and honorable intentions, those 112 emails, and next year's budget always seem to eat completely into our 'Day After Tomorrow' time.

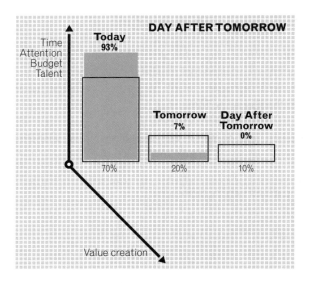

THE ISSUE IS VALUE

But don't let me tell you that Today is not important. It is, it is hugely important. Because it generates the *current* value of your activities. And Tomorrow is huge as well. Because that takes care of your *future* value.

But that incredibly small wedge of 'Day After Tomorrow' ideas, concepts, notions or inspiration, can generate *huge* amounts of *long-term value* for you, your company and your people.

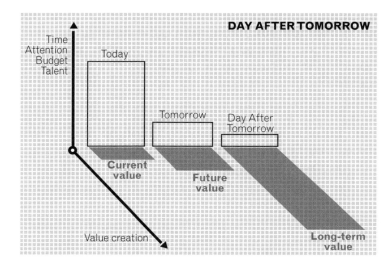

So, my thesis is quite simple: if you don't make sure that the 'Day After Tomorrow' becomes a part of how you organize yourself as an individual, if you don't embed it into the DNA of your organization, then the odds are that you won't even make it to the 'Day After Tomorrow'.

ORGANIZING FOR THE 'DAY AFTER TOMORROW'

I have observed hundreds of organizations in the past 15 years on how they tackle this exact problem of handling this 'Day After Tomorrow Deficit'. I have examined all the different ways to *organize* for the 'Day After Tomorrow', and have been able to spot patterns, and find structures and approaches that work. There is no simple solution, there is no silver bullet, but depending on where you are, who you are and what you want to do, I do believe that there is a right way to tackle the 'Day After Tomorrow'.

SOY

When I started to use this 'Day After Tomorrow' model in workshops and lectures, I noticed how it stuck in people's minds. I was told how this deceivingly simple framework helped others to start thinking more actively about the challenges ahead. They realized they had to allocate more time to reflect on their 'Day After Tomorrow'. It helped them focus on the essentials of radical change. Suffice to say that made me feel quite pleased with my ingenious contraption.

Until that ill-fated workshop with one of the largest Japanese automobile organizations in the world, I was invited to perform a day-long workshop with its top management.

The automotive industry is undergoing vast and rapid disruptive changes, from self-driving autonomous vehicles to electric cars, from the car-sharing economy to global competitive forces. It will see more change in the next ten years than it has in the past fifty. I was eager to jump in and investigate, debate and converge their thinking with this top leadership group. I was expecting to learn as much from them as they would from me, engaging in discussions on radical innovation with such a world-leading pioneer.

And I did. After a fruitful, intense and satisfying day, I was exhausted. After all the participants had thanked me for the work, I was left in the meeting room with the CEO. He pointed to the 'Today, Tomorrow, Day After Tomorrow' model that was still on one of the flip-charts, and said: "Unfortunately Mr. Hinssen, your model is incomplete".

I was stunned. How could one of the simplest models in the world possibly be wrong?

"You forgot something. Something essential." I'll never forget when he went over to the flip-chart and added a big red box to my diagram, and wrote 'SOY' in big red letters on top of it.

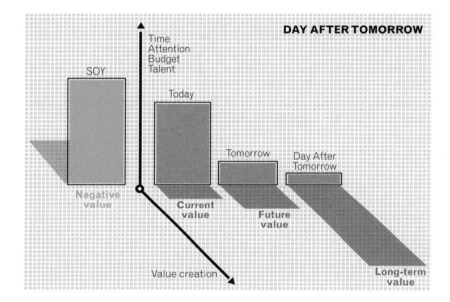

"That is the 'Shit of Yesterday' that we have to clean up every day in our organizations", was his comment as he drew steadily on. "And that creates negative energy."

When I went back to my hotel room that evening, I knew he had done me a great favor. And since then it has become a standard addition to the model.

Indeed, how much 'Mess of the Past' (MOP being the more polite term), are we trying to handle in our organizations? What is the relationship between Day After Tomorrow-thinking and the Mess of Yesterday-reality of our everyday lives? How much negative energy is drained into cleaning up the 'Mess of Yesterday'?

I'm not naive. You cannot erase the SOY in many organizations. But when we observe how disruptive (platform) players are escalating and skyrocketing away from the traditional competition, it is often because they can concentrate solely on the 'Day After Tomorrow', and are completely unbound by any legacy, SOY or MOP.

That's because disruptive startups have no past to speak of. They're brand-new, not needing to shovel away the enormous pile of crap that they have gathered over the years. And if there is any garbage to clean up (there always is), of course, startups have to throw away and clear out a lot of the failed experiments, the energy it takes is not slowed down by a worried group of tie-wearing onlookers who are trying to stop them from doing so because "we should not rush into anything we cannot turn back" or some crap (pun intended) like that.

This 'Day after Tomorrow' model forms the backdrop of this book. We will examine what types of ideas, technologies, models and concepts are shaping the 'Day After Tomorrow'. We will explore how to be relevant to customers in the 'Day After Tomorrow', and how we will devise Business Models and cultures that will thrive there. But, above all, we will study patterns, organizational arrangements and frameworks that will help you and your organizations prepare for the 'Day After Tomorrow'.

Fasten your seatbelts. It's going to be a bumpy ride. And it will be a real one. Not one where we'll be misled by 'EisenBahnScheinBewegung'.

I have another weird word for you (I collect them, I'm thinking about dedicating a museum to them): 'esprit d'escalier' or 'staircase wit', which is a French term used in English for the predicament of thinking of the perfect reply too late. Like when someone is rude to you and you have absolutely no idea how to respond, but you come up with something exceedingly witty 5 minutes after they are gone.

Well, let this 'Day After Tomorrow' model be your cure for a corporate 'esprit d'escalier' so that you won't be standing with both feet on the smoldering remains of your company's ashes, thinking "I should have done *that*". Instead, let it help you to start imagining now what you need to do to avoid that awful scenario.

Let's get cracking.

THE 'DAY AFTER TOMORROW' MODEL:
WHAT YOU NEED TO REMEMBER

Increased Speed
The rate of change is speeding up. There may be some nay-sayers out there, but if we can believe geniuses like Klaus Schwab, Peter Diamandis and John Thomas Chambers - or simply our own intuition - we are making the transition from a mostly linear business world to one that's exponential in nature.

Radical Thinking
Now, when evolution happens this fast and this profoundly, I believe that companies will only survive if they adapt the kind of long-term radical thinking that will be able to withstand the outside acceleration. I believe that the optimal division of your organization's time, talent and investments should be 70% on Today, 20% on Tomorrow and 10% on the 'Day After Tomorrow'.

When to Act?
But when should you stop thinking about your 'Day After Tomorrow' and *act* on it? When should you start cannibalizing yourself? At the time when it feels the least necessary. At the time when everything is going absolutely great: your customers are loyal, revenue is streaming in, you keep scaling successfully and the only competition is that insignificantly small disruptor that just appeared on the horizon. Just then. That's the moment you need to shift gears, because you still have the *time* (the disruptor is merely apparent, but gathering speed) and the *money* (since you're at the top of your game).

3

THE ENGINE OF OUR FUTURE

Technologies for the 'Day After Tomorrow'

This is not so much a chapter about technology as one about the driving force behind all of our futures. If you want to understand where you – as an individual and as (a part of) a company – are going, then you must be able to grasp what's driving you there.

As this is a book about radical innovation and 'Day After Tomorrow' thinking, I will obviously not focus on the technologies of 'today' - like Big Data, mobile apps, cloud computing, etc. - but on those that have the most potential for radical impact. I believe that these five below are the ones that will evolve exponentially in the coming years and completely change the name of the game. If you're not keeping an eye on them and are not investigating what they could mean for your business, you will be in trouble quite soon:

1. Artificial Intelligence (AI)
2. The Internet of Things (IoT)
3. Networked Logic: Blockchain & Smart Contracts
4. Augmented and Virtual Reality (AR & VR)
5. Quantum Computing

THE 'WRIGHT' TIME

Now, it's not because I call these 'Day After Tomorrow' technologies that they are brand-new. Those of you who are 'into' technology like me, will know that some of them have been around for quite some time now.

The field of Artificial Intelligence research was first introduced at a conference at Dartmouth College back in 1956. Not exactly new. 'Father of computer graphics' Ivan Sutherland, with the help of his student Bob Sproull, designed the very first virtual reality and augmented reality head-mounted display in 1968. Not so recent either. Richard Feynman was the first to propose a basic model for Quantum computing in 1981. The concept of a network of smart, connected devices was discussed as early as 1982 with a modified Coke machine at Carnegie Mellon University becoming the first internet-connected appliance, able to report its inventory and whether newly loaded drinks were cold or not.[1] Both slightly more recent, but still 'ancient' in terms of computing. Actually, the newest (and only new) kid on the block (pun intended) is the blockchain that was conceptualized by Satoshi Nakamoto in 2008 and even that is almost 10 years old.

What makes these 'old' technologies the engine behind our 'Day After Tomorrow' has to do with timing. The 'Wright' timing, to be precise.

The analogy I really like is the story of the Wright Brothers. They were the first humans to achieve controlled, human operated and sustained flight with a heavier-than-air machine. Their Wright Flyer made its first successful trip on the 17th of December 1903, at Kitty Hawk, North Carolina. For most people, that is the moment when we humans learned how to fly. Not really. The theory behind the heavier-than-air flight had already been developed all the way back in 1738, by Daniel Bernoulli. That is 165 years before the Wright Brothers made it happen on the beaches of North Carolina.

If you're an engineer, you will certainly have studied Bernoulli's principle. It explains how the flow of air over the shape of a wing can create enough lift to make an airplane take off. But when Daniel Bernoulli wrote it down in his book *Hydrodynamica* in 1738[2], it was just a theory: pure and beautiful mathematics and physics. A long time would pass before anyone could prove that it was correct. Bernoulli did not conceive the airplane. But he did describe the fluid dynamics principles that would be needed to build carburetors and airplane wings. It took the brilliance and guts of the Wright Brothers to apply it.

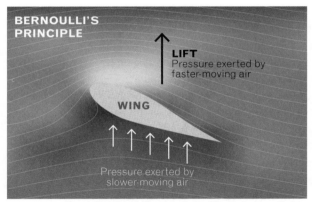

Source: 'How Does A Wing Actually Work?' by Veritasium on Youtube

The Wright Brothers had been trying to make airplanes work for years. The problem was that they needed an engine - a very powerful one - to drive the propeller that could 'pull' the plane forward fast enough to create enough air-flow over the wings and generate enough lifting power to get it off the ground. Gasoline engines were available thanks to the burgeoning automobile industry. But powerful engines were still too heavy at the time and would make the con-traption impossible to get off the ground.

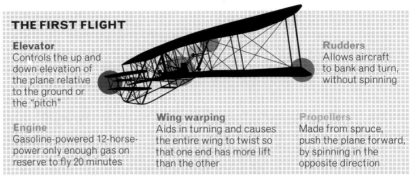

THE FIRST FLIGHT

Elevator
Controls the up and down elevation of the plane relative to the ground or the "pitch"

Engine
Gasoline-powered 12-horse-power only enough gas on reserve to fly 20 minutes

Wing warping
Aids in turning and causes the entire wing to twist so that one end has more lift than the other

Rudders
Allows aircraft to bank and turn, without spinning

Propellers
Made from spruce, push the plane forward, by spinning in the opposite direction

Inspired by the infographic: The First Flight by Katie Schmitty (2013)

The real breakthrough that was key to the Wright Brothers' success came in the form of aluminum (which was still very rarely used for engine blocks at the time): an extremely powerful, efficient and lightweight custom-built engine made of aluminum, to be precise. The impressive 12 horsepower output that it produced was just enough to make the Wright Flyer take off. All it took was perseverance, guts and the use of a new material.

In the world of these 'Day After Tomorrow' technologies, I believe we are exactly at that Kitty Hawk, North Carolina, 1903 moment. For the past few years, we have understood the theory behind them, as well as their mathematics. But they all lacked the equivalent of the 12-hp aluminum engine to make them work. Until now that is… With the advent of cloud computing – where we can stitch together the power of thousands, or even hundreds of thousands of machines – we are finally arriving at producing the tools powerful enough to make smart, connected machines that can think independently and create new worlds.

We now take a plane like we take a bus. Imagine what the next twenty years will give us in the worlds of VR, AR, AI, IoT and quantum computing. Then you probably understand why you'll need to know about them.

#1 DAT-TECH:
Artificial Intelligence and Machine Learning
When Machines Start Thinking for Themselves

Computers are getting smarter. Much smarter. Much faster. While a 'smart' computer system like the one in *Star Trek* was still science fiction a short while ago, we are seeing rapid development in the world of Artificial Intelligence. An evolution that is turning science fiction into reality faster than you can say "I'm sorry Dave, I'm afraid I can't do that" (as 'Hal' said in *A Space Odyssey*).

The concept of 'Artificial Intelligence' has been around for quite some time, though. In 1956, the first conference on the subject was organized on the campus of Dartmouth College: a gathering that is now widely considered to be the birth of AI. It is where the field got its name, received its mission, and where the major players gathered for the first time to address the challenges ahead.

Those who attended – amongst whom tech rock stars Marvin Minsky and Claude Shannon – would become the leaders of AI research for decades to come. These geniuses did not get everything right, though. They, for instance, forecasted that by 1985 "machines will be capable of doing any work Man can do", and, in *Life Magazine*, Marvin Minsky, predicted that, by the end of the 20th century, "We will have a machine with the general intelligence of an average human being".[3]

Well. Not really.

By no means have computers reached a 'general intelligence' today. The majority of us humans are still baffled by how incredibly stupid they are and how horribly slow to understand our commands. We're frustrated by the ignorance when we have to instruct a computerized system in a bank or an airline what we want to do. But we're getting there. Slowly but steadily. In March 2016, the neural network[4] DeepMind (owned by Google) defeated the best Go player in the world, Lee Sedol. That was a true landmark in the history of Artificial Intelligence, because of the utter complexity of this board game.

But back to the Dartmouth conference. Afterwards, a massive amount of money poured into the field. The government, the military and the industrial players all loved the idea of computers that could think. Overexcited at the prospect of machines that could be like human beings – but better and cheaper – they started sending truckloads of cash to the researchers, engineers and universities.

WINTER IS COMING

But then disappointment followed. The reason was simple: there was simply not enough computing power nor memory to run all the advanced ideas and radical concepts of the AI researchers. These were the days when companies like Atari and Commodore started building home computers that had 64 kilobytes of memory, and the systems that the AI researchers had at their disposal were not that much more powerful. Tackling the challenges of AI with the computers in that time was like trying to get to space with sticks and bones. No go.

That's when the first 'AI winter' occurred in the late seventies: a period in which Artificial Intelligence research made horribly slow progress, and frustrated many scientists in the field. Pessimism in the AI community was followed by criticism in the press, followed by severe cutbacks in funding, leading, ultimately, to the end of fundamental research. Backers felt misled, deeming that the AI researchers had grossly over-promised and massively under-delivered.

But Moore's law was on their side. Since the first AI winter was caused simply because there was not enough computing horsepower, it was just a matter of time before there would be enough of it. This had the exact same dynamic as the second half of the chessboard we talked about earlier. Computers were getting more powerful every day, computer chips started to become incredibly strong and we were able to build 'parallel' computers that worked in harmony. Big computer manufacturers like IBM understood this. They had not given up, and dedicated even more resources to their genius teams working on the dream of computer intelligence. One of the highlights happened in 1997 when IBM's Deep Blue finally defeated Kasparov, the best chess player in the world. Since then, no grand-master has been able to win from a computer.

So, the AI winter thawed into spring again. Only eight years after Deep Blue defeated Kasparov - in 2005 - a Stanford Robot on the Grand DARPA Challenge drove a car autonomously over an unrehearsed desert trail of more than 130 miles. Two years later, a team from Carnegie Mellon University drove a car autonomously through an urban environment for more than 50 miles whilst tackling traffic hazards and adhering to all traffic regulations.

A SYSTEM THAT PROGRAMS ITSELF

The year 2014 was another highlight: Google acquired DeepMind, a British Artificial Intelligence startup from the University College of London for about USD 500 million. Not bad. The massive neural network DeepMind is truly fascinating: it combines the very best of machine learning and systems neuroscience into an incredibly powerful machine that can learn from experience as we humans do, but much faster: their system is not pre-programmed. It 'programs' itself. We're beginning to see the rise of true artificial intelligence.

Today we see that companies like Facebook are deploying chat-bots that are essentially machines carrying out conversations. We see companies like Disney using algorithms to engage with users on social media who want to travel to Disney theme parks, and the customers have no idea that they are talking to a computer instead of a human. Artificial Intelligence agents can even invent their very own language to communicate how to best get a job done.[5]

In 2016, Google unveiled their Google Home product, which is essentially an AI interface to the internet. It understands natural language and simple English questions like: "What is the weather forecast for tomorrow?". But it can also handle more complex challenges like: "Book me an Uber to get to the cinema". Soon, we'll be able to throw complex tasks to these AI interfaces like: "Check the timing of my upcoming flight to Houston, and make sure there is an Uber to pick me up on time". The AI device will not only understand our questions, but will make sure to calculate the traffic on the way to the airport.

Products like Amazon Alexa, Google Home and others will bring AI towards a mainstream audience. At one end of the spectrum you have the Self-driving Ubers and Autonomous Drones, that will trigger a huge breakthrough in the coming years. And, at the other end, sit back and watch AI become the main-stream interface for consumers. In just a short period we have seen 'digital first' emerge as the preferred way to communicate as customers evolve towards 'mobile first'. But as my nexxworks Partner Steven Van Belleghem says, very soon 'AI first' will replace 'mobile first' as the preferred consumer-facing inter-action. Just think of the impact this change in interface will have for traditional search engines and their advertising models in the coming years.

But the possibilities are truly mind-blowing when we think of a world where machines can be as smart as humans. Or even smarter... Nick Bostrom, of the 'Future of Humanity Institute' in Oxford, is studying exactly that: what will happen when machines become smarter than human beings?

His research shows that we are on a path where eventually machine brains will surpass human brains in 'general intelligence'. When this happens, they will reach 'superintelligence' and learn better, faster and more efficiently than humans. These super intelligent machines will 'evolve' faster than humans and improve their own capabilities much faster than any human computer scientist. Superintelligence could create an evolution at a scale and speed unlike anything we've ever seen as humans. Neat.

Oh yeah, and it could also mean the end of human beings. Less neat. According to Bostrom, the outcome of superintelligence could put the fate of humanity in the hands of machines that are a lot smarter than us, which could potentially be an existential catastrophe for us humans.

Today we see more and more concern. In 2015, an open letter – signed by more than 1,000 eminent scientists and thinkers, including Stephen Hawking, Steve Wozniak and Elon Musk at the 'International Joint Conference on Arti-ficial Intelligence' – urged for a global ban on the use and development of fully autonomous weapons. Imagine how 'killer robots' could become super-intelligent! The world of science fiction suddenly becomes extremely existential.

WINTER IS LEAVING

Many scientists have come to believe that in these recent years the 'Winter of AI' is truly coming to an end. Moving into a 'Springtime' euphoria in the field, we see a revival of interest and real tangible progress. AI has learned how to bluff at poker, analyze financial deals in seconds (while this used to take 360,000 human hours[6]), discern cats from dogs in pictures, paint, write source code, make music, write books, create films (the latter two need some fine-tuning, agreed), cook, perceive people with suicidal tendencies on Facebook, make cars drive by themselves, and that's merely a fraction of what's going on. If the history of Artificial Intelligence was written by George R.R. Martin, the creator of *Game of Thrones*, the one-liner would clearly be: "Winter is leaving". As I stated in the introduction, we are at the 'Wright' time of AI. In 2016, DeepMind could beat Lee Sedol, the best Go player in the world, because, for the first time, we had enough computing power to make that happen. But we knew *how* for a long time.

I'm a very big fan of Google X's recipe for innovation They take a *huge* problem, find a *radical* solution, and then apply a *breakthrough* technology to achieve that. That's how they invent 'moonshot' technologies, which they hope might someday make the world a radically better place. In the Google X paradigm, the *huge problem* AI-researchers are trying to solve is to make machines that think. The *radical* solution is the use of layered neural networks with deep reinforced learning. But the *breakthrough* technology to make it all work is the advent of cloud computing. Imagine what the next twenty years will give us in the world of Artificial Intelligence now that we have the computing power to make it work.

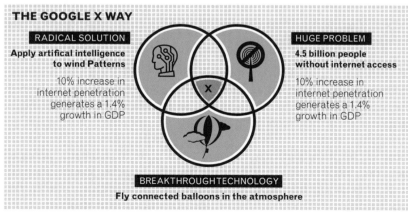

Source: Google X

Andrew Ng – formerly in charge of the 'Google Brain' project and former chief scientist of Baidu (the largest Chinese competitor to Google) – perhaps describes it best: "AI is the new electricity. Just as 100 years ago electricity transformed industry after industry, AI will now do the same."[7] Do you know how it can power your company in the coming years? If not, it's the 'Wright' time to investigate it.

#2 DAT-TECH
Internet of Things,
and the Fourth Industrial Revolution
When Things Wake Up

> *"Eventually everything connects - people, ideas, objects. The quality of the connections is the key to quality per se."* **CHARLES EAMES**

But it's not just our computers that will become smart, even smarter than humans. We are at the threshold of the 'Internet of Things' (IoT) where all devices will become intelligent, connected and communicative. Cars, washing machines, street lights, televisions, glasses, desks, door locks, thermostats, kitchen appliances, water pipes, clothes, food packages: name any device, one day they will all probably start seeing, hearing and talking.

The ever-smiling design thinker and Autodesk Chief Pollutant Mickey McManus is one of the smartest people I know. He believes that the IoT is 'just' a part of an ultra-complex and highly organic trinity that will have a massive impact on the way we work and live:
1. the Internet of Things;
2. digital manufacturing;
3. and machine learning.

TRILLIONS OF CONNECTED THINGS

Mickey believes that the number of intelligent connected devices in the IoT will completely shift the scale of 'things' to a level that is unprecedented in human history. Today we're used to millions and billions. We have just under 10 billion people in the world, and we've even built organizations that have more than a million employees for example. But soon now, the unbounded complexity and scale of the IoT, will open up a world of trillions.

The only way we will be able to manage that scale, according to McManus, is by copying nature. Nature has been running *massive* mature, ultra-complex, resilient information systems for (ironically) billions of years. These have the most effective memory, storage and communication systems for handling this scale of trillions. Just to give one small example: our human body has approximately 37 trillion cells that seem to be working together pretty well (most of the time). Nature can teach us how to design an ecology of things that can handle trillions.[8]

DIGITAL MANUFACTURING – IF YOU CAN THINK IT, YOU CAN MAKE IT

The advent of fast (we're not completely there yet) and efficient 3D printing will allow us to create objects in ways that were completely impossible before. It allows us to transform atoms into bits. Basically, we're pretty close to the point where we will be able to materialize what we think.

Just like the world of word processing revolutionized our offices, and the advent of laser printers allowed us to unleash our own creativity onto the world, we now have the possibility to build anything we want using 3D printers. We can print retainers, organs, DNA-strands, even large structures like bridges and buildings. It allows us to completely rethink supply chains, where instead of shipping products, we can ship materials that can be stored and transported a lot more efficiently.

This collision between the IoT world of trillions and digital manufacturing will have a huge impact. We'll be able to manufacture whatever we want ... and then, in the next phase, we'll wake them up: they will become connected and smarter.

MACHINE LEARNING & THINGS WAKING UP

That's where machine learning comes in. One of the best examples are Qualcomm's 'Zeroth' processors, which mimic the human brain and nervous system: these make machine learning and deep learning available into all sorts of small devices and objects. They allow devices to have 'embedded cognition driven by brain-inspired computing' which basically means that IoT devices will all have tiny little brains connected to one another into a big brain. Qualcomm is embedding these neural processing chips into 3D-printed robotic assemblies that could dynamically detect patterns and shapes.

This trifecta of trillions of IoT devices, digital manufacturing and machine learning is bringing digitization to a whole new level. Mickey believes that "Once things get connected, and wake up, we will all live in this sea of information.

Instead of having information that lives 'inside' computers, we will now have us living 'in' a sea of information all around us."[9]

INDUSTRY 4.0

This combination of the IoT, digital manufacturing and machine learning will usher us into the era of the Fourth Industrial Revolution.

Surprisingly, a big part of the 'Industry 4.0' discourse did not originate in Silicon Valley. Instead, it emerged in Berlin. That's because the German economy has been built on making things: cars, toys, turbines, trains, power plants, high-end power tools, etc. If the world of 'making' is going to be disrupted, the Germans understood that they had better think of a new strategy.

Industry 4.0 could digitize the entire manufacturing sector, which would be driven by four disruptions:
1. the spectacular rise in computing power and connectivity;
2. the emergence of analytics and big data capabilities;
3. new forms of human-machine interaction, such as augmented reality;
4. and breakthroughs in transferring digital instructions to the physical world, such as advanced robotics and 3-D printing. Bits to atoms, in other words.

While Industry 3.0 had a clear focus on the automation of single machines and processes, Industry 4.0 is about the end-to-end digitization of all physical assets and the integration of all partners in the value chain into a vast digital ecosystem. It's what happens when manufacturing meets the era of the network, where computers and automation come together in entirely new ways. Robotics will be connected remotely to computer systems equipped with machine-learning algorithms that can learn and control the robotics with very little input from human operators.

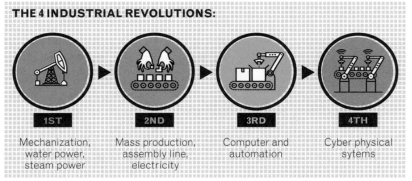

THE 4 INDUSTRIAL REVOLUTIONS:

1ST	2ND	3RD	4TH
Mechanization, water power, steam power	Mass production, assembly line, electricity	Computer and automation	Cyber physical sytems

Source: https://en.wikipedia.org/wiki/Industry_4.0

The benefits could be vast. In very dangerous working environments for example, the health and safety of human workers could be improved dramatically. Supply chains could be more efficiently controlled when there is data at every level of the manufacturing and delivery process. Computer controls could produce much more reliable and consistent productivity and output. And the results for many businesses could be increased revenues, market share and profits.

Personally, I can't wait for the world of Trillions to arrive.

#3 DAT-TECH:
Networked Logic
The Internet of Trust

BITCOIN

Today the term 'bitcoin' is widely known. This new currency has spawned a whole new field of technology, that will completely transform the way we view the world of transactions. The underlying mechanism that makes cryptocurrencies like bitcoin possible, is called the 'blockchain', and it holds the potential to revolutionize our world of business.

Let's start at the very beginning. A very good place to start. When you read you begin with ABC. When you talk about blockchain you begin with Satoshi,… Satoshi. (Ten points if you get the reference. No idea why this popped into my head, though.) In 2008, an anonymous scientist and hacker with the nickname Satoshi Nakamoto described the concept of bitcoin, and blockchain, for the very first time. He published a paper, and in an accompanying email he said: "I've been working on a new electronic cash system that's fully peer-to-peer, with no trusted third party."

The statement would be the equivalent of Isaac Newton e-mailing his friends: "Just came up with an interesting idea this afternoon after an apple fell on my head. Calling it 'gravity'".

WHAT'S UNDERNEATH THE ICEBERG

In his paper, Nakamoto described an electronic cash currency he called bitcoin that could be used like any other currency, like a Euro, or a Pound or a Dollar. Today you can pay with bitcoin on many e-commerce sites. You can convert dollars into bitcoins, and use them. And you can convert bitcoins back into whatever currency you like. But the beauty of this seminal work was not bitcoin. It was the blockchain, the part of the iceberg below the water line. If the tip of the iceberg is bitcoin, then everything underwater is blockchain.

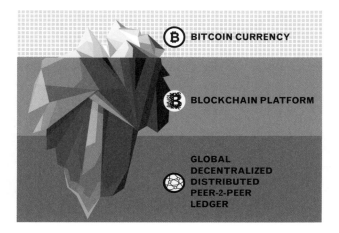

The blockchain is a mathematical concept, a continuously growing list of ordered records, called blocks. And it is essential to understand its fundamentals in order to grasp its implications. The blockchain allows the creation of trusted mechanisms that are incredibly safe, robust and secure. And it solves the mathematical problem called the 'The Byzantine Generals' Problem'.

This riddle was first described in 1982, and centers around a group of generals, each commanding a portion of the Byzantine army that encircled a city. They want to attack the city, but the complication is that not all generals trust each other: there are traitors amongst them. The important thing is that *every* general has to agree on a common decision, because a half-hearted attack by just a few generals would cause everything to fall apart.

The puzzle is a difficult mathematical conundrum, and it deals with a fundamental problem of how to build trusted networks that allow for secure decisions to be made. Like when to attack a city, or how to trust a financial transaction.

Satoshi Nakamoto solved the Byzantine Generals' Problem with the concept of a blockchain: a chain of blocks, that keeps on growing, and contains all the records of all the transactions. Every block has a time stamp, so you know when the block has been added, and a link to a previous block. If the blocks are distributed to all the parties involved in what is known as a peer-to-peer network, you can make the blockchain extremely fault tolerant. Peer-to-peer means that everyone in the network is connected to everyone else, and that there is no *central* repository. If you were to have a central database, and someone tampers with that, trust would be lost. But because everyone in the peer-to-peer network has a copy of all the blocks on the blockchain, it is almost impossible to compromise.

I'M GOING ON A TRIP AND I'M GOING TO BRING

Let me illustrate this by the best way that I had the blockchain explained to me, ... by means of a silly game. If you have children, at one point you will have entertained them on a seven-hour drive to the mountains with this kind of triggering phrase "I am going on a trip and I'm going to bring, ... an umbrella". And then the person next to you in the car says: "Ah yes ! I am going on a trip and I'm going to bring, an umbrella, and ... a suitcase.". The next person continues the list, and says: "I am going on a trip and I'm going to bring, an umbrella, a suitcase, and ... a cat". You know the drill. The list of items grows, and grows, and the moment that someone makes a mistake, they're out, and leave the game.

Blockchain is exactly like that. All parties in the peer-to-peer network have a copy of the database of records, the blockchain, which grows with a new block every time. And every new block incorporates all the transactions that have occurred in the past in a clever mathematical way. Were someone to compromise a node in the network, say hack the database of transactions, all the others would immediately notice this. They would be sure to eliminate this node from the game, and kick them off the blockchain network.

I also like the definition that Arno Laeven, the chief blockchain thinker of Philips uses: "Blockchain is an immutable, tamper-proof and transparent shared record of events". [10]

In essence, the blockchain is a Global, Decentralized, Distributed, Peer-to-peer Ledger. Let's chop this up to make it easier to understand:

Global. Just like the internet, the blockchain knows no boundaries. You can implement private blockchains, say for a particular company, or for a particular industry. But the blockchain that is used to run the bitcoin cryptocurrency is a global phenomenon.

Decentralized and Distributed. The blockchain has no central database, no central repository. It's a true network of nodes, and the fact that it has no 'center' means that it's not as easily compromised or hacked.

Peer-to-peer: the various nodes of the network communicate with one another. They are constantly humming to the rhythm of "I am going on a trip and I'm going to bring my umbrella, and my ...". All nodes are connected, peer-to-peer, so that when there is a wrong note, they can understand that this could indicate a false transaction.

Ledger: essentially, the blockchain is a system of records. It 'keeps' a ledger of transactions, meticulously logging which bitcoin goes to which node in the network. It's a bookkeeper's dream.

A BLOCKCHAIN COMPANY

Very soon after the introduction of bitcoin, some clever people started to realize that, in theory, you could use the mechanism of the blockchain to transfer a lot more than just money. You could use the blockchain to securely move stocks and bonds. In theory, you could put the deeds to a house on the blockchain. You can also track physical goods – like diamonds – via the blockchain. Blockchain cuts out the middlemen: it enables value to be exchanged without unnecessary and perhaps untrustworthy intermediaries.

And why stop there? You could actually put a lot more complex agreements and functionalities on something as solid as the blockchain. One of the most interesting developments comes from a company called 'Ethereum'. Its founders realized that you could actually put a piece of code on the blockchain: a program, a piece of logic. Just like records of bitcoin transactions are kept securely on the blockchain, Smart Contracts would allow you to put 'logic' on the blockchain, and then execute them.

Let me explain. In essence, Ethereum turned the blockchain into a programmable platform. It aims to become the 'operating system' of the world for logic.

If you want to understand this evolution, it's like the very old first versions of websites which just had text and images. You could only look at a website. But when we introduced the programming language JavaScript, we were able to build all sorts of fascinating and interactive online applications, and the web became a lot more interesting and alive.

In essence, Ethereum is a scripting language for the blockchain to develop new applications. You could use Ethereum to build entirely new supply chain applications, or make a blockchain to reassemble the stock market, or even build completely new digital corporations and run them beyond the jurisdiction of any government entity. Once placed on a blockchain, these applications called

'Smart Contracts' could exist in an environment where software, data and financial assets interact without friction.

Actually, anything for which we now use 'written agreements' could become logic. Every legal agreement could become a 'smart contract' that lives on the blockchain. Just imagine what would happen if they all become logical code that can be checked, matched and automatically executed as smart contracts. What would that mean for the armies of lawyers raking in substantial sums of money by writing documents that hardly no one (except for them) can understand?

A LAYER OF TRUST

William Mougayar wrote an excellent field guide to the wonderful world of the blockchain in his book *The Business Blockchain: Promise, Practice, and Application of the Next Internet Technology*[11]. He wrote: "The blockchain is the second significant overlay on top of the Internet, just as the Web was that first layer back in 1990. That new layer is mostly about trust, so we could call it the 'trust layer'."

This is exactly why *The Economist* put the blockchain on the cover as 'The Trust Machine'[12]. The blockchain has the potential to transform how people and businesses cooperate. A shared, trusted, public ledger that everyone can inspect, but which no single user controls.

According to Mougayar: "Blockchains loosen up trust, which has been in the hands of central institutions like banks, policymakers, clearing houses, governments and large corporations. It essentially allows people to evade these old control points."

He makes a strong point: "Today, we Google for everything, mostly information or products. But tomorrow, we will perform the equivalent of 'googling' to verify records, identities, authenticity, rights, work done, titles, contracts and other valuable asset-related processes on the blockchain." In essence the blockchain could become the New Google. It's the internet, plus trust: The Internet of Trust.

We're witnessing a historic pivotal moment in the still very short-lived history of the internet. The emergence of the blockchain is of the same level of importance as the introduction of the World Wide Web in 1995. It will make the internet more decentralized, more open, more secure, more private, more robust and more accessible.

But it can, and probably will, bring with it the complexity of radically new technology and the dangers of unbounded malignant complexity when falling into the wrong hands. And, no doubt, it will bring a period of radical disruption for those who choose to ignore it.

#4 DAT-TECH:
Extended Reality: AR and VR
Altering the Fabric of Reality

The way we experience and 'see' the world is fundamentally going to change. Technologies like Augmented and Virtual Reality have the potential to completely change the way we interact with customers and with our environment.

But it's not an easy path. The road of extending our reality as humans seems to be paved with commercial failures. As recently as 2015 we witnessed the epic failure of the first version of Google Glass – an optical head-mounted display designed in the shape of a pair of eyeglasses. Back in 2012, it was ballyhooed as the 'smartphone for your eyes', and the launch happened in grandiose Google style: a group of skydivers wearing Google Glass jumped from a zeppelin above San Francisco, and streamed their visual experiences to the World Wide Web.

GLASSHOLES

Originally, the team at Google X who devised the glasses wanted to develop a 'ubiquitous computer' – a computer that would always be with you, but without hindering your normal interactions with the world. They wanted to build a system where you didn't have to carry a bulky laptop, a tablet or even a smartphone. They wanted to have a computer available for your every wish and demand. Something you wouldn't notice, but that would enhance your reality.

The hype was immense: Google started selling a prototype of Google Glass to qualified 'Glass Explorers' in the US at the beginning of 2013 for the hefty price of USD 1,500. For a while, you would see all the Google executives donning a Google Glass in their public performances. And the other early adopters were very eager to show them off at parties, receptions and conventions. These obnoxious posers were quickly dubbed 'Glassholes'.

But the product was a disappointment. It was released way too early to the general public. It lacked power, its batteries ran out very quickly, the interactions were clumsy and awkward, and the overall experience, well, 'sucked'. The product quickly faded from view and became somewhat of a mockery, one of the first few visible failures of the infallible Google.

I personally believe that the Google Glass experiment was a marker for the future. It was truly an embryonic product, but to dismiss the context of augmented reality by dissing Google Glass is pure foolishness. When you saw a Commodore 64 back in 1981, it would have been easy to dismiss it as a toy, a trivial trinket, and completely miss the development that would lead to the explosion of smartphones on this planet 30 years later. Ditto for Google Glass. True, it was flawed because it was so young, but the promise of Augmented Reality is not going to die down because of that minor hiccup.

In the past few years, the field of Virtual and Augmented Reality has been alive with new startups, and an enormous amount of venture capital has been thrown at them in this domain.

'Google Glass' was just the beginning of the 'Extended Reality' progression. Microsoft is betting big time on its 'HoloLens' Augmented Reality technology: it makes the company look pretty sexy with its amazing demos. Google, and particularly the Google executives are betting big time on 'Magic Leap', the brain-child of Rony Abovitz who founded the startup in South Florida, and raised more than USD 1.4 billion to fund its development (though the company has been shrouded in extreme secrecy since it was founded in 2011). Besides these juggernauts, many smaller niche players have emerged, companies like Meta Spaceglasses, zSpace and Daqri.

But the biggest splash in the Virtual Reality pool was caused by the massive cannonball of Mark Zuckerberg when he plunked down USD 2 billion for Oculus Rift to focus on Virtual Reality.

Zuckerberg is a true believer: "Imagine enjoying a court-side seat at a game, studying in a classroom of students and teachers all over the world or consulting with a doctor face-to-face—just by putting on goggles in your home. Virtual Reality was once the dream of science fiction. But the internet was also once a dream, and so were computers and smartphones."[13]

A (POKE)MONSTER SUCCESS

The general public got a taste of the world of Augmented Reality when, in the summer of 2016, the world suddenly went absolutely nuts about the 'PokemonGo' game – a collaboration between Niantic Labs and Nintendo.

PokemonGo took the world by storm: it was freely downloadable, and the players were required to react with the real world in order to play. Overnight we suddenly saw hordes of people running around streets, parks, beaches and even people's yards with their phones out 'looking for Pokemons'. I believe this was a pivotal moment. PokemonGo showed the world what Augmented Reality could do for gaming, but that was just the beginning.

Essentially the concepts of Augmented and Virtual Reality were conceived many years ago, but we lacked the horsepower to make it happen. We needed the power of smartphones to make Pokemon Go a reality, and even then, we were pushing the boundaries of what these phones could do.

AUGMENTING THE INDUSTRY

But perhaps the real power of extended reality will not come from the consumer world, although the applications in the realm of gaming are truly incredible. No, the biggest growth might come from industry. Constantly giving workers an extra layer of information on their activities might prove to be the killer application for extended reality.

Just imagine that employees in an industrial process have 'overlays' that show them which items are to be inspected, which items should be picked and where they should be placed. Augmented Reality could guide employees, make them much more efficient, and provide them with information in the 'blink of an eye' instead of 'at their fingertips'. No more need for clumsy interfaces like computer screens, or a mouse, but just constant and relevant information wherever you look.

I believe we are just about to enter a new paradigm where our reality will be altered significantly, and permanently. The way we will interact with the world, and with technology, will never be quite the same again. Companies such as Microsoft with the HoloLens, Google with Magic Leap and Facebook with Oculus Rift will transform how we perceive, and how we interact in society and with customers. And it will make the time where we thought a computer mouse was a revolution seem like ancient history.

UTOPIA OR DYSTOPIA?

I'm convinced that there are two sides to this evolution. A utopian future for sure. Telepresence will allow us to communicate as if we are in the same room, although we could be continents away. Traveling to remote places will happen from the comfort of our own homes, and we will experience nature, culture, art and architecture like never before in history. Imagine how we could redefine education by showing our kids exactly what we mean. How we could transform their understanding of geography, history and even sciences. Just imagine how we could experience sports and games, like we are actually part of the action. I can't wait!

But the dystopian side is there as well. If I see how addictive the Minecraft game – with just its crude 8-bit graphics that look like something from the 1980s – is to my 13-year old son, can you imagine how habit-forming the complete immersion of Virtual or Augmented Reality will be? It could create a pandemic addiction to these extensions of reality unlike anything we've ever encountered.

There is no way back, though. Our realities will be altered and extended in the 'Day After Tomorrow', more profoundly than ever before. It will allow us unlimited creativity to conjure up any world, and experience it to the fullest. But the winners won't be the ones who just focus on technology. The winners will be the ones who understand that the design of the human-computer interaction will be key.

#5 DAT-TECH:
Quantum Computing
When Digital Becomes Quantum

> *"If quantum mechanics hasn't profoundly shocked you, you haven't understood it yet."* **NIELS BOHR**

Perhaps the most jaw-dropping 'Day After Tomorrow' technology is the world of quantum computing. It could completely transform the way we think about technology, unleashing computing power that is several magnitudes bigger than any device we have today.

But it could also utterly and completely fail. The jury's still out on this one …

FAITH NO MOORE

The chips inside our computers and smartphones have used the very same fundamental transistor technology ever since the 1960s. It's pretty crazy when you think of that. Yes, their capacity has grown immensely, doubling every 18 months as described in Moore's law. But the problem is that Moore's prediction seems to be hitting a dead end. At the very least it's running out of steam.

First of all, the physical limits are getting in the way. The current state of the art is producing transistors that are only 14 nanometers wide: billionths of a meter. We will probably be able to shrink the transistors on a chip to just five nano-meters, about the thickness of a cell membrane, but that's probably the limit. The problem is not just getting the things to be smaller and smaller, it's also more and more difficult to get rid of the heat that these processors produce.[14] Ever noticed that your laptop heats up in your lap, and its fan starts spinning like crazy, as you're playing more and more YouTube videos on your screen? More processing means more heat, and it's very tricky to remove this heat from processors that are getting ever more powerful.

If we'd shrink transistors even more than five nanometers, let's say to two nano-meters, the transistors would only be 10 atoms wide. And when things get this small, it's unlikely that they'd operate reliably. Any disturbance greatly affects the reliability of the system. That's because, once we get to this scale, we start to get close to the world of quantum physics. Quantum physics is essentially the 'science of the very small'. Normal physics (or classical physics, if you may), has been essentially untouched since it was put in its definitive form by Isaac Newton. It worked quite nicely to describe most of the things around us. Apples falling from trees, cars crashing into walls, engines and gears, people playing tennis. All the normal things could be described without a flaw.

THE MOST AMAZING COMPUTER IN THE WORLD

But when things go really, really fast (near the speed of light), the 'classic' rules of physics don't work anymore. And this field led to the development of the 'Theory of General Relativity', as pioneered by Albert Einstein. Now, when things are very, very small, the world of physics is fundamentally different. That's the world of Quantum physics, one of the most mysterious and counter-intuitive branches of science out there.

Some believe that this 'crazy weird' science could be used to build a computer, the most amazing computer in the world. Richard Feynman was the first to come up with a basic model of a quantum computer when he introduced the concept in 1981, during a lecture at the California Institute of Technology in Pasadena, California.

The field of quantum prequired a whole new set of mathematical constructs in order to get a grip on the interactions of subatomic particles. It required a whole new 'language' to understand the dynamics when you break apart an atom. And, according to Feynman, it would also require a completely new kind of computer, a quantum computer.

As with so many examples in 'Day After Tomorrow' technologies, the result of the research into quantum computers has been a string of colossal failures and incredibly slow progress. As a matter of fact, the rate of progress was so painfully slow that sceptics often compared quantum computing to fusion energy: a truly revolutionary technology that is 20 years away, and always will be.

But what is it exactly? Well, the essence of quantum computing consists of two fundamental concepts in the world of quantum mechanics, namely 'superposition' and 'entanglement'. It gets a bit complex here, but bear with me. It will be worth it. (And don't worry if you don't completely understand it. You'll be in good company with geniuses like Richard Feynman, Seth Lloyd and Niels Bohr).

The first property, quantum superposition, is the cornerstone of quantum mechanics.

ONE AND ZERO AT THE SAME TIME

Traditional digital computers work by manipulating 'bits' that exist in one of only two states: a 0 or 1. But quantum computers are *not* limited to just two states, they encode information in 'quantum bits', called 'qubits' in the parlay of quantum computers: these are a superposition of both one and zero. Simply put: they can be a 1 AND a 0... at the same time.

Quantum computers can store much more information in those 'qubits' than bits, which are just 1 or 0. A qubit can be conceptualized like an imaginary sphere. Whereas a classical digital bit can be in two states – at either of the two poles of the sphere – a qubit can exist at any point on the sphere. This means a computer using qubits can store a huge amount more information than a classical digital computer, while consuming a lot less energy than the latter. Since a quantum computer made of qubits can contain all these multiple states simultaneously, it has the potential to be millions of times more powerful, even more so than today's most powerful digital supercomputers like Sunway TaihuLight and Tianhe-2.

The second property, quantum entanglement, is a phenomenon that occurs when pairs or groups of particles interact in such a way that the quantum state of each particle cannot be described independently of the others. It essentially means that there is a 'connection' between the particles, and the quantum state must be described for the entire system as a whole.

In order to follow Feynman's dream, the extremely bizarre concepts of super-position and entanglement are giving us some new avenues to think about in computing, with some unique characteristics.

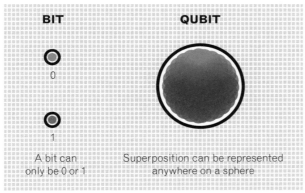

Source: Tahmid Mostafa 'Classical computer & quantum computing' via www.emaze.com

In short: the superposition concept allows qubits to have a value of not just 0 or 1, but both states at the same time, thus enabling simultaneous computa-tion. The entanglement concept enables one qubit to share its state with others separated in space, creating a sort of super-superposition, where processing capability effectively doubles with every qubit.

Say you want to run a computing algorithm with five entangled qubits in a quan-tum computer, then this quantum computer can do 32 (two to the power of five) computations *all at once*. In comparison: a classical (digital) computer would have to perform those 32 computations in succession. That is an enormous, and exponential, increase in computing power.

If you had a quantum computer at your disposal of just 300 entangled qubits, then you could, theoretically, sustain more parallel computations than there are atoms in the universe.

DARTH VADER'S FRIDGE

At the end of 2016, the Canadian D-Wave systems announced that they would start the development of a quantum computer with 2,000 qubits. One that would be 500 to 1,000 times faster than any computer on the planet today.

The quantum computer they developed looks a bit like a really big deep-freezer, as if it had been commissioned by Darth Vader. It's a huge black box, ten feet high, with big futuristic white letters that spell out 'D-Wave'. Inside, there's a massive refrigeration system to cool the D-Wave chip to 0.015 degrees above absolute zero. In the very heart of the machine is a chip made up of a grid of hundreds of tiny niobium[15] loops. These serve as the qubits – the soul of the machine.

The rest is basically high-end engineering to keep the outside from disturbing the quantum interactions. The shielding of the machine is such that inside the black box, there is a vacuum at a pressure 10 billion times lower than atmospheric pressure and the Earth's magnetic field has been reduced by less than a 50,000[th]. Surrounding the chip is an inverted pyramid of gold-plated copper disks to draw off any heat, and to keep vibration and any other energy from disturbing the quantum heart.

Oh, and they cost between USD 10,000,000 and USD 15,000,000 a piece, in case you were wondering where you could buy one.

D-WAVE'S 'QUANPETITION'

Google has been using the D-Wave quantum computer to train image-recognizing algorithms, to make better AI-algorithms, and to help in the fine-tuning of the driverless car algorithms. But Google is also working on a quantum computer of its own.

There's actually a massive race going on between the big players. IBM has been working on quantum computing for a long time. In 2017, it released a 5-qubit quantum computer accessible through the cloud for the general public to run experiments and test applications. IBM calls it the Quantum Experience, and it is making quantum computing available via the cloud to anyone interested, thus making it easier for researchers and the scientific community to discover new applications for this technology. That's a lot less than USD 15,000,000.

Microsoft has been hiring some of the brightest minds to put an all-star team together, including Leo Kouwenhoven of the University of Delft in the Netherlands. This University is one of the leading hotspots of quantum innovations. In 2015, researchers from Delft University of Technology were able to teleport quantum information between two diamonds (Yes, diamonds. Pink diamonds actually) that were 1.3 km apart.

Intel, the largest chip maker of the digital era, also wants to reinvent itself for the quantum age. Intel made one of the biggest bets by announcing in 2015 that it would invest USD 50 million into research at QuTech, a spinoff from Delft

University of Technology. QuTech is focusing on silicon quantum dots, often called 'artificial atoms'. Intel reported that they can now layer the ultra-pure silicon needed for a quantum computer onto the standard wafers used in chip factories. It makes sense. Intel made its fortune by making computer chips for the digital age based on silicon, the same material as ordinary sand. Now they want to use that same material to make Silicon Qubits.

QUANTUM KILLING THE DIGITAL STAR

It's an arms race, that much is sure. But it's not just Google vs. D-wave, or Microsoft vs. IBM or Intel. It's quantum computers against the Digital computers. Singularity University showed the comparison quite nicely: The most powerful 'classical' digital computer on the planet is the Tianhe-2, which is stationed in Guangzhou, China. This monster of a machine costs USD 400 million, and burns about 20 megawatts of electricity, enough to power 20,000 households, in order to run. The Tianhe-2 is about half the size of a football field, and has 3.2 million Intel core chips inside. At the end of the Obama administration, the US announced that it would build an even bigger computer, 30 times more powerful than the Chinese Tianhe-2. But with today's digital technology, such a device would cost a billion dollars and it would require a nuclear power plant to run the supercomputer.

A fully entangled, truly Universal quantum computer with just 100 Qubits, would be more powerful than the entire Tianhe-2.

The technology blog *TechTarget* described the potential of quantum computing in a brilliant way: "Development of a quantum computer, if practical, would mark a leap forward in computing capability far greater than that from the abacus to a modern-day supercomputer, with performance gains in the billion-fold realm and beyond."[16]

Quantum computers could hold our future. If they finally deliver what they promise (unlike cold fusion) they will help us tackle 'Day After Tomorrow' issues in machine learning and Artificial Intelligence, help us deliver personalized medicine and crack future healthcare. They could help us understand ecology and climate change. They will enable fundamental breakthroughs in both material science and engineering.

Just imagine what they could do for you.

'DAY AFTER TOMORROW' TECHNOLOGIES: WHAT YOU NEED TO REMEMBER

Artificial Intelligence (AI)

AI's winters are over. Both of them. In just a short period 'digital first' became 'mobile first' and is now quickly becoming 'AI first'. As Andrew Ng puts it: "AI is the new electricity. Just as 100 years ago electricity transformed industry after industry, AI will now do the same."

The Internet of Things (IoT)

Together with digital manufacturing and machine learning, the IoT is 'just' a part of an ultra-complex and highly organic trinity that will have a massive impact on the way we work and live. It's about scale, and how we will need to 'copy' natural systems in order to manage them. But it's also about 'things' waking up and transforming our 'muted' surroundings into a sea of information. This trifecta of the IoT, digital manufacturing and machine learning will usher us into the era of the Fourth Industrial Revolution.

Blockchain & Smart Contracts

'A blockchain is an immutable, tamper-proof and transparent shared record of events' as Arno Laeven puts it. The impact of the blockchain goes way beyond its financial facet (bitcoin). It could be used to manage contracts, stocks, bonds, tracking of goods and even a company. The emergence of the blockchain is of the same level of importance as the introduction of the World Wide Web in 1995. It will make the internet more decentralized, more open, more secure, more private, more robust and more accessible. It will create an 'Internet of Trust'.

Augmented and Virtual Reality (AR & VR)

Our realities will be altered and extended in the 'Day After Tomorrow', more profoundly than ever before. VR & AR will allow us unlimited creativity to conjure up any world, and experience it to the fullest. The winners won't be the ones who just focus on technology, but those who understand that the design of the human-computer interaction, of the interface will be key.

Quantum Computing

Quantum computing is as crazy as it sounds. And by no means is there a certainty of success. But *if* quantum computers deliver what they promise, they will be millions of times more powerful than traditional computers, even more so than today's most powerful digital supercomputers like Sunway TaihuLight and Tianhe-2 (and a lot cheaper). And this will drive unseen breakthroughs in machine learning, artificial intelligence, healthcare, ecology, science, engineering and many more domains.

4

NETWORKS, PLATFORMS & BITS

'Day After Tomorrow' Business Models

> *"Without order nothing can exist.*
> *Without chaos nothing can evolve."*
>
> **OSCAR WILDE**

HEALTHY PARANOIA

The long and colorful history of economy and business is loaded with juicy sto-ries of how large, well-established institutions got the future completely wrong, how they utterly failed to see fundamental changes coming, or completely underestimated the impact it would have on their business, especially in the fast-moving sector of technology. You would think otherwise since they exist in a fast-changing flux of innovations. But, strangely enough, hi-tech companies have a nasty habit of utterly dismissing and ridiculing new innovative players, and then act terribly surprised when these new kids on the block steal and eat their lunch.

Not Andy Grove, though. He was all too aware of the ever-lurking dangers. Under the able leadership of this legendary CEO, Intel became the world's biggest chip maker. In 1997, *Time* magazine chose him as 'Man of the Year' for being "the person most responsible for the amazing growth in the power and the innovative potential of microchips". Being one of the greatest business leaders of the 20th century, Grove realized that Intel would not stay on top of their game merely by the merits of their technical skills.

So, he established a culture of 'healthy paranoia' inside his company.

A true student of Austrian-born American economist and political scientist Joseph Schumpeter, Grove pointed out that "Business success contains the seeds of its own destruction". He was extremely vigilant about not falling into the trap of being complacent and he wanted his engineers to remain fully alert to any changes that could disrupt their industry. Grove explained: "Success breeds complacency. Complacency breeds failure. Only the paranoid survive."[1]

The CEO understood that the core element of enterprise agility lay in the culture of the organization. He encouraged a culture within Intel that allowed innovation to flourish. He relentlessly urged his executives to allow their people to constantly test new techniques, new products, new sales channels, and chase new markets and new customers. He wanted them to be ready for unexpected shifts in business and technology. He wanted his managers to always stimulate experimentation and be prepared for changes. Grove turned 'healthy paranoia' into a sustainable value.

A LIVING ORGANISM

In Grove's words: "A corporation is a living organism; it has to continue to shed its skin. Methods have to change. Focus has to change. Values have to change. The sum total of those changes is transformation." He fostered a culture of open communication. His dialogue method was known throughout the company as 'constructive confrontation', which sometimes meant blatant screaming spells in the hallways. Craig Barrett who succeeded Grove as CEO explained: "It's give and take, and anyone in the company can yell at him. He's not above it."

Andy Grove was smart enough not just to focus on the 'paranoia', side. He knew that he needed a counterbalance if he wanted his organization to work. Therefore he fostered an open and frank atmosphere of constructive dialogue, and insisted that people be intellectually demanding to one another, which created an atmosphere of 'ruthless intelligence'.

But in my opinion, the true brilliance of Andy Grove was to take this constructive dialogue, this sense of experimentation with new ideas, this challenging ruthless intelligence and then turn that into focused action. My favorite Andy Grove saying is: "Let chaos reign, then rein in chaos." He would allow his teams and engineers to be as creative as can be, to experiment with novel concepts and ideas, and then he focused their future vector into a coherent strategy. Order from chaos, over and over again.

The cocktail of 'healthy paranoia', 'constructive confrontation', 'ruthless intelligence', 'creative chaos' and 'focused action' paid off handsomely. Andy Grove was the very first hire at Intel, and became Intel's president in 1979. Under his leadership, the company successfully transformed itself from a maker of memory chips to the world's biggest manufacturer of semiconductors, growing revenue from USD 1.9 billion to USD 26 billion.

But after Grove had retired, Intel ran into serious challenges. Where Grove's healthy paranoia had insured a top position in the world of personal computers, the new direction of the industry in the world of mobile computing, smart-phones and tablets proved to be a struggle for Intel. New players like the British ARM holding, and Qualcomm based out of San Diego were eating Intel for lunch in the incredibly fast-growing mobile revolution.

It is incredible to see how, in corporate history, the ability to remain agile and the capability to reinvent oneself, are so often tied to venerable leadership. For more than 20 years, Grove's 'healthy paranoia' catapulted Intel to world dominance. But then the mobile revolution came so swiftly that it took almost everybody by surprise. Corporate Myopia of the worst kind.

A LOUSY EMAIL MACHINE

In recent times, no product has had such an impact on a market as the intro-duction of the iPhone by Apple in 2007. Having been around since 1976, Apple wasn't exactly a new kid on the block. But in the mid-nineties, Apple Computer was virtually wiped out as a company, though it had been miraculously saved by the return of the prodigal son, Steve Jobs. Despite this, the competition no longer took Apple seriously: it was seen as a has-been that had somehow managed to escape bankruptcy, but would never again play a leading role on the global technology scene. They considered Apple a footnote in the history of computing, a relic of a past long gone. Not quite right.

When Apple introduced the iPhone in 2007, essentially the first smart mobile phone, the competitors had a field day in ridiculing the product, and the company.

The CEO of Palm, which had developed handheld personal digital assistants at the time, was a man called Ed Colligan. Palm was a highly successful player in the world of handheld devices, and they had been trying to get into the mobile phone game. This is how Colligan reacted when the iPhone was introduced: "PC guys are never going to figure out how to make a decent phone. Apple is not going to just walk in."[2] Not quite right.

Nokia was, at the time, the absolute world-leader in the mobile phone business. The Finnish company had started to make some 'smart' mobile phones, but they were clumsy and not user-friendly. The Chief Strategy Officer of Nokia, Anssi Vanjoki, said of Apple's ambitions to enter the world of smartphones: "Just as in the computer business, Apple has always remained a niche manufac-turer. That will be their role in mobile phones as well."[3] Not quite right.

But my top favorite view is that of Steve Ballmer, the very flamboyant CEO of Microsoft at the time. His company was the global technology leader for consumers, with an almost complete stranglehold on the PC business. Ballmer was never known for his diplomatic or subtle rhetoric. When the iPhone was introduced, Ballmer laughed it away: "Apple just launched the most expensive phone in the world. And it doesn't appeal to business customers because it doesn't have a keyboard. Which makes it a lousy email machine."[4] Blackberry made the same mistake of dismissing the iPhone as a mere toy with no business value. Not quite right, either.

We all know what happened next. The iPhone became the all-star product that catapulted Apple to become the world's most valuable company. In 2016, just eight years after the launch of the iPhone, it had the highest stock valuation of any company on the planet. Its product almost single-handedly defined the entire category of smartphones, and would dominate the scene for years to come. In 2007, the five major mobile phone manufacturers, Nokia, Samsung, Motorola, Sony Ericsson, and LG collectively controlled 90% of the mobile industry's global profits. By 2015 the iPhone had single-handedly overtaken 92% of the entire global profits in this sector.[5]

Palm went south in the most spectacular way and was sold to HP in 2010 for a fraction of what it was once worth. Nokia completely folded by 2012, the stock which traded at a price of USD 250 just a few years earlier had dropped to below USD 2, and the company was virtually bankrupt by 2012. Microsoft picked up the pieces of Nokia's phone business, but was completely incapable of building even a marginal market share with their Microsoft Mobile offering. Apple had crushed all of them in the most spectacular way possible.

It was clearly a foolish mistake to dismiss the capability of Apple to change the rules of the game in mobile phones, and to think that only the established competitors could innovate. But this kind of miscalculation is more the rule in this sector than the exception.

In the beginning of this book, you'll recall me asking a number of 'Big Questions'. This was the first one:

Big Question #1:

"Why is it almost impossible for large organizations to spot new and radical technologies quickly, and develop their potential? What explains this organizational blindness to new opportunities?"

I'm not sure that Palm, or Nokia, or Microsoft didn't see smartphones coming their way. They weren't blind, and probably had very smart people in their organizations who understood the threat. But they certainly *underestimated* the growth, the acceleration and the size of the opportunity. Or, as often happens, Management just did not want to listen to the warnings of those in the field. Even Google almost missed out on the mobile revolution. It had had the insight to quietly acquire Android for a mere USD 50 million back in 2005. Android was a young small startup founded by Andy Rubin who, after the acquisition, ran the Android division of Google until 2013. Under his reign, Android grew to a market share of more than 80%, and with Apple iOS taking another 15%, the rest becoming utterly insignificant.

In hindsight, Google admitted that buying Android was perhaps Google's 'best deal ever'. Google successfully transformed from a web-centric company into a mobile-centric company, with Android and Andy Rubin being crucial in that metamorphosis. But even Google almost missed it.

The combination of Google with Android and Apple with iOS crushed every single competitor, including Nokia, Palm, Blackberry and Microsoft. Steve Ballmer, Microsoft's CEO, did not only ridicule the role that Apple could play in smartphones, he was also highly skeptical of Google, not hiding his frank disdain when he said: "Google is actually not a real company. It's just a house of cards."[6] Well…

We'll discuss the strategy of Google to reinvent itself later in this book at length, as this relatively young company is constantly challenging itself to rethink what they do, to focus on being able to rewrite their mission, and to reboot their focus. Google remains constantly alert to the fact that there could be totally new radical players, aka 'disruptors', on the horizon, who are out to eat their lunch. They want to avoid Corporate Myopia at all cost. They balance on the verge of paranoia so they won't miss the next 'Android', which will allow them to write the next chapter of their corporate story. The Google execs keep the very same mindset as Intel's late CEO Andrew Grove.

It's an extremely wise attitude to never underestimate the power of a small startup to completely shake things up and disrupt an entire market.

THE OFFERING MEMORANDUM

Apple became the most valuable publicly quoted company on the planet in 2016, surpassing the General Electrics and Exxon Mobiles of this world. But even the most valuable enterprise on Earth had extremely humble startup roots.

One of the most amazing documents in the history of Apple can be found in the 'Computer History Museum' in Mountain View, right in the heart of Silicon Valley[7]: it's the preliminary draft of the 'Offering Memorandum' of Apple Computer Inc. which was donated by Mike Markkula. This document is now a part of the online collection of the Computer History Museum and you can simply download it from their website.[8]

Markkula was actually the very first investor in Apple. He was the marketing manager at Intel, working for Andy Grove, and had successfully made a modest fortune for himself with stock options in his company. At the age of 32, he had already retired, and was looking for a more quiet life for himself and his family.

One day he received a phone call that he should check out this little startup called 'Apple Computer' that might be interesting to invest in. Markkula drove up to the famous garage of the parents of Steve Jobs where Apple had set up shop in 1976. He parked his Corvette in front of the garage and saw Steve Jobs come out to greet him with cutoff jeans, sandals, shoulder-length hair and ragged beard. He sat down in the garage with the two Steves, Jobs and Wozniak, and the first thing he asked them was to see their business plan. They looked puzzled; they didn't know what a business plan was.

Still, Markkula was intrigued by what he observed in the garage. He worked diligently with the two Steves for the next two weeks to put a business plan together for Apple Computer Inc. Markkula put up USD 80,000 of his own money as an equity investment in the company and a further USD 170,000 as a loan, and so became one-third owner of Apple and employee number 3. It was by far the best investment he had ever made in his life. Markkula was instrumental in shaping the startup into a real company, and Steve Wozniak, who designed the first two Apple computers, actually credits Markkula for the success of Apple more than himself.

When Apple was growing like crazy in the next couple of years, Markkula was the business-savvy leader who would coach Apple through its growing pains.

He would also be instrumental in helping the company prepare for their listing on the stock exchange, the fabled 'IPO': Initial Public Offering.

Now, the document that Markkula donated to the Computer History Museum is the draft of the document that propelled Apple onto the stock exchange: the 'Offering Memorandum'.

When I took one of my former companies public, in 2006, I had no idea how incredibly important the 'Offering Memorandum' actually was. When you start a company, you spend all your time and effort on making it grow, putting together a great team, delivering amazing products and services, and doing everything to please your customers. You work like a dog to grow your business. You know the ins and outs, the opportunities and obstacles, the potentials and the pitfalls.

But when you have to sell your company, at least the shares in your company, to the general public, you have to pen all of this down. You have to write a book, basically, that 'sells' your company: the 'IPO Offering Memorandum'.

Of course, you don't have to record all of this alone. There will be a team of lawyers and investment bankers to help you in this process, but I'm not exactly sure this really makes it any easier. The first thing you need to write down in the Offering Memorandum are the 'Risk Factors'. In this section, you basically cover your ass, and write down all the risky things about your company. Not quite enough to scare off potential investors, but just enough to legally protect yourself if the venture were flop.

The 'Risk Factors' of the 'Offering Memorandum' of Apple Computer[8] read like this:

Risk Factors

Operating History: Apple Computer Inc. is a new company which has not established a long history of operation upon which to base opinions of accuracy of forecasts, financial projections or operations efficiency.

Manufacturing: Apple has experienced extreme difficulty in obtaining its custom injection molded cases. There is no assurance that this problem will be solved through establishing additional sources of supply.

Cash Flow vs Rapid Growth: Apple management expects that rapid growth and potential market fluctuations may present severe cash flow management difficulties.

Management: Apple Computers' Management team is young and relatively in-experienced in the high volume consumer electronics business.

Look at the words: 'new company', 'extreme difficulty', 'severe cash flow management difficulties', and the management team that is 'relatively in-experienced'.

Just wonderful. Would you have invested if you read these risk factors?

You should have.

THE APPLE AND THE PHOENIX

In the beginning of 2017, Apple Computer was the most valuable company on the planet. If you had invested in the IPO of Apple in 1980, at the offering price of USD 22 a share, 100 shares would have cost you USD 2,200. Since then the stock has split four times, including three 2-for-1 splits and one 7-for-1 split. That means your 100 shares would have multiplied into 5,600 today, and your initial investment would be worth USD 736,568 in early 2017. That's a return of 33.48%. Imagine what your return would have been if you had invested in Apple before the IPO, or as the very first investor like Mark Markkula.

At first, as we all know, Apple went through a truly meteoric rise. Through the roof. And then it all collapsed. Apple became a corporation. It grew large, bloated, big, bureaucratic. After the Lisa debacle and the Mac Pirate shenanigans[9], they fired Steve Jobs, who went on a personal crusade to clear his name and fame by starting NeXT computers. But Apple carried on under the reign of John Sculley and a number of horribly bad CEOs to become a dying giant. It morphed into a company that was producing mediocre, boring, beige products that no one really felt any excitement about. And just when the company was puffing out its dying breath, they brought back the prodigal son and he turned the company around in the most spectacular way. It was the biggest resurrection since Jesus Christ 2,000 years earlier.

Wired magazine, at that moment probably the journalistic exponent of the burgeoning dot.com era, and the 'voice' of the technological diaspora from Silicon Valley, put Apple on its cover in June of 1997. The cover had the Apple logo, with a crown of thorns wrapped around it, and beneath it just the letters: 'Pray.' That issue of *Wired* even had an article named '101 ways to save Apple'. The number one suggestion was: 'Admit it. You're out of the hardware game', with the suggestion to scrap their hardware production entirely. Suggestion #22 was: 'Sell yourself to IBM or Motorola'. The tone of the article was very clear: Game over Apple. Everyone in the valley believed they were dead. They had been shopped around to IBM, who turned them down. To Sun Microsystems who turned them down. To Oracle, who didn't want them. Apple was left out to die in the desert, vultures overhead.

Exactly ten years later, in April 2008, *Wired* magazine featured an almost identical magazine cover but, this time, the black sleek Apple logo was adorned by a barbed wire crown, and beneath it the words: 'Evil/Genius'. The references to the Messiah were blatantly clear. The magazine apologized for being so completely wrong 10 years earlier: 'Our Bad. *Wired* Had Some Tips For Apple — We Were Wrong.' At that point Apple had not even launched the iPad yet.

© Tony Klassen

As fascinating as the story is, it is, first and foremost, a sign that it *can* happen. Companies can radically reinvent themselves. Companies can dramatically turn around and even from the near dead, come back to greatness. Apple did. Haier did (as we will see later in the book). And so did General Motors, Netflix, Disney, Lego and others before and after them.[10] But, they are the rarest of beasts.

Another Big Question I had at the beginning of the book ties into this:

Big Question #4

"How can corporates accelerate their 'Day After Tomorrow' thinking? Why do large organizations – who understand the fundamental challenges coming at them, because of disruptive technologies, business models or concepts – seem to be paralyzed to move fast enough to respond? How can companies become agile in their 'Day After Tomorrow' thinking, and be successful in developing an approach that works?"

Apple is a fascinating story because it has exemplified *both* of those Big Questions. They disrupted the microcomputer industry from the extremely humble beginnings of a fledgling startup, and became huge. They lost it all, were nearly dead in the water, and then disrupted the mobile revolution all over again. They are a perfect example of those rarest of beasts, capable of reinventing itself, over and over again, like a phoenix burning up and rising again from its own ashes.

Unfortunately, Apple does not provide a playbook that any other company can just successfully duplicate. The leadership style and innovation culture of Apple cannot just be copied and pasted somewhere else. It gives us a proof-point that corporate resurrection is possible, but it does not provide a guideline or a roadmap.

EATING THE WORLD

Too bad. Because many companies will need a roadmap for fundamental change in the coming years.

In August 2011, Netscape founder and VC Marc Andreessen wrote the seminal piece *Why Software Is Eating The World* for the *Wall Street Journal*.[11] If you haven't read it yet, you definitely should. Back then, we still had no idea of the power of companies such as Uber, or the rise of phenomena such as Airbnb. We were only just beginning to see the first mentions of driverless cars, or the rise of the world of Artificial Intelligence. Yet Andreessen perfectly described what would happen in the next few years. He did not focus on the technologies, but on the impact that technology would have on business models, and on society.

Andreessen said: "We are in the middle of a dramatic and broad technological and economic shift in which software companies are poised to take over large swathes of the economy. Over the next 10 years, I expect many more industries to be disrupted by software, with new world beating Silicon Valley companies doing the disruption in more cases than not."

I've had the pleasure to visit Marc Andreessen's organization Andreessen Horowitz – or A16Z for short – many times. It's an amazing place and, in my opinion, one of the most professionally-run venture capital firms in the world.

In the world of venture capital, it seems there are two fundamental philosophies on how to invest in startups. On the one hand, you have players like '500 startups', which started in Silicon Valley and are the exponent of the 'spray and pray' philosophy. You invest in as many startups as you can, you 'spray' them with venture capital, you give them the chance to grow and if a few of those turn out to be a unicorn with a billion dollar valuation, then you are in luck. The philosophy is not entirely absurd, since the mortality rate of a startup is extremely high. There are a million things that can go wrong, and therefore players like '500 startups' want to spread their cash over a very wide portfolio of startups. The initial idea of 500 startups was to create a fund that would invest in 500 startups, but they have been so successful that to date they have invested in more than 1,500 startups. Spray and Pray.

At the complete other end of the spectrum of venture capital lies the firm of Andreessen Horowitz. They're almost the 'NASA scientist' of venture capital. Every year in Silicon Valley alone more than 4,000 startups are created, of which only 15 are high performers, that will produce more than 95% of all economic returns. Those 15 are the needle in the haystack, and A16Z wants to use the 'scientific' method to zoom in on those 'golden' 15.

Because both Andreessen and his business partner Ben Horowitz abhorred the behavior of the financially driven venture funds that had invested in their companies Netscape and LoudCloud, they decided to adopt a fundamentally different philosophy. They hated sitting in a boardroom as founders with a bunch of pencil-pushers and Excel-heads who didn't 'grok'[12] technology. They decided that they wanted to become a completely founder-centric venture capital firm. They would only invest in a company where the founders and leaders of the companies they invest in understand the bits and bytes and can even write source code. And they take the founder-centric approach very seriously. In all of the meeting rooms where the partners of A16Z meet with the startups, there is a square card reader that the partners use to swipe their credit cards when they are late for a meeting: A16Z believes that the time of a startup founder is very precious, and if a venture partner is late for a meeting, *they* will have to pay the startup. Brilliant.

When you visit A16Z and they present their corporate philosophy, they always show the 'Boom!' slide.

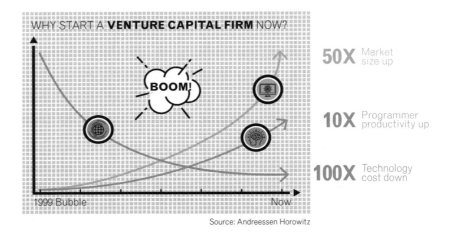

Source: Andreessen Horowitz

So, what does that slide mean? It actually wants to show how this is the perfect 'booming' moment to start a VC or - by extrapolation - a company, because of the 3 exponential driving forces below.

Technology costs are falling like a brick. Since 1999, over a 20-year period, A16Z claims that technology costs have fallen 100-fold. That's quite impressive, and perhaps a little over the top. Still. First, there is the natural transition rate of Moore's law, where computing capacity doubles every 18 months, and costs drop by 50% every 18 months. But there's more. Because today we can procure any computing power in the cloud, and the economy of scale of mega-vendors such as Amazon Web Services is so immensely huge, the costs to 'enter' the world of technology have become virtually zero.

When I started my companies at the end of the 20th century, I still had to raise huge amounts of capital just to get started. It took a lot of money to build infrastructure, set up networks, procure servers and install software. It cost time and money, and therefore the hurdles to set up a hi-tech company were astronomical. Today, any kid with a good idea can use a credit card to go to Amazon Web Services (AWS) and in less than 15 minutes, (s)he has enough computing power to start building a company. If they need to scale, they only need to pay for what they use. Technology is no longer the hurdle to start a venture.

At the same time, programmer productivity is up by a factor of 10 according to A16Z. Programmers today can stand on the shoulders of giants. A clever coder can leverage the enormous amount of work available on open source frameworks. They don't need to start from scratch, they can immediately zoom in on their own specific focus, because the groundwork is already available. You can access open source websites like GitHub where developers share their work in an open way. [13]

And then there is the market size. Venture capitalists like A16Z are betting on exploding, exponential growth in core markets. As Marc Andreessen wrote in *Why Software Is Eating The World*: "In the next 10 years, I expect at least five billion people worldwide to own smartphones, giving every individual with such a phone instant access to the full power of the internet, every moment of every day."

He saw this as a natural progression, a 'staged approach', like the stages of rockets, each one lifting it one step further into space. In his words: "Six decades into the computer revolution, four decades since the invention of the microprocessor, and two decades into the rise of the modern internet, all of the technology required to transform industries through software finally works and can be widely delivered on a global scale."

'30 30 30'

Andreessen is not alone. Recently, Jack Ma, the founder and CEO of Alibaba, said something very similar at the World Economic Forum in Davos. Alibaba is the most exciting digital phenomenon in the Far East. It grew extremely rapidly both as a Business-to-Business platform connecting (Asian) manufacturers, as well as a Business-to-Consumer platform and as a payment platform called Alipay. When Alibaba introduced its IPO on the New York Stock Exchange, they commanded a USD 250 billion valuation, and according to Jack Ma, they're only getting started.

But at Davos, in 2017, he used the concept of '30 30 30' to describe what would come next. He outlined that most technological revolutions take 50 years. In the first 20 years of those cycles, the technology players are established. According to Jack Ma, that's where we are right now in the world of digital. "Pay attention to the next 30 years. They will be critical for the world. The true implications of the digital developments will become evident in the next 30 years". Then he talked of the next '30': "Pay attention to the 30-year-olds. They are the internet generation and will change the world. They will build a new tomorrow". And, finally, he touched on the final '30': "Pay attention to companies that have less than 30 employees, they have the agility"[14]. At the World Economic Forum, Jack Ma quoted from his favorite Hollywood movie, *Forrest Gump*: "Nobody makes money catching whales. People make money catching shrimps."

Marc Andreessen with his *Software is Eating the World* and Jack Ma with his '30 30 30' both outlined the battle that is to come, the coming of the 'War of Ones and Zeroes': "Companies in every industry need to assume that a software revolution is coming. Over the next few years, the battles between incumbents and software-powered insurgents will be epic."[15]

Joseph Schumpeter, the economist who coined the term 'creative destruction,' would be proud.

PLATFORMS ARE EATING THE WORLD

Since the *Software is Eating the World* piece was written, we have seen an epic acceleration of the evolution. We've seen the rise of Global Platforms, which are benefiting from the network effects, as I described in my former book *The Network Always Wins*.

But today, we're at the stage that '*Platforms* are eating the world'. We've had crucial 'platforms' in the past, but these used to be seen as infrastructure, and mostly 'invisible infrastructure'. The platforms were a means to *enable* business models, now - with companies like Uber, Youtube and Airbnb - it seems like platforms *are* becoming the new business models.

Let me illustrate this. Two great examples of 'invisible platforms' are SWIFT and GS1. Both are great massive, systemic platforms and amazing companies, yet hardly known by the general public.

SWIFT is the 'Society for Worldwide Interbank Financial Telecommunication' and the biggest go-between when you wire money from one country to another. It is the financial backbone of the world, connecting virtually any bank in the world to each other in order to allow financial messages to flow. But it remains 'invisible' infrastructure: most people have never heard of SWIFT. Yet if it would stop operating, the financial ecosystem would grind to a halt overnight.

The other example is GS1, one of my favorite organizations in the world. It's the global provider of barcodes for use in retail and healthcare. Every single barcode that is on a carton of milk, or on a cereal box, has been handled by GS1. A barcode is the link between the manufacturers (the Nestlés and Danones of this world) and the retailers (the Walmarts and Amazons of this world). It's the common 'Global Language of Business' between them to understand which product is which. And GS1 is the global platform that holds this all together. Without GS1, the world of manufacturing, distribution and retail would be a complete Biblical 'Tower of Babel' chaos, and it would come crashing down. Yet most people in the world have never heard of GS1.

Platforms have been instrumental in shaping society, but they used to be discrete infrastructures, unseen to the eye. Today, the power of 'visible' platforms transforming entire industries is evident all around us. Uber is not an 'invisible' platform that connects the cab companies worldwide. Instead its business model *is* the platform, and the consumers are an essential part of it. So how does it work?

PLATFORM ECONOMICS

It turns out that 'platform economics' are a whole new ball game. For most of the 20th century we've built companies that were focused on 'efficiency'. They would enter a market and optimize the 'value chain', trying to control as much as possible the efficiency to get a product developed and out to the consumer. The most successful companies were those that focused on their 'competitive advantage' which was often the sum of all their efficiencies.

But in the networked world it's quite different. Competitive advantage seems to no longer be the sum of all efficiencies, but rather the sum of all connections in the network. In a networked economy, platform businesses bring together supply and demand (producers and consumers) in high-value exchanges, and the chief assets are information and the interactions on the platform.

Platforms grow in value as their number of network nodes grow. They exhibit similar network effects according to Metcalfe's law, which states that the value of a telecoms network is proportional to the square of the number of connected users in the system. Simply put: if you are the only owner of a telephone in the entire world, you can't call anyone and it has no value. At all. Yet as the number of other telephone owners grows, so does the value of your phone's use. Because two telephones can make only one connection, five can make ten connections, and twelve can make 66 connections. It's quite the opposite of the economic factor of 'scarcity' value which states that an item's relative price increases based upon its relatively low supply. Networks and platforms have completely redefined the concept of value, and therefore of ownership.

Platform Revolution is a book written on this topic by Geoff Parker, Marshall Van Alstyne and Sangeet Choudary in 2016[16]. They outlined their thinking in a *Harvard Business Review* article called *Pipelines, Platforms, and the New Rules of Strategy.*[17]

The fundamental change they see today is that digital technology has significantly reduced the need to own physical infrastructure and assets. Instead, building and scaling digital networks is vastly cheaper and simpler, and therefore can generate much faster growth.

The 'pipeline' businesses of the past created value by controlling a 'linear' succession of activities: the 'value chain'. Today, many industries that used to be controlled by pipeline business are being transformed into 'platforms'.

There are three fundamental shifts. First, instead of 'controlling' resources, the platform players 'orchestrate' the resources. Airbnb grew like crazy because it did not have to 'own' the assets on its platform, but merely orchestrate the supply and demand. Another good example is Waze: instead of investing enormous amounts of money in traffic sensors – like Nokia did, when it bought Navteq for USD 8.1 billion in order to launch itself in mobile navigation – it crowdsourced location information from the GPS-sensors in the phones of its users.

The second shift is from 'internal optimization' to 'external interaction'. Pipeline companies try to optimize their entire value chain, from the sourcing of materials to the sales distribution and service. But platform businesses focus on facilitating the interactions between producers and consumers.

The third shift they see is the creation of value. Instead of a focus on customer value and maximizing the lifetime value of customers in a pipeline business, the platform ecosystems focus on expanding the total value of the ecosystem as a whole.

Pipeline organizations	Platform players
Control resources	Orchestrate resources
Optimize internal value chain	Facilitate external interaction
Focus on customer value	Focus on the total value of the ecosystem

THE 'POSITIVE FEEDBACK' LOOP

This is where the network effects really become visible, and an ecosystem can get a 'positive feedback' loop: it gets stronger with every interaction. These explosively scalable network processes are disrupting traditional, buy-make-sell competitors. This positive feedback loop was famously illustrated on a cocktail napkin that was recently tweeted by David Sacks, the co-founder of Yammer and one of the investors in Uber:

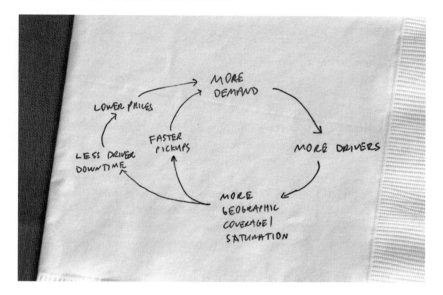

Let's start at the top. More Demand. Should you have a surge in people wanting to use Uber, you'd need more drivers. If you have more drivers, then you have more geographical coverage which, in turn, will mean faster pickups and less driver downtime, which will mean lower prices, which would make the service more appealing, and create more demand.

In electronics, these types of 'positive feedback' loops can cause a circuit to overload and burn up. Positive feedback in chemical reactions can increase the rate of reactions, and may lead to explosions. Positive feedback loops on a cocktail napkin can ensure that you ping an Uber and it magically arrives immediately, at your service.

Brilliant. But, beware. Positive feedback in economic systems can also cause boom-then-bust cycles. That's because their ability to enhance or amplify changes tends to move a system away from its equilibrium state and make it more unstable.

THE WINNER TAKES IT ALL

It seems today that the economics of platform businesses is still an unexplored field, but one of the early signs of this phenomenon is that it leads to 'category kings'. Because the positive feedback loops of platform businesses result in almost unlimited growth, it seems like the concept of 'winner takes it all' seems to push everyone except the undisputed leader – the 'category' king – out of the market. Look at Alibaba, which accounts for more than 75% of all Chinese e-commerce transactions[18], or the complete dominance of a platform like Facebook.

Greater scale generates more value for the network which, in turn, attracts more participants, which creates more value: this is how the positive feedback loop produces the monopolies of 'category kings'.

Sangeet Choudary, one of the co-authors of *Platform Revolution*: "Platforms win, not just by facilitating new interactions, but also by aggregating and analyzing the data of it all. The explosion of data, and its use by platform businesses to keep learning is perhaps the most significant." He frequently uses the idiom 'data is the new oil' to describe the 'engine' behind the participative business models of the platform businesses. Platform business models are more explosive, more virtual, more dynamic, and more intelligent than the 'pipeline business' of the past, but they rely on information in a most spectacular way.

THE DISRUPTION RULE BOOK

It would be foolish to dismiss the rise of platforms as a fad. I truly believe that the 21st century will play out as the 'network century'. Although the digital foundations were laid in the 20th century, the real impact of this 'age of networks' is still in its infancy.

So yes, 'Platforms are eating the world' is truly the logical evolution of Marc Andreessen's' prediction. And the world seems to be moving along faster and faster, as in the good 'VUCA' tradition: more Volatility, more Uncertainty, more Complexity and more Ambiguity. The VUCA world is spinning around faster thanks to the positive feedback loops of network effects. This time around, it's not just new products, like the iPhone, that are disrupting markets and companies. Today we have fundamentally new business models that seem to be hitting even harder than new products to shake up entire industries.

So how do these new players, these disruptors think?

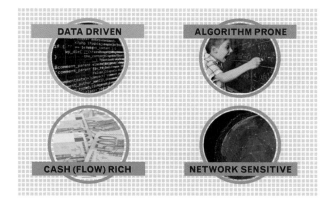

DATA DRIVEN · ALGORITHM PRONE · CASH (FLOW) RICH · NETWORK SENSITIVE

Network economy disruptors are data hogs. They collect information at every step of the way. Imagine what Google-owned Waze knows about what happens on our streets every day. A *lot* more than our governments. Imagine what a company like Uber knows about our cities: what people do, where they need to go, how the flow of humans is evolving. Data truly is the 'new oil' for these network disruptors, and the discussions going forward about data governance, privacy and the regulatory aspects of this collection of data will be fierce.

Data makes these disruptors in the network economy very smart. They build algorithms to navigate the data they collect and develop intelligence to mine the oil. The network disruptors 'understand' the evolution of supply and demand. Imagine a city, where Uber needs to 'understand' when cars will be needed, when concert halls will spill out spectators who need a ride home, when baseball games will end and where fans will need mobility, when movie theaters will generate demand for their services. Algorithms make the network disruptors 'smart'.

Disruptors love to play the network effects. This helps them scale and grow exponentially. It's the positive feedback loop I referred to above. Tagging and liking makes connections, you 'infect' other users with your reactions. The network grows stronger with every single use and interaction. My favorite part of Uber is where you can send someone your 'ETA', and they can follow exactly where you are and when you'll get there. You can see the network connections spread like a virus. Exponential growth.

About 20% of every Uber transaction in the world flows back to the mothership in San Francisco. Who would have thought that the taxi business would be so cash rich? That it could create such a stream of money for Uber? With the network effects, once you scale the network, and take a piece of the transactional value, these little cuts become massive cash flow streams. Networks make *big* money catching shrimps, as Jack Ma would say.

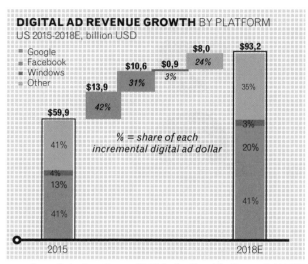

DIGITAL AD REVENUE GROWTH BY PLATFORM
US 2015-2018E, billion USD

- Google
- Facebook
- Windows
- Other

$59,9
41%
4%
13%
41%

$13,9
42%

$10,6
31%

$0,9
3%

$8,0
24%

$93,2
35%
3%
20%
41%

*% = share of each
incremental digital ad dollar*

2015   2018E

Source: Technology - License: CC Attribution-ShareAlike License - Oct 24, 2016

BUT HOW DO THEY DO IT? WHAT IS THEIR MAGIC?

First of all, the network disruptors excel at bypassing rules and conventions. That's because the market rules were created for the 'pipeline' businesses of the past. The regulators that developed the governance for the current markets developed their ideas in the 20th century, and the network players operate in the 21st century. That's why many platform businesses are illegal when they start. Uber is illegal in many countries, but gradually it is convincing – or should I say forcing – city by city to legalize it.

Network disruptors also try to remove every single service friction. They excel at 'customers first, without compromise' and want to make their customers' experiences as smooth as possible. The killer argument where Uber won over

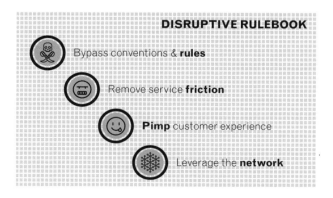

DISRUPTIVE RULEBOOK

Bypass conventions & **rules**

Remove service **friction**

Pimp customer experience

Leverage the **network**

the hearts of their customers, was to remove the number one source of friction for taking a taxi: paying. Not that people don't want to pay. It's more the horror of paying in taxis *all around* the world. In many countries you can't use a credit card, or the machine to take your card is not working. In Switzerland, one of the most developed countries in the world, very few taxis accept credit cards. Instead, they will drive you to an ATM so you can get Swiss francs out of the wall. Uber removed that friction completely. You step out of the car, while paying automatically. Frictionless.

Network Disruptors aim to pimp the customer experience to unparalleled heights. Take the Uber example again when finding a ride is reduced to swiping your finger on a piece of glass. I heard a colleague recently talk about a city where Uber did not operate and where he felt the 'adrenaline' again of trying to hail down a cab in the middle of the street. Network disruptors replace this anxiety by flawless customer experiences.

These network disruptors obviously also leverage the network, and allow people to build on top of their network. Often, they will open up their infrastructure, and allow others to connect, and build new businesses. Network disruptors know that if they open up their APIs (Application Programming Interfaces), more users will find their way to the network, more traffic will flow on their platform, and more value will be created on the ecosystem. It's all about the positive feedback loops.

The Uber platform has been used to allow other markets to take advantage of the new infrastructure. Look at 'Uber Flu' where – at the start of the flu season – you can 'order' a nurse to give you a flu-shot. Or the rise of 'Uber Eats' where you can have meals delivered via the Uber platform.

The platforms are rising in popularity. They stop being invisible and become business models. New business models pile on top of each other. It's about standing on the shoulders of giants to keep on innovating in the 'age of networks'.

THE NEW ROMAN EMPIRE

Not everyone is happy about all of this. On the contrary.

Kevin Maney wrote the cover story for *Newsweek* in June 2016, and its title reads: *Why The World Hates Silicon Valley*.[19]

The opening lines of the article provide an interesting analogy: "Silicon Valley is the new Rome. As in the time of Caesar, the world is grappling with an advanced city-state dominating much of the planet, injecting its technology and ethos everywhere it lands and funneling enormous wealth back home."

Where I live, in the north of Europe, we still feel the presence of the Roman Empire, two thousand years later. The main street in the town where I live is still called 'Romeinse Heirbaan' which translates to 'Roman Road': built with superior Roman technology to carry their troops to occupied lands and bring the riches and wealth they amassed back to Rome. The network of roads they built was so vast, and so vital, that this was one of the pivotal elements of Roman success. And with Rome clearly entered in the middle, it gave way to the expression: 'All roads lead to Rome'.

Today, all roads seem to lead to Silicon Valley. In his *Newsweek* article, Maney clearly describes the parallel. The Roman Empire exported its 'technology' (aqueducts, viaducts, roads, bridges, etc.) and its culture to a vast Empire, and then hauled the loot back to Rome, a tiny little city-state. It wasn't the Italian Empire, it was the Roman Empire. It lasted for a really long time, and when it collapsed, it plunged the better part of Europe into the deep abyss of the Middle Ages, where it seemed like time went backwards.

Today, with the rise of the network disruptors, we see a very similar pattern. Uber is a clear example of how this works. Every time someone in the world uses an Uber, about 20% of the fare for this ride flows back to San Francisco, in the heart of Silicon Valley. Where previously 100% of that money spent in a country would remain there, now 20% of that fare will be channeled to the center of the new Roman Empire. As Maney points out: "Now imagine that happening in industry after industry, country after country." The same goes for a lot of the money amassed by the likes of Netflix, Airbnb, Upwork or eBay.

The concentration of power is unlike anything we've ever seen before. Alphabet for example, the parent company of Google, controls 12% of all money spent on media advertising globally, according to a recent study by *Adweek*.[20] There has never been a company on this planet that has had such a control over ad spending. And the Category Kings only seem to become more powerful, and more dominant. A study by Activate, a media research firm, at the end of 2016, estimates that Google and Facebook are expected to command 73% of each additional digital ad-dollar over the next three years. For every extra dollar spent on advertising in the next three years, 73% will flow back to these two Category Kings in the New Roman Empire.[21]

Kevin Maney talks of 'two Americas', as a result of the forces of these network disruptors: 'Atoms America' and 'Bits America'. The world of 'Atoms America' is the world of manufacturing, retail, services, restaurants, hotels. It's the old-school business that you can see, feel and touch. On the other side is 'Bits America', with people who write source code, analyze data, build apps and leverage the network. In his words, Atoms America is in trouble, and Bits America is making the divide harder and harder to swallow. But Bits America got a big wake-up call after Donald Trump was elected, because Atoms America voted clearly with a Luddite[22] voice. Not that they will be able to stop the evolution from atoms to bits, but they could cause serious damage while trying.

ATOMS WORLD VERSUS BITS WORLD

In my opinion, what Maney describes on an American scale is very much a global phenomenon. What we're experiencing here, is the Atoms World versus the Bits World.

Silicon Valley is mostly the birthplace of the network disruptors. Remember the popular term GAFA, denoting the four exponents of this network explosion: Google, Apple, Facebook and Amazon? All of them are headquartered on the Californian West Coast. Only Amazon is not based in California. The spectacular rise of their respective network reach fueled a whole new mercantile term: 'GAFAnomics': the network economic models of these 'digital attention' unicorns.

They are huge and hugely successful. Worldwide, Google has a 90% share of the search market and reaches an audience of billions globally every single day: with search, and with Android. Amazon has created an empire around the world growing its network of distribution, both physically and digitally. Apple with iTunes has reached a vast global audience of listeners, viewers and digital consumers. And Facebook has an empire of its own: with almost 1.9 billion users of Facebook in 2017, more than 1 billion on WhatsApp, more than 1 billion users on Messenger, and half a billion on Instagram.

Explaining GAFAnomics is easy as pie: it's about scaling the network. Network effects allowed the GAFA to grow exponentially, become Category King, focus on keeping attention and 'stickiness', and monetize their user base. In the US alone, by 2016, Google and Facebook commanded more than 50 billion minutes of digital attention every *week*. Google and Facebook monetize only digital assets on their networks, while Amazon and Apple monetize atoms (from iPhones to Amazon Fresh groceries), but the economic driver behind their success is clear: network effects.

There's a reason why these companies are on the US West Coast, in my opinion. Sure, there are really innovative companies all over the US, and on the East Coast, with hubs like New York and Boston attracting a lot of talent and great startups. But the beating heart remains in Silicon Valley. It's 'Hollywood for Geeks'. A magnet for talent and ambition. It's hypnotizing to be there and to be swept off your feet by the enthusiasm for the future. "450 square miles surrounded by reality" is what people outside of Silicon Valley call them. The people inside Silicon Valley refer to the rest as 'The Paper Belt', people still stuck in the days before digital.

So why are most startups in Silicon Valley? Many books have been written on this subject. Most think it's about the intoxicating mixture of talent (with Stanford and Berkeley as the main suppliers of extremely smart people), money (with the ultra-concentration of venture capital) and – maybe most of all – the risk-taking culture of entrepreneurship and unbridled ambition. The spirit of Silicon Valley, is as elusive as it is cardinal to the success of its inhabitants.

Frederick Jackson Turner was an early 20th century American historian who coined the term 'Frontier Thesis' or 'Turner Thesis'. He took the moving 'frontier' line going from the US East Coast to the 'Wild West' as his study subject, and observed the 'pioneering' spirit of the people who kept on moving that line. At that time, Chicago was considered to be the outskirts of the Wild West. Anything to the West of the 'Windy City' was considered to be pioneering country.[23]

Now, the 'Turner Thesis' states that this moving frontier line was the place where pioneers would build the future, based on their unbridled belief that there was a brighter tomorrow out West. The settlers who left Europe for the 'New Continent' were ambitious people who wanted to get away from standing armies, established churches, aristocrats, noblemen and landed gentry who controlled most of the land. Above all, they wanted to believe in a brighter future. The people in Europe who stayed behind were the ones who did not want to take the risk.

Imagine that of those bold believers who crossed the Atlantic Ocean looking for a brighter future, only a handful dared to venture out West. And when you've crossed all the way over the Rocky Mountains and eventually come to the Pacific Ocean, and can go no further, that's where Silicon Valley is.

There's another Silicon Valley theory I love. How the alternative culture of California's 'Summer of Love' worked as a magnet for all kinds of weird, creative and divergent thinkers, many of whom stuck around afterwards. It's the children and grandchildren of these paradigm-shifting hippies and artists, who would be tantamount to the daring, hopeful and risk-averse culture of the Silicon Valley companies.[24] Whether it's Turner's theory, or this one, or a combination of both, there is no denying the unique spirit of this part of the world.

EUROPEAN QUESTIONS

When I take groups of European business executives on tours to Silicon Valley with my company nexxworks, I often get a call back from the startups that we visited. Often, they will tell me that they got a lot of 'European questions'. The people in Silicon Valley, you see, *want* to believe in a brighter future, they are fundamentally optimistic about the things that *can* happen. But our busload of European executives tends to be sceptic about that. They will ask questions about what could go wrong, how a company could fail, about how an idea could backfire. These Europeans can't help it, they are the genetic descendants of the people who stayed behind on the Old Continent and thought it was too risky and scary to get on those ships to the US.

I'm probably pushing the 'Turner Thesis' a bit too far, but out into the 450 square miles of La-La-Land surrounded by reality, there is an almost contagious optimism about the future, and risk-taking is fully embedded into the culture of doing business.

It is one of the reasons of the success of this new Roman Empire. Risk-taking is deeply embedded in its culture and 'Fail Fast, Fail Often' became a true mantra. I love Facebook's early days' motto: 'Move Fast and Break Things'. It meant that new tools and features on the platform might not be perfect, but creation speed was key, even if there were some mishaps along the way. If you fail quickly and learn from your mistakes, then you will be able to move faster. That's the pioneering spirit of the 21st century, the epitome of the 'Turner Thesis' for the network age.

GAFBAT AND BEYOND

In the age of networks, the 'Turner Thesis' is not limited to the West anymore, though. The compass has lost its meaning in the network. Today you see an explosion in 'Bits believers' all over the world. Whereas the GAFAnomics had a focus on the US West Coast, the reality of the network age is that we see new hubs of the network expanding globally. In the past few years, I've had the intense pleasure of spending more and more time in Asia, and what you see happening there is perhaps even more spectacular than the GAFAnomics.

In China, we talk of the 'BAT-men': Baidu, Alibaba and TenCent. These network disruptors are more recent than the GAFA players, and are therefore already using much more advanced technology. And they have a *big* advantage: the Asian population of consumers is immense in terms of scale and reach.

Baidu owns the 'search' business in Asia. It is the Chinese equivalent of Google, and is only one year younger that its Silicon Valley counterpart. Baidu grew extremely rapidly, and this helped fuel its expansion and research. Just like Google, today Baidu is betting big on the world of Artificial Intelligence (AI), and the autonomous world.

TenCent dominates communication in Asia. It is the owner of WeChat – the most popular messaging service in Asia. In 2017, WeChat had one billion users. But the really impressive part is that WeChat is much more than messaging. It represents a unique combination of content, messaging and applications, and has essentially become the *de facto* mobile operating system for building network applications in Asia. In terms of functionality, it's leaving Facebook Messenger and WhatsApp biting the dust. TenCent has an enormous portfolio of content, services and applications in the network, with WeChat at the center of its networking universe.

Alibaba 'owns' e-commerce in Asia. As we mentioned earlier, they have grown to become a global commercial platform controlling business-to-business exchanges in Asia to Business-to-Consumer activities worldwide. Their online payment activities, AliPay, grew to dwarf the online and mobile payments activities in the US, for example. The *Financial Times* estimated that Chinese mobile payments were nearly 50 times greater than those in the US in 2016, with the value of Chinese third-party mobile payments rising to USD 5.5 trillion.[25]

The US West Coast GAFAs are getting kicked around by the BAT-men.

Today we see an explosion of new network hubs. It's not just Palo Alto anymore. It's Shanghai, Shenzhen and Beijing. But it's also Berlin (for Internet of Things startups, for example), London (for FinTech startups), or Tel Aviv (for security startups), and so many others. More and more we see 'Bits Believer Hubs' in the network, wanting to claim and carve out a space in the 'Day After Tomorrow'. So, if you want to thrive in the 'Day After Tomorrow', it's not just important to keep an eye on these platform players, but to see how your company can become a network disruptor too. How *you* can become a data hog, bypass conventions, remove service friction, pimp the customer experience and leverage the network. Standing by and watching will no longer do.

But Is It Disruption ?

Clayton Christensen is the absolute 'Pope of Disruption'. It was his book *The Innovator's Dilemma*, that introduced the theory of 'disruptive innovation' in 1997.[26] He defined it as "an innovation that creates a new market and value network that will eventually disrupt an existing market and replace an existing product". No wonder that this latter-day *Schumpeter* has been profusely revered in Silicon La-La-Land. Everybody loved Clayton.

Or at least until 2015, when he wrote an article in the *Harvard Business Review* entitled *What Is Disruptive Innovation?*.[27] In it, he stated that while Uber is innovative, it wasn't a truly 'disruptive' innovation. He had every Silicon Valley granola-breath tech hipster choking on their kale smoothies. Clayton claimed that Uber's business model merely represented a 'sustaining innovation' as it only produced an incremental improvement on the existing taxi industry.

While Uber toppled from its disruptive pedestal, Christensen did reinforce Netflix's position. According to him, it was a good example of disruptive innovation when it toppled Blockbuster – the largest US home movie rental company that went bankrupt in 2010. Netflix came in as the low-cost challenger at the bottom end of the market, tapping a new market that Blockbuster had failed to notice. Instead, Blockbuster concentrated on improving products and services for its most discerning customers, while Netflix saw an opportunity to serve the unserved: sending mail-order DVDs to remote areas where there was no Blockbuster outlet.

In the eyes of Christensen, true 'disruption' happens when the incumbent's mainstream customers start taking up the startup's products or services in volume. That's exactly what started to happen when, all of a sudden, Blockbuster customers stopped going to the (expensive to maintain) Blockbuster retail outlets, and switched *en masse* to the Netflix alternative.

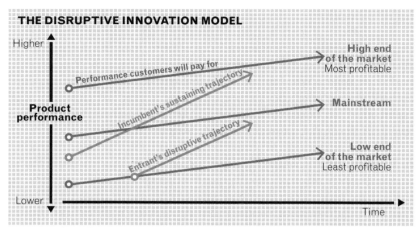

Source: Clayton M. Christensen, Michael Raynor and Rory McDonald, from 'What is disruptive innovation?'
(December 2015) · © HBR.ORG

This illustration is the very heart of Christensen's disruptive philosophy: the incumbent (Blockbuster) goes for the profitable customers – the high-end market – while the challenger (Netflix) goes for the low end of the market, and then 'Boom!' goes mainstream.

In the eyes of Christensen, the fact that Blockbuster went belly up because Netflix started mailing DVDs in brown envelopes was a truly disruptive innovation. The fact that Netflix reinvented itself in the world of streaming, and became the biggest digital network provider of video content on the planet, is a mere 'sustaining innovation'.

When the CEO of Blockbuster, Jim Keynes, was asked about Netflix in 2008, two years before they went belly up, he said: "Netflix is not on our radar screen in terms of competition. It's Walmart and Apple we should be worried about."[28] Remember what the people of Palm, Nokia and Microsoft said about the iPhone when it was launched? There is a pattern here, right? Intel's Andy Grove would have told them they weren't paranoid enough.

FROM NETWORKS TO NEW MARKETS AND BUSINESS MODELS

The very heated debate about what is 'disruptive' and what isn't in the eyes of hard-core academics like Clayton Christensen is perhaps a little moot. *TechCrunch*, the online voice of all disruptive things, wrote: "Uber unlocked an entirely new source of supply that created an entirely new market within for-hire transportation. It also brought into the market many consumers who wouldn't regularly use traditional taxis. In many cities, the market that Uber created is several times the size of the original taxi market. This is new market disruption in action."[29]

I believe this is the real discussion. Network effects will create entirely new markets. Business models will fundamentally change, shift and warp. And companies that want to take advantage of this, will have to take notice. Or disappear. The move from 'pipeline' to 'platform' is actually not an option. And it certainly won't be the last shift we'll experience.

FROM PRODUCT-CENTRIC TO SERVICE-CENTRIC

One of my favorite people in Silicon Valley is Jeremiah Owyang. This founder of 'Crowd Companies' is one of the most connected digital strategists in the Bay Area. When the new economic models started to flourish, he was one of the first to focus on the 'collaborative economy': what happens when the network is a place where we can share, participate and collaborate in ways that were previously impossible. He started to study the effects of network collaborative economies in many sectors and markets, and is the chief architect of the 'Collaborative Economy Honeycomb' model. In this model, he describes the frenzy of startup activity trying to reinvent entirely new business models in no fewer than 16 different markets.

It is clear that in the 'ground zero' of business model disruption, right in the very heart of Silicon Valley, we are witnessing how startups are out to eat your lunch. Fueled by some of the most powerful VCs in the world, talented digital pioneers are attempting to fundamentally alter well-established businesses, trying to trigger a fundamental shift in the world order, as profound as that caused by the Industrial Revolution 150 years ago: a shift from atom-bound pipeline companies to bit-driven, agile, small and networked platform companies.

But even Jeremiah Owyang – who's a collaborative economy ninja – does not have a magic formula. There is no 'silver bullet' for the age of network economies. But in his innovation council, where 'incumbents' share their ideas on how to attack this business model challenge, a few interesting approaches emerge.

Many companies are driving a transition from a product-centric business model to a service-centric business model. In the automotive industry, where 'selling cars' was the business model for a long time, we have seen that the influence of network thinking is forcing companies like BMW and Volkswagen to rethink that. Instead of selling cars, they are now providing 'mobility-as-a-service'. BMW launched 'Drive-Now' to provide cars for every occasion, as a service

Collaborative Economy Honeycomb Version 3.0

The Collaborative Economy enables people to get what they need from each other. Similarly, in nature, honeycombs are resilient structures that enable access, sharing, and growth of resources among a common group.

In the original Honeycomb 1.0, six distinct categories of startups were represented by the inner track of hexes. After a short period of time, Honeycomb 2.0 expanded to include six additional categories, placed on the outer perimeter.

In the new Honeycomb 3.0, four hexes are added on the corners of the graphic for a total of sixteen: Beauty, Analytics & Reputation, Worker Support, and the large Transportation hex is split into two distinct hexes.

By Jeremiah Owyang
jeremiah@CrowdCompanies.com
@jowyang, March 2016

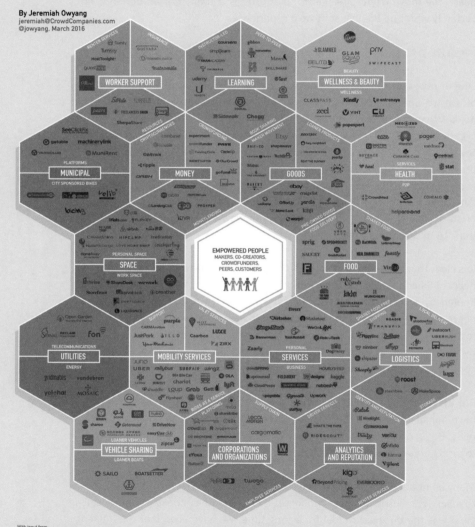

With input from:
Carl Bohlin, Matt Case, John Cass, Emily Castor, Shelby Clark, Lisa Gansky, Julie George, Neal Gorenflo, Greg Hedges, Bill Johnston, Karen Khounthavong, Alex Lassar, Gregory Leproux, Angus Nelson, Andreas Pages, Shervin Pishevar, Augie Ray, April Rinne, Jeff Rodman, Alexandra Samuel, Jamie Sandford, John Sheldon, Arun Sundararajan, Brian Solis, Julie Viola, Mike Walsh, Jonathan Wichmann, and Vision Critical.

Design by Vladimir Mirkovic www.transartdesign.com Creative Commons license: Attribution-NonCommercial.

CROWD™ COMPANIES
www.crowdcompanies.com

and, in 2016, Volkswagen launched 'Moia.io' as a way to position themselves as a mobility provider.

But that is just the beginning. As Owyang says: "TOMS shoes now offers a marketplace selling other people's products beyond their own. Nokia voluntarily gave up their specs to their phone cases to allow 3D printing to occur. U-Haul allowed the crowd to fund their own vehicles." Startups are going to attack almost any market with the full force of network effects, it is up to incumbents to act. As Owyang points out: "Corporations have one of two choices: one, fight the network, with regulations, or bombastic marketing, or two: collaborate with this new category of crowd-based startups and wield new business models."[30]

In my mind it is evidently clear that we will be facing a massive shift in business models over the next few decades. The combination of network effects with the advent of the 'Day After Tomorrow' technologies will afford huge opportunities for the Bits World to disrupt any industry. 'Software Is Eating The World' was just the beginning. The 'Day After Tomorrow' will re-arrange the world.

In these changing times, unless we can make sense of how the network economies and 'Day After Tomorrow' technologies evolve, companies will be in deep trouble. One of the slogans on the wall at A16Z is quite revealing: "The battle between every startup and incumbent comes down to whether the incumbent innovates before the startup gets distribution."

'DAY AFTER TOMORROW' BUSINESS MODELS: WHAT YOU NEED TO REMEMBER

Healthy Paranoia

Paranoia can sometimes be a good thing. Companies should make sure they never become complacent, but always remain aware of the lurking dangers of disruption. To make sure this paranoia does not turn sour, they can combine it with an open company culture, one that encourages ruthlessly honest dialogue. This is how companies can stay on their toes, and can avoid Corporate Myopia.

From Pipelines to Platforms

Today we have moved from Marc Andreessen's 'Software is eating the world' to 'Platforms are eating the world'. Platforms are no longer the invisible infrastructure they used to be. They have become ruthless business models. Today, atoms are becoming bits. Products are becoming services. Slow 'pipeline' companies find it increasingly difficult to compete against the agile network disruptors out there. If your company has not yet investigated how to become a platform company, it ought to.

The Disruptive Rule Book

DISRUPTIVE RULEBOOK

 Bypass conventions & **rules**

 Remove service **friction**

 Pimp customer experience

 Leverage the **network**

Passion & Risk

Disruption thrives on risk and passion. That's exactly the reason why it started first in Silicon Valley, home of those daring pioneers who left their status-quo addicted relatives back home to chase their belief in a better future. Disruption is as much about guts, grit and 'love' as it is about smart ideas. If you don't 'grok' that, you will never be a true innovator.

5

IT'S A CULTURE THING

The Secret Ingredient
of 'Day After Tomorrow' Organizations

WE HAVE MET THE ENEMY, AND HE IS US

The first thing new employees receive at Facebook is a little red book. It is a crystal clear and beautiful - almost poetic even - listing of the main aspects of its company culture. The reason why they created it is because Facebook keeps growing into an increasingly large corporation and they know they should do everything in their power to try to preserve their culture.

I spend most of my time with large organizations that are terrified that they have lost their agility, their speed, their capability to move swiftly and quickly. They're terrified that, somewhere along the road, they have lost their 'soul'. I love to show them Facebook's little red book to calm them down.

It's easy to be agile and swift when you're a startup. But as you grow to become a large enterprise, it's also remarkably easy to lose those capabilities: to build management structures that only seem to make things harder, to lose your sense of purpose as a company, and to attract employees who see working with you as just a 'job' and not a pursuit of their passions.

That's why culture matters.

That's why Facebook has a little red book.
That's why Peter Thiel told the Airbnb founders "Don't fuck up the culture" when they asked him for advice.
That's why Southwest Airlines' core values are "Warrior Spirit; Servant's Heart; Fun-LUVing Attitude".
That's why Dropbox operates on the principle of "you're smart, figure it out".
They understand that culture is the true engine of an organization: it can accelerate it, or slow its pace.

I could not describe it any better than Airbnb's co-founder Brian Chesky did in a letter to his entire team: "The thing that will endure for 100 years, the way it has for most 100-year companies, is the company culture. The culture is what creates the foundation for all future innovation. If you break the culture, you break the machine that creates your products."[1]

Wow. "If you break the culture, you break the machine that creates your products."

HOW CAN WE DESIGN FOR SPEED?

If you see the avalanche of technologies hurtling at us at warp speed, and if you see the maelstrom of business model flux that companies are going to face in this age of networks, the fundamental question is: how should we build companies that can handle their speed and radical change? How can we design organizations that have this 'agility' built in, and what are the blueprints of organizational design for the 21st century? This is, in my opinion, the number one issue that should be top of mind of executives today. But in many cases, the very opposite is true.

Today many companies still have Human Resources structures, processes and organizational patterns that are direct descendants from the industrial age approach. One of my favorite sayings is: "We have met the enemy… and he is us.". This is sadly very true for most large organizations. They often have plenty of really brilliant, incredibly innovative and extremely passionate people, but their management structures, corporate governance, processes and bureaucracy make it virtually impossible for all that brilliance, innovation and passion to shine through.

A 'TAYLORED' CULTURE

These days, most organizations still use the same methodology for managing people as advocated by Taylorism. The term comes from Frederick Taylor, who was probably the first 'management guru' in the early 20th century's burgeoning industrial revolution. He was the author of one of the very first business best-sellers *Principles of Scientific Management*[2] and was the one to turn management into a science. Taylor would have thought empathy, culture, passion and little red books to be a waste of time and money. He essentially saw workers as cogs in the vast, industrial machine. Henry Ford was a big fan, and his revolutionary River Rouge car plant was chiefly based on the ideas of Frederik Taylor.

Taylor's view on management was clear and simple and these are three important aspects of it: the first is to break all complex jobs into a series of simple ones, the second is to measure everything that workers do and to optimize operations accordingly, and the third is to convert those measurements into incentives: linking pay to performance. It worked wonders for the industrial age. Fine. But today, the influence of Frederik Taylor is still very present in how we run organizations. We still often hire people for a 'job', tack them onto an 'organization chart', and give them a stack of business cards with their 'title' on it: 'Junior Research Planning Assistant for the North-West US Sales Organization'.

The aspect of breaking down complex jobs into simple ones, meant that we started to build (and still do build) organizations with divisions, silos, branches, departments and subsidiaries, and to orchestrate all that we developed in rigidly boxed org-charts and matrices.

Taylor also wanted everything measured. Everything is reviewed. Even today, not just the performance metrics of laborers on a production line, but everyone is 'assessed' from managers to service workers to knowledge workers. From a yearly chat with your 'supervisor' we've gone to 360-degree feedback reviews from your superiors, your peers and your team. It is turning the Taylor philosophy of measurements from an annual ritual into a seemingly never-ending trial. And still, by far, we incentivize people based on output performance.

A lot of companies still cling to this outdated approach. The labor techniques of Amazon, for instance, even seem to make those of Henry Ford pale by comparison. Reports on how Amazon treats its employees in the picking warehouses and sorting lines of their operation facilities seem to indicate they maxed out Taylorism to the extreme with their 'rank and yank' approach: workers are regularly ranked by productivity and the weakest are ruthlessly eliminated.

PUTTING A DENT IN THE UNIVERSE

There is clearly a massive backlash happening today. Many young people simply refuse to become 'meatware' for large enterprises that still run on Taylorism. They have been raised in the online and networked age where the social web turned our environment into an open, transparent and fast meritocracy. They are critical and demanding. They won't take crap from their bosses. They laugh in the face of 'we do this because we have always done this'. They mock the siloed thinking, knowing that sharing information is the fastest way to success. They abhor classic, fixed-time assessments.

Young people eat Taylor's rules for breakfast.

That's exactly why the startup scene has become so intriguing and alluring for young talent. They think "Why join a slow, boring and rigid company when I could join a startup with a flat structure, direct communication, rapid learning from peers, clear common goals and a chance to feel the passion of collectively trying to 'put a dent in the universe'?". Why not, indeed.

Many large organizations are starting to feel that Taylorism might be at the end of its lifecycle, and rightly so. It worked brilliantly for the early industrial revolution and the period of globalization thereafter. Taylorism can work wonders if you only need to focus on growth, scale and efficiency. That's how large enterprises such as Exxon, Nestlé and General Motors could achieve global dominance with Taylor-made machines humming to perfection. But in the age of disruption, the age of networks, the age of VUCA, things are changing: the need for creativity, innovation, agility and flexibility is becoming a core asset for any organization. And that's not exactly the stuff of Frederik Taylor.

Vladimir Lenin was one of the biggest supporters of Taylorism. In the 1920s and 1930s, the Soviet Union enthusiastically embraced Taylorism to develop the infrastructure for the industrialization of the country after the Russian Revolution. The historian Thomas Hughes has extensively studied how the Soviets used Taylorism to develop their concepts of the centrally planned economy, and the use of the '5-year plans' that became widely established under Joseph Stalin. The collapse of the Soviet Empire in 1991 is testament to the fact that Taylorism is not the answer when changing circumstances require a focus on creativity, innovation, agility and flexibility. I wouldn't dare to compare many large organizations today to the Stalinist, centrally controlled machines inspired by Frederik Taylor, but nonetheless, companies will have to adapt in a major way.

THEORY X AND Y

The clash of cultures above can be clarified by the gap between theory X and theory Y, as brilliantly described by MIT Sloan School of Management professor Douglas McGregor in 1960. Theory X, basically, has a very low opinion of human nature. It supposes that the average employee has little to no ambition, shies away from work or responsibilities, and is individual-goal oriented. Generally, Theory X style managers believe that employees are dumb, lazy and work solely for a sustainable income. The only way to make sure they do what they have to do, is to monitor them and reward or reprimand them accordingly. Truly heartwarming. That would have made a wonderful little red book.

Theory Y is the complete opposite. Theory Y managers believe that employees are internally motivated, enjoy their labor, thrive on challenges, and work to better themselves without needing a direct 'reward' in return. Theory Y employees are considered the most valuable assets to the company, as its beating heart. Theory Y companies empower their employees and forego of Theory X's constant supervision.[3]

While most startups clearly advocate Theory Y (even if they probably haven't heard of it), Theory X's approach is the one still used in many large organizations. For them it's exactly like this: "we have met the enemy, and he is us". The biggest obstacle to the coming avalanche of change is their own internal organizational structure that served them so well in the 20th century.

The challenge for the age of networks, is to re-design our companies in terms of structure and culture: both of which must withstand the need for speed and agility in order to thrive in the 'Day After Tomorrow'.

ABANDON ALL HIERARCHIES

For centuries, the tried-and-trusted mechanism to run large organizations was the military command and control model. The Roman Empire grew to greatness thanks to its amazing military discipline and training, concentrated on instilling teamwork, group cohesion and effective communication top-down from the general to the troops. When the Roman troops fought the Gauls – who were fierce individual warriors – the former systematically won because their command and control systems had forged them together into highly effective fighting units.

In my previous book, I wrote at length about General Stanley McChrystal, who was the Commander of the US Armed Forces in Afghanistan. After horrible losses and terrible defeats, McChrystal came to the conclusion that his 'Command and Control' tactics had failed miserably with an enemy that was organized in a completely different way. He realized that the enemy he was fighting was not a 'structure' but rather a 'network' that was pumping information around faster than his hierarchically led troops. General McChrystal eventually decided that he needed to copy his adversary's methods and turn his organization into a network as well in order to be successful. This dramatically reduced allied losses and eventually his troops neutralized the jihadist mastermind, Abu Musab al-Zarqawi.

In his words: "It takes a network to defeat a network", which is now known as McChrystal's Law.

Today, the retired General has set up a business consultancy called the McChrystal Group, which helps companies become smarter, faster and flexible based on his own experiences in Afghanistan. He teaches them to 'unlearn' command and control and build a self-governing, cross-organizational warrior and intelligence network. He shows them how to redefine leadership and culture to enable quick action with little or no oversight. It's was a huge step for the military back in his General days, but it's no small step for large corporations either.

UNLEARNING COMMAND AND CONTROL

According to McChrystal, many people working in large corporations lack a clear idea of what is known as 'commander's intent': the directional guidance that helps everyone understand what leadership is trying to achieve and what the entire company should be 'fighting' for. Instead, many people lose track of the big picture and get distracted by the daily flow of information.

If you want to introduce true agility into a team, you must have leadership that is capable of monitoring rapidly changing situations while trusting others to make decicions about front-line actions. His motto is 'eyes on, hands off'.

But this only works when the troops are true members of a cohesive, trusting network comprised of skilled, problem-solving, collaborative people. And when they are all acting in unison for a clear and inspiring common cause.

General McChrystal learned the hard way how difficult it was to 'unlearn' command and control, and build his organization into an effective network. But, in his words: "I also learned that leading that network — a diverse collection of organizations, personalities, and cultures — is a daunting challenge in itself."[4]

The lessons from McChrystal show that it is possible, though. That a rigid structure *can* become a network if there is a clear, common cause. That a network can 'defeat' a network. In these changing times where the outside world seems to behave more and more like a network, where we see the huge network effects on business models, we have to understand how to turn our organizations into effective networks in order to be ready for the 'Day After Tomorrow'. But it requires a completely different way to train, develop and nurture this type of fast and connected ecosystem than to build the skills and tactics needed for a traditional organization. And it will require a whole new set of leadership skills to 'lead a network' than to 'lead an organization'.

Soooo. Let's burn all the org charts then?
Hold your horses. Maybe not so fast.

HOW ZAPPOS GAVE BOSSES THE BOOT

One of the best-known experiments in 'rethinking' organizational structures was the radical and highly visible 'Holacracy' experiment that was run at Zappos, headquartered in Las Vegas. Zappos is the online shoe shop that Amazon acquired in 2009 for USD 1.2 billion. It was initially founded in 1999 and run by Tony Hsieh. Hsieh had already made a fortune for himself when he started an advertising network called LinkExchange back in 1996, which he sold to Microsoft for USD 265 million only two years later.

From the very start, Zappos did things differently. They had a focus on customer service that was unparalleled in the world of retail and online business. Customer service reps were given initiative and freedom to help customers in any way they thought made sense, without having to ask their 'supervisors' first. The chain of command was uncoupled around the customer so that there would be a direct line between employees and customers and the former could go above and beyond to please the latter. One of my favorite examples is how a Zappos employee once conducted a customer-service call that lasted for almost 11 hours (and was only interrupted by a short bathroom break).[5]

We visited Zappos, with the nexxworks 'Innovation Tours', to understand their 'extreme customer centricity' approach. It is inspirational to see how such a company preserved this core vision while it kept growing, even when it was acquired by Amazon.com. Hsieh wrote the book *Delivering Happiness*[6], which tells the story of how he made customer service the responsibility of the entire company, not just a single department. He focused on the company culture as the number one priority to build his organization.

And then he took it one giant step further.

Zappos already had a rather extreme HR philosophy from the outset. Almost since the beginning of the company, they had had a policy of giving 'The Offer' to any new hire: "take USD 2,000 in cash instead of starting the job". They believed it was better to weed out those that weren't 100% thrilled about working at Zappos from the start. They only wanted people who were passionate about their work. People with a 'just a job' mentality were not welcome.

MAILING THE CHANGE

Then Hsieh went all the way when he pushed Zappos into 'Holacracy' in March of 2015. Holacracy is the ultimate antipode of command and control, because it eliminates traditional workplace hierarchy. Instead of being assigned a 'job' and giving you a reporting line to a 'boss', the system of Holacracy works completely differently. Everything is organized around 'circles', and employees are free to 'join' the circles they would like. And, in every circle, there is a system of 'self-organization' to make sure that the goals of the circle are met.

IN **TRADITIONAL** COMPANIES	WITH **HOLACRACY**
Job Descriptions Each person has exactly one job. Job descriptions are imprecise, rarely updated, and often irrelevant.	**Roles** Roles are defined around the work, not people, and are updated regularly. People fill several roles.
Delegated Authority Managers loosely delegate authority. Ultimately, their decision always trumps others.	**Distributed Authority** Authority is truly distributed to teams and roles. Decisions are made locally.
Big Re-Orgs The org structure is rarely revisited, mandated from the top.	**Rapid Iterations** The org structure is regularly updated via small iterations. Every team self-organizes.
Office Politics Implicit rules slow down change and favor people "in the know".	**Transparent Rules** Everyone is bound by the same rules, CEO included. Rules are visible to all.

Source: http://www.holacracy.org/how-it-works

Hsieh did not introduce the concept gently. Instead, he sent an email to all 1,443 Zappos employees. It started like this: "This is a long email. Please take 30 minutes to read through the email in its entirety." After a couple of paragraphs talking about 'Teal management' and 'self-organizing' entities, he said: "As of 4/30/15, in order to eliminate the legacy management hierarchy, there will be effectively no more people managers."

Bosses. Gone. Boom.

It was a radical experiment. The first results were not so encouraging. Reports leaked to the press talked about confusion in the workplace, chaos and uncertainty, employees who didn't understand how to get anything done anymore in the company. In his email, Hsieh had given a deadline of the last day of April for people to opt-out if they didn't want to join the Zappos journey into Holacracy. On that day, 14% of the company walked out. The entire staff turnover of Zappos in 2015 was over 30%.

By the end of that year, Zappos had fallen off *Fortune's* 'Best Companies to Work' list for the very first time in eight years. For Hsieh, the move to self-management was not just about following the latest management hype, it was his deep belief that this was the way to go, in business, but also in society. In the past few years, he spent a substantial part of his personal fortune, to the tune of USD 350 million, in building a work-life community in Las Vegas, which he calls the Downtown Project. He strongly believes in the power of grassroots communities[7], and compares self-management to the interactions that spring up organically in a city rather than the top-down bureaucracy of a typical organization. In an interview with *Fortune* magazine, Hsieh said: "The one thing I'm absolutely sure of, is that the future is about self-management."[8]

TEAL, THE LIVING COLOR

In his famous email that dazzled the Zappos workforce, Hsieh said he wanted to move Zappos from 'Green' to 'Teal'. He also asked all 'Zapponians' to read *Reinventing Organizations* by Frederic Laloux which is, to this day, known all over the company as 'The Book'.[9]

Frederic Laloux is a fellow Belgian, living in Brussels, the same age as me, who engaged in groundbreaking research on new organizational models at McKinsey. His view on traditional organizations is harsh and unforgiving: he describes them as "for the most part, places of quiet and pervasive suffering, places inhospitable to the deeper yearnings of our souls". Laloux wanted more.

He wanted to help build "truly soulful organizations that invite all of our human potential into the workplace".

Laloux's model assigns a color to each type of organizational design that has evolved over human history. 'Red' organizations are the oldest format: they are managed by control, power and fear and act like a wolf pack with a predatory leader. The mafia and street gangs are perfect examples of this approach. 'Amber' organizations, then, are the real 'command and control' structures, with formal roles. Cases of amber management are to be found in the military, but also still in most government organizations today. Most contemporary companies are 'Orange' – ruled by Taylorism – and focus on growth, efficiency and building a competitive edge. A lot of banks, insurance companies, or retailers such as Walmart, are examples of 'Orange' organizations. The next stage of evolution, according to Laloux are the 'Green' organizations that focus on culture and empowerment. He describes Starbucks as an example of such a 'Green' culture.[9]

EXHIBIT 1: EVOLUTIONARY BREAKTHROUGHS IN HUMAN COLLABORATION

Color	Description	Guiding Metaphor	Key Breakthroughs	Current Examples
RED	Constant exercise of power by chief to keep foot soldiers in line. Highly reactive, short-term focus. Thrives in chaotic environments.	Wolf pack	· Division of labor · Command authority	· Organized crime · Street gangs · Tribal militias
AMBER	Highly formal roles within a hierarchical pyramid. Top-down command and control. Future is repetition of the past.	Army	· Formal roles (stable and scalable hierarchies) · Stable, replicable processes (long-term perspectives)	· Catholic Church · Military · Most government organizations (public school systems, police departments)
ORANGE	Goal is to beat competition, achieve profit and growth. Management by objectives (command and control over what, freedom over how).	Machine	· Innovation · Accountability · Meritocracy	· Multinational companies · Investment banks · Charter Schools
GREEN	Focus on culture and empowerment to boost employee motivation. Stakeholders replace shareholders as primary purpose.	Family	· Empowerment · Egalitarian management · Stakeholder model	Businesses known for idealistic practices (Ben & Jerry's , Southwest Airlines, Starbucks, Zappos)
TEAL	Self-management replaces hierarchical pyramid. Organizations are seen as living entities, oriented toward realizing their potential.	Living organism	· Self-management · Wholeness · Evolutionary purpose	A few pioneering organizations (see "Examples of Teal Management")

Source: Frederic Laloux, Reinventing Organizations, Nelson Parker, 2014

134

THE DAY AFTER TOMORROW

I've had the pleasure of diving into the Starbucks culture many times at its Seattle headquarters. They fundamentally work around cultural values, and their mission "To inspire and nurture the human spirit – one person, one cup and one neighborhood at a time" is not just a hollow slogan on the wall. It shows a dedication to the community they are trying to build. New recruits at Starbucks' headquarters are not allowed to 'work' during their first month. They are urged to take the time to understand the company, and meet as many people as possible. During those 30 days, their 'job' is to build their own network inside the organization, over a cup of coffee, and establish the relationships that could take their career to a higher level.

But even 'Green' is not the highest level in Laloux's view on the evolution of organizations. One step beyond it we can find 'Teal' entities. Decentralized Teal companies are characterized by self-management, creative potential, bringing one's 'whole' self to work, and having a purpose beyond making money. They operate effectively, even at a large scale, with a system based on peer relationships, without hierarchy or the need for consensus. Their strategy emerges organically from collective intelligence, not from 'bosses' or even individuals. Organizations that are 'Teal' - like Patagonia, FAVI, Sun Hydraulics, Morning Star, Heiligenfeld and Buurtzorg – become a living organism, instead of just a structure.

What strikes me the most is how neither the concept of Teal organizations, nor Holacracy are entirely new.

The Holacracy system was introduced at Ternary Software, a Pennsylvania startup launched in 2001. It had been experimenting with democratic forms of organizational governance based on the principles of (among others) agile software development, the lean movement and sociocracy. Its founder Brian Robertson distilled the best practices of Ternary into an organizational system that later became known as 'Holacracy'. In early 2007, the Ternary experimentation shifted to 'HolacracyOne' – a new organization formed by Robertson and entrepreneur Tom Thomison to further mature Holacracy and assist companies with their respective transformations. Robertson also developed the 'GlassFrog' software that organizations could use to set up the circles of work and manage the transition towards Holacracy.[10]

JUST A FAD?

But neither 'The Book' by Laloux nor GlassFrog software could save Zappos from the serious trouble that lay ahead. The press had a field day with its struggles: there were numerous reports of the Zapponians leaving the mothership after the introduction of Holacracy and stories of chaos and confusion at the workplace. *The Economist* ran an article titled: 'The holes in Holacracy'. It quoted Jeffrey Pfeffer from Stanford University who argued that "hierarchy is a fundamental principle of all organizational systems."[11]

In an interview with *Harvard Business Review*, John Bunch – who was the Holacracy Implementation Lead at Zappos – reflected on the hyperjump to 'Teal': "You would say maybe that Holacracy is chaotic. But there's actually probably more structure in a holacratic company than there is in traditional companies. All the work that is going on across the organization is extremely well-defined, it's transparent. You can look it up anywhere across the company."[11]

Zappos transitioned from an 'org chart' to a 'work chart'. It strived for employees to become more productive because they're more passionate about being able to select the work they want from the work chart, as opposed to selecting a job description from the org chart. In 2016, there were about 500 circles at Zappos, with most employees typically functioning in two or more circles. The mission of a circle can change, sometimes frequently, to reflect the evolving needs of the firm. Tony Hsieh himself, the CEO of the company, became the 'lead link', in an overarching company-wide circle, with the powers of the final arbiter, in case of a deadlock situation in one of the circles.

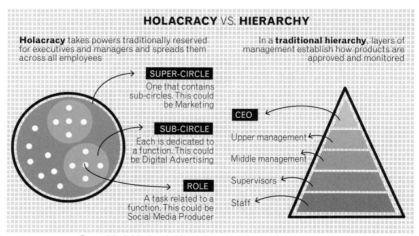

Source: http://uk.businessinsider.com/zappos-ceo-tony-hsieh-on-misconception-about-holacracy-2016

In the same *Harvard Business Review* interview, Ethan Bernstein, Professor of Leadership in Organizational Behavior at Harvard Business School, said this transition was probably inevitable going forward. "It makes perfect sense in our image of the trend towards the millennial generation. Not every organization, obviously, is going to take the big step that Zappos has taken, but I do think that if you look over the next 10 or 20 years, most organizations are going to take a small step or several small steps this way." He argued that organizations that are increasingly thinking about structure as an advantage and a way to make their employees more productive, will continue to evolve and innovate in the direction of self-management.

Perhaps Hsieh's mega-jump all the way to a 'Teal' culture was somewhat too bold and impulsive. Maybe baby steps towards new organizational patterns that deviate from the Imperial command and control would have made it easier for those poor Zapponians to adopt. Also, it seems a little off to introduce such a flat, inclusive and empowered approach in such a top-down manner. After all, he emailed everyone something that conveyed "I, the boss, have decided that there will be no more bosses and I don't give a damn what you, employees, want or think". Pretty ironic, if you ask me, though I'm sure he never meant it that way. But his pressure-cooker approach will yield valuable lessons going forward, for any company.

When the rumors about the 'Teal' troubles at Zappos started to surface, the press was quick to paint 'Holacracy' as a foolish fad, a cult-like frenzied hype and a pipe dream of self-organization. I do *not* agree. We have to move past this and recognize Zappos' endeavor for what it truly is: a grand-scale and bravely radical experiment on rethinking organizational structures. We all stand to learn a lot from how people responded, reacted and learned during this very bold test. True, 30% of the Zapponians dropped out during year one, but the ones that have stayed are the ones that fit the new culture like a glove and are truly excited to participate in one of the largest experiments to rethink 'the firm' of our times.

WHY DO COMPANIES EXIST?

But why do companies exist at all? That bold question was posed and studied in the 1930s by Ronald Coase, a young student at the London School of Economics. He had the chance to travel abroad and spend time researching large booming companies in the US: the likes of Ford and General Motors. He was duly impressed by how they were run, in the true Taylorist manner, but he kept asking himself why they existed in the first place. He wrote his theory down in the short article *The Nature of the Firm*, which very few people paid attention to. Until three decades later, when the American scholar Oliver Williamson rediscovered it. Coase received the Nobel prize in Economics in 1991, and Williamson would receive the same prize in 2009.[12]

So, what did Ronald Coase discover in *The Nature of the Firm*? In his time, companies were still considered to be 'black boxes' that transform inputs into outputs. Coase, however, wanted to peek inside, find out how they tick, and understand the mechanics of the internal organization of firms. In doing so, he discovered a whole new area of economic theory.

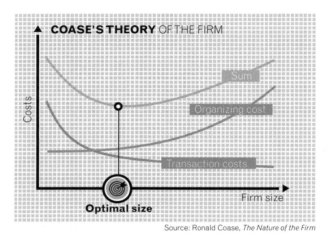

COASE'S THEORY OF THE FIRM

Costs

Sum

Organizing cost

Transaction costs

Optimal size

Firm size

Source: Ronald Coase, *The Nature of the Firm*

The well-established economic theory of the time – based on the 18th century theory of Scottish economist Adam Smith – advocated that markets were 'efficient'. Coase did not completely agree and introduced the concept of 'transaction costs'. He argued that if markets were efficient, and everyone who was best at providing goods or services most cheaply was already doing so, no one would ever 'hire' anyone. In a perfectly efficient market, Coase argued, we could all just do business through a bunch of contracts with suppliers and freelancers, and we wouldn't have to establish ourselves in formal 'companies'.

So why don't we all have one-man companies and a load of freelancers? Why do we have corporations like Exxon or Google? Because Coase discovered markets are not frictionless. There are 'transaction costs' associated with the interactions: the cost of finding the right supplier, for example. Imagine how difficult it is to find the right plumber to come to your house, how much time it takes you to find the guy, to arrange a visit, to keep calling him to come back and finally fix that leaking sink. Transaction costs: not just in finding the right suppliers, but in bargaining, making sure that you keep your intellectual property and trade secrets, and 'protecting' you in the transaction. Also: the cost of enforcing your rights when something goes wrong, the cost of litigation, of lawyers and trials. Coase discovered that, in many cases, the cost of obtaining a product or service via the market actually exceeded the price of the product or service: meaning the cost of hassling with your plumber was higher than the plumber's final bill.

WHEN TRUST IS CHEAPER

These transaction costs disappear if you internalize them into a 'firm'. If you have an in-house legal team, then you don't need to worry about the trans-action costs of having to find the right lawyers when you need them, you just use the ones inside the firm. The reason why the internalized transactions are cheaper is because of 'trust'. You 'trust' that the internal legal team is competent and knowledgeable, and that they will fight for the cause of the 'firm' and not try to rip you off. Coase perceived that a 'firm' is just a network of people who saw their costs decline when they conducted business with each other on a regular basis. The bigger the company, the more you can drive down the inter-nal transaction costs, and the more efficient you become.

So why don't companies just keep on growing, with lower and lower transaction costs? Aha, well that's the interesting part. Coase discovered that as compa-nies grow larger and larger, the cost of 'organizing' the firm starts to increase. As companies grow larger and larger, they build management structures and overheads. They create committees and subcommittees. They make mistakes in allocating and planning for resources. The bigger the companies become, the less you 'know' the other party, or trust them the way you did when the com-pany was smaller. As companies grow, the 'organizing cost' starts to increase, and often very rapidly.

There are two conflicting costs in companies as they grow: the larger the firm, the lower the transaction costs, the cost of doing business. Great. But also, the larger the firm, the higher the organizing cost, the cost of the structure. Not so great.

If you combine these two opposite forces and find an optimal balance, that is the 'optimal size' of the firm.

Interestingly, the basic element to be reckoned with here is 'trust'. The reasons why 'the firm' exists in the first place is that - out on the open market - you can't 'trust' a lawyer, and this costs money. If you internalize them, it becomes easier to 'trust' the internal legal team to do a good job.

But as companies grow too large, the 'trust' in the internal people fails com-pletely. The bureaucracy, red tape, governance, review and audit processes actually destroy any 'trust' in the internal mechanisms. The result is that people in the firm would rather hire external help, consultants, or outsource their busi-ness than trust the internal functions, structures or people.

I cannot tell you how many times in my career I have visited companies where business executives would rather work with a young agile, external digital agency than with the internal IT department. Sadly, this is not necessarily because the IT department has fewer skills or less knowledge. It's just faster, simpler and cheaper to work with the bearded and short-panted hipster crowd from the agency, than with the internal structure of IT-Business Liaisons and IT-Business Alignment frameworks. The 'organizing cost' grows very large, very quickly and annoys people in companies even more than dealing with unknown 'plumbers' at home. We have met the enemy, and he is us.

And that is what Coase discovered back in the 1930s in his little article that almost nobody noticed called *The Nature of the Firm*. An article that also answers my Big Question number 3.

Big Question #3:

"How is it possible that large corporations – even when they understand their own challenges and the directions they need to take – are incapable of moving on their own, without external help and guidance?"

Because of organizational cost and the erosion of trust that come with growth and scale. But there is a way to 'cheat' these seemingly unavoidable evolutions. Eckart Wintzen proved it could be done.

THE 'HIVE' IS THE NEW NETWORK

Trying to overcome the innate problem of the organizing cost became the quest of the second half of the 20th century. Companies built 'divisions' to break the firm into more manageable chunks. They built 'branches' to maintain more trust at a local level. They built 'compartments' where they could curb the run-away cost of organizing the firm as it grew.

One of my favorite ideas to solve this huge challenge of large organizations comes from the firm that is now called 'Atos': a giant in the technology services industry which originated as the largest Dutch IT services provider of the time, called 'BSO/Origin'[13], founded by the eccentric entrepreneur Eckart Wintzen.

By all standards Eckart Wintzen was a hippie. A billionaire hippie. He was characterized by his grey slightly unkempt shoulder-length hair, scraggly beard, John Lennon-style glasses, and apparent allergy to formal suits. Tony Stepanski, who ran the US operations for Wintzen, recalled that when he met him for the first time he looked "like he'd just fallen off the back of a garbage truck."[14]

Looks can be deceiving.

Eckart Wintzen grew his company to a global staff of more than 11,000 employees before he sold it to Atos and they merged into Atos Origin. The transaction made him immensely wealthy. At the time of the sale, his privately held company had over 100 offices in 24 countries, with global revenues exceeding USD 500 million.

CELL DIVISION 101

But BSO/Origin was not a traditional 'firm' as we know it. It was a collection of 'cells' that was the result of a deliberate strategy to optimize the effectiveness and agility of the organization, while keeping the 'organizing costs' low.

The concept of 'cell division' was the fundamental principle that Wintzen lived by. It was his baby.

When Wintzen started the fledgling IT services company, it grew rapidly to 100 people. But then he surprised his number two with a divorce proposal: Why didn't they each take charge of different yet connected companies by splitting their present firm into two halves? His number two agreed, and set up shop with half of the company in a new building almost 50 kilometers away.

It was Wintzen's first 'cell division'. It worked beautifully: each half would function as a lean, competitive unit. He then succeeded in repeating this process over and over again: every-time one 'cell' would grow beyond 100 people, he would split it and make them separate entities within a corporate 'network'.

The results were spectacular: overheads stayed low, the 'organizational cost' remained minimal, but the entrepreneurial instincts thrived. The very best new people handled virtually any challenge Wintzen threw at them, knowing that they could rise through the ranks quickly and perhaps, one day, head up their own cells.

A FRIENDLY BUT COMPETITIVE HIVE NETWORK

Wintzen called it "friendly competition between peers". As he put it: "Every guy who started a new cell wanted to show his former boss that results could be obtained better, faster."[14]

Wintzen had found a way to cheat on the organizational cost of Coase, by using a 'hive' network of cells, and a 'cell division' approach to grow fast and large, without losing the agility, the flexibility and, above all, the entrepreneurial 'hunger' of the original cell. The different cells would often compete for the same business. Although it might seem strange, Wintzen would actually fuel this type of internal competitive pressure because, in the end, he didn't care: whichever cell won the business, the network would always win. The 'hive' of cells would prevail.

In Wintzen's view, the key success factor was to keep the *culture and purpose* of the entire organization identical. While he built a network of cells, he made sure that all the people in the cells had exactly the same spirit, the same mission and the same passion. As Wintzen put it: "The stronger the company culture, the more people will want to belong to our collective, the more they will want to be part of our journey. If the company culture becomes 'meh', then the whole thing falls apart".[14] He also hated Human Resources. The entire company grew to more than 4,000 employees before he finally felt the need to set up a global HR department. Until then, all the HR activities were done entirely witin the cells.

For the people inside the cells, working there could be a combination of chaos and order at the same time. But there was never a dull moment. And, year after year, the firm that Wintzen had created came out on top of the 'Best Companies to work for'.

You could argue that the nature of the IT services business allowed Wintzen to set up this 'hive' structure of cell-division. All of the entities in his network did *exactly* the same type of business: he could use a 'cookie-cutter' approach to replicate the cells and grow the business. That would be much more difficult to replicate in other industries.

Or would it?

CHAORDIC

Have you ever wondered why your credit cards have your name embossed in them the way they do? The history behind that is actually quite fascinating. Back in the 1930s, the precursor of the plastic card in your wallet was called a 'charga-plate'. These 'charga-plates' were small rectangles of sheet metal, very similar to a military dog tag, that were embossed with the customer's name, city and state. On their backs, was a small paper card with a signature. Regular customers of merchants – who made frequent purchases – could use the plates so that copying errors would be reduced when orders were manually processed. The 'charga-plate' was placed in a little device, with a paper 'charge slip' positioned on top of it, and an inked ribbon pressing against the charge slip would capture the correct name and address from the embossed 'charga-plate'. If you're lucky, you can sometimes still see your credit card being run through a 'credit-card' machine to ink your card details onto a paper slip. That's the old 'charga-plate' legacy.

The Diners Club card was the first real 'general purpose' credit card that was introduced in 1950, followed by the American Express card. In September 1958, Bank of America launched the BankAmericard, which became incredibly successful because they licensed their card to many other banks. But the latter almost created a financial crisis of unprecedented proportions.

The early credit cards in the US, of which BankAmericard was the most prominent example, were mass produced and mass mailed in an unsolicited manner to bank customers. The cards were thought to be a safe bet when it came to credit risks. Yes, you understood that right: not the application was mailed, but the actual credit card itself.

Unfortunately, the banks didn't do their homework properly. Children were receiving credit cards in the mail. Pets had cards sent to them. Convicted felons were getting cards. They had been mailed off to unemployables, drunks, drug addicts, gamblers and to compulsive debtors, without any proper background checks. These mass mailings were known as 'drops' in banking lingo, and were outlawed in 1970 due to the financial chaos they caused. However, by the time this law came into effect, the damage had been done and more than 100 million credit cards had been dropped into the U.S. population. If you want to understand where the obsession of the US population with 'credit card debt' came from, look no further. Fraud was rampant, the banks were hemorrhaging red ink.

By 1968, the entire credit-card industry had become so self-destructive that Bank of America called its licensees to a meeting in Columbus, Ohio, to find a solution. This meeting resulted in giving Dee Hock the reigns to solve this debacle. The situation was so dire, it called for desperate measures, and Dee Hock saw his chance.

The story of how he saved Visa, the new name of BankAmericard, is beautifully written in his book *One from Many: Visa and the Rise of Chaordic Organization*.[15]

AN ENABLING ORGANIZATION

Visa – with the many banks that had licensed the card and all the financial institutions that were involved – was an organizational nightmare. Dee Hock realized that he had to think completely out of the box: "It was the time for change. Command and control organizations were not only archaic and increasingly irrelevant. They were becoming a public menace, antithetical to the human spirit and destructive of the biosphere. I was convinced we were on the brink of an epidemic of institutional failure."

Dee Hock designed the new Visa organization in a highly decentralized and collaborative manner. Everything that could be pushed out to the edges of the organization was pushed out as far as possible: authority, initiative, decision making, ... The members of the Visa network, would have to work together (to accept the cards issued by one bank by another for example), to agree on standards (like the layout and format of the card), but would also fiercely compete with each other for customers and business.

Hock realized that no 'dictate from headquarters' would possibly work. Instead, he looked to nature for inspiration. From the beginning, Hock had designed Visa as a deliberately un-centralized organization. As he puts it: "The Visa organization had to be based on biological concepts to evolve, in effect, to invent and organize itself." Visa has been labelled "a corporation whose product is coordination." Hock prefers to call it "an enabling organization".

It worked. Visa grew phenomenally during the 1970s, from just a few hundred members to tens of thousands. By the early 1980s, Visa had surpassed MasterCard as the largest in the world, and today it controls more than 50% of the world's credit card market. Since 1970, Visa has grown by something like 10,000%, and it still continues to expand at roughly 20% per year.

Don't be mistaken, just because Visa was decentralized, it does not mean that it was an organization without bosses. Far from it. But the nature of the organization that Hock built was constantly balancing on 'the edge of chaos': it encouraged as much competition and initiative as possible throughout the organization – 'chaos' – while building in mechanisms for cooperation — 'order.' Hock even conceived a new word to describe this kind of tension: a system that was both chaotic and ordered, was 'chaordic'.

It's not absurd to consider Visa, "the corporation whose product is coordination", as a model for how networked organizations of the future could be managed. In Hock's words: "Inherent in the Visa experience could be the archetype of the organization of the 21st century."

NATURE IN THE LEAD

Hock took a lot of inspiration from nature. He built a system of guiding principles to grow the Visa network. One principle was that decisions should be made by bodies and methods that included all relevant and affected parties and were dominated by none. As he says: "Just like there is no dominant part of nature, no organ in your body dominates any other. Get rid of your liver and your brain dies just as certainly as your liver will without the brain."

Hock's view is reminiscent of another nature-inspired organizational model which is described in the book *The Starfish and the Spider: The Unstoppable Power of Leaderless Organizations* by Ori Brafman and Rod Beckstrom.[16]

Starfish represent decentralized organizations while spiders are like hierarchical command and control structures. The principle is deceivingly simple. Starfish have a decentralized neural structure, which allows for regeneration in case of trouble. If you cut off a starfish's leg it will not die. On the contrary, it will grow a new leg *and* the severed leg can grow into an entirely new starfish too. If you 'hurt' it, it grows and multiplies. Spiders, on the other hand, have a centralized neural structure. Cut off a leg and it will grow slower and be more vulnerable. Cut off its head and it dies. Traditional top-down organizations are like spiders and natural inspired organisms like Visa and BSO/Origin thrive like starfish.

Another guiding principle of Hock was that participation and ownership should be open to all relevant and affected parties in the Visa network. In his words: "A rainforest doesn't choose which seed will sprout. They're all eligible to belong." I love his analogy. Just like his organization, rainforests are beautifully emergent, fecund and productive places. And Victor Hwang and Greg Horowitt feel the exact same way.

THE PLANTATION AND THE RAINFOREST

Ah. Those wretched organizing costs of Coase. Without those, we could build Taylorism-inspired entities that could grow forever and keep becoming more and more efficient. Well-oiled, lean and mean product machines. Instead, we have to look into the inherent messiness of nature to think about hives and networks, we have to look at cell-division, at Teal colors and starfish, and observe natural systems on the edge between order and chaos.

We may even have to really understand the rainforest.

One of the most inspirational insights into building organizations for the 'Day After Tomorrow' came from a book called *The Rainforest: The Secret to Building the Next Silicon Valley*, written by Victor Hwang and Greg Horowitt.[17]

Both Hwang and Horowitt are venture capitalists. They started a successful firm called T2 Ventures out in Silicon Valley. During the course of the last decade, they were asked over and over again by governments all around the world to explain how they could 'build the Next Silicon Valley'. How could Kazakhstan become the Next Silicon Valley? How could Milan or Munich become the next startup capital of the world?

Hwang and Horowitt got a little tired of hearing that same question *ad nauseam*. They kept telling people that it's not about just putting all the 'ingredients' together to make a miracle happen.

We've established, in the previous chapter, that Silicon Valley is indeed a special place: a cocktail with all the right ingredients. The concentration of smarts and experience flowing out of talent-factories like Stanford and Berkeley. The concentration of money and VCs with Sand Hill road at the very epicenter of Silicon Valley. The enormous experience of previous ventures and models flowing freely towards the next generation of startups, where the older generation of entrepreneurs can act as catalysts, business angels and network nodes. And let's not forget the adoption of risk-taking, 'fail-fast-fail-often-learn-from-mistakes' attitude of the serial entrepreneurs that 'Frontier Theory' founder Frederick Turner would be so proud of.

Those were a given. But there is more. There is something special.

GOING BANANAS

Hwang and Horowitt compared that magical mix to the ecosystem of a rainforest, which they feel is completely different to the concept of a plantation, which is how traditional companies tend to function. But what is the difference between the two?

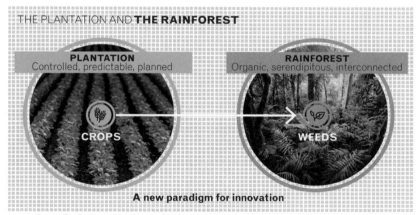

Source: The Rainforest: The Secret to Building the Next Silicon Valley, written by Victor Hwang and Greg Horowitt.

The plantation is a metaphor for the business and management model that emerged from the Industrial Revolution. The notion of the firm as dictated by Taylorism, and this agricultural comparison, are primarily focused on growing one thing: you cultivate one crop, to perfection. The company or plantation uses all the technologies, talents and tools, to calibrate accuracy, precision, quality and the productivity of this particular crop.

Let me put it like this. If you run a banana plantation, bananas are all that you care about. You wake up every morning energized, thinking: "bananas!". You spend all day in your plantation thinking about more bananas, about more productivity in your plantation to produce even more bananas. You will make PowerPoints about bananas, and write memos about bananas, and spend a lot of time putting emails about bananas into folders. You will have off-sites with your key people in your plantation, talking about more bananas. You will have slogans on the wall about banana quality, and warn your executives about possible moves in the banana world.

Plantations are brilliant. If you want more bananas.

But the chances that you'll ever think about anything else but bananas is virtually nada. Zilch. Zip. Bupkis.

GROW WEEDS EVERYDAY

Then there's the wild and seemingly disorganized messiness of the rainforest. There are no 'crops' in the rainforest. The rainforest has 'weeds'. It's messy and chaotic. Hwang and Horowitt see Silicon Valley as a 'rainforest ecosystem', an inherently dangerous place to start with. You can get killed by a snake in the rainforest and die instantly. The mortality rate of a startup is nearly 95%, even in Silicon Valley. But the startups don't mind. You can get killed by the venom of a snake, and perish instantly, but that same venom could be the cure for cancer, that's the lure of the rainforest.

As the authors say: "Think of companies such as Google and Facebook today, they were indistinguishable from weeds only a few years ago. The oddballs are the game-changers in innovation systems. In rainforests we want to nurture the weeds to grow." Plants are best harvested from plantations, but weeds sprout best from rainforests.

According to them, Silicon Valley is unique because it functions as a rainforest. It's not just about smart people, the world is filled with smart people. But smart people out in Kazakhstan trying to build a startup might fail because they are like a lone flower in the desert, without a rainforest around it to help it grow and bloom. You need the hustle and bustle, the 'thickness' of the jungle to foster interactions: innovation is a 'body contact sport', where you need the interactions that are natural in such a fertile and connected environment.

The right balance of 'trust' in an ecosystem like Silicon Valley gives an ideal mix of 'transaction costs' and 'organizing costs'. If you build a rainforest ecosystem, innovation can skyrocket. It explains the rise of Amsterdam in the 17th century where the rainforest of shipbuilders, sailors, risk-taking capitalists, merchants and adventurers created the Dutch 'Golden Age'. It explains the rise of Florence in the renaissance, the rise of Hollywood in filmmaking, the rise of Wall Street in the age of capitalism. And it explains Silicon Valley today.

The authors challenge us that if you want to build a new Silicon Valley today, you don't just need to bring all the ingredients together: talent, money, startups, etc. It goes far beyond that. The most important thing is to facilitate the growth of supportive networks, hives of trust and to reduce the 'transactional costs' of building new ventures. It's about building a community where ideas can have sex, and bear amazing results.

I've often found out myself that if you are in Silicon Valley, you are approached by every single entrepreneur who will start pitching their idea and story to you right away. They trust that speed is more important than caution. It's more important for them to receive direct feedback from you about their idea, than to wait for any legal safeguarding. But when I come back to Europe, and some fledgling startup with an idea wants to pick my brains, they will first send me a four-page Non-Disclosure Agreement before sending me any information.

IDEAS FLOURISH BY SHARING

It's all about trust. Behavioral scientist Janet Crawford understands how hard it is, though: "Attention has a negative bias. It's much more useful (for your survival) to notice the tiger lurking in the tree, than the tasty fruit on its branches". We are evolutionarily wired to avoid loss more than to seek gain. Distrust is easier than trust." But that's mostly the 'safe' European way. Those who were brave enough to cross the Atlantic to unknown lands – who crossed the Rocky Mountains to end up in the rainforest of Silicon Valley – see things differently. For them surviving was just as much about seeing the tiger as it was about seeing the fruit. Hwang and Horowitt put it like this: "Rainforests like Silicon Valley have developed ways to foster communication, trust and collaboration among very different kinds of people." That's what makes them truly unique.

I loved their book. It describes how you could build an innovation ecosystem somewhere else and mimic the 'magic' of Silicon Valley. And today we see that happening. Tel Aviv is a vibrant rainforest for the world of cybersecurity and intelligence. China has numerous rainforest-style innovation clusters that are building the next generation of Alibabas, TenCents and Baidus. Berlin is turning into a pulsating rainforest with a strong focus on the Internet of Things and the Fourth Industrial Revolution.

You can also apply the plantation and rainforest metaphor to the world of corporate innovation.

For the past few years, I've used the 'banana plantation' example in my speeches to large organizations around the world. And when I talk about 'PowerPoints about bananas', and 'Three-day off-sites about more bananas', I can often see these corporate executives reflect with a perplexed look on their face.

I can hear them think: "My God. It's true. We're only worried about the bananas." Corporate Banana Myopia. There could be creatures in the rainforest, tiny startups that you might still consider weeds, that could one day rise up and swallow you alive like an ivy would choke a large and powerful tree.

The natural reaction of many corporates is a very understandable one: "We have to get some of the 'rainforest' magic into our banana plantation right away". Yes! Brilliant! "So, let's buy one of those rainforest startups!" No! Horrible!

I've lost count of how many times I have seen this disaster scenario play out. A large banana plantation feels that it must become more like a 'rainforest': so, it fiercely flashes a huge amount of cash to the rainforest inhabitants and eventually 'buys' the startup that took the bait. The plantation buyers will feel very smug after that and will tell everyone how they were smart and rich enough to buy their very own trophy rainforest startup.

I can predict, with almost total certainty, what will happen next. It's not rocket science if you think about it: a creature that has lived in the rainforest all its life, suddenly gets yanked out of its ecosystem, and is planted in a plantation. There is a chance – a great chance – that it will die, lacking, as it does, the connectedness, temperature, soil and humidity of its familiar environment.

Remember:

Big Question #2:

"Why are large corporations so eager to acquire new startups, and why are they capable of screwing them up so profoundly in such a record time?"

Rainforests and plantations are why. Because plantations have no idea how to foster rainforest magic.

I've had this experience myself in my first startup. When Alcatel acquired my company, we were well used to the 'startup rainforest' life but were suddenly thrown into the living hell of the rules, regulations, governance and politics of a huge banana plantation. We died almost overnight.

The *real* trick in my opinion to getting more 'rainforest magic' in your plantation is to focus on culture. Not that this will be easy. It will be very hard because there is a *fundamental* difference in culture between the plantation and the rainforest.

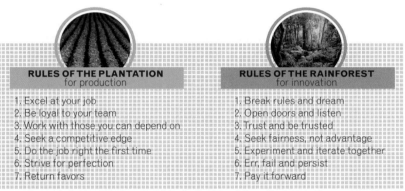

RULES OF THE PLANTATION for production	RULES OF THE RAINFOREST for innovation
1. Excel at your job	1. Break rules and dream
2. Be loyal to your team	2. Open doors and listen
3. Work with those you can depend on	3. Trust and be trusted
4. Seek a competitive edge	4. Seek fairness, not advantage
5. Do the job right the first time	5. Experiment and iterate together
6. Strive for perfection	6. Err, fail and persist
7. Return favors	7. Pay it forward

Source: The Rainforest: The Secret to Building the Next Silicon Valley, written by Victor Hwang and Greg Horowitt.

Let me give you a few examples. One of the most important rules (yes, I'm aware of the irony) of the rainforest is: "Break rules and dream". Startups, by nature, have to drive radical changes. They have to apply 10x thinking and produce moonshots. But they must also be a little naive. They have to believe in a brighter future, and in a positive outcome. They need people who are allowed to dream up the 'Day After Tomorrow'. The plantation, on the other hand, has a very different approach. They tell their people "Excel at your job". People in the plantation were recruited for productivity, for efficiency, for being able to scale and to deliver profitable results.

Another example is the rainforest rule: "Experiment and iterate". The capability to learn from your mistakes is a well-documented, fundamental, cultural aspect of a startup. They know they have to fail, and fail fast in order to accelerate their learning. This results in a culture of trying, experimenting and iterating ideas. The whole philosophy of *The Lean Startup* by Eric Ries[18] is based on exactly this concept: the Minimum Viable Proposition or 'MVP'. You build something that you can get into the hands of first consumers as quickly as possible so that you learn from their feedback and iterate. It will not be perfect, but then again perfection is always just an assumption until the consumer gets to actually use it. The concept of MVP is the mantra of the rainforest. The rule of the plantation is quite the opposite: "Do the job right the first time." Plantations have proven methods, established processes and elaborate governance mechanisms. People often don't have the freedom to experiment, and they often don't have the patience for iteration.

ASK AND YE SHALL RECEIVE

A final example of these opposing rules is the rainforest "Pay it Forward" rule. This is one of my favorites. "Pay it Forward" is a common sentiment in Silicon Valley, and in many startup ecosystems. It basically means you can ask for help, and people will try to assist you without wanting something in return. The idea is to pass on knowledge, as a gift, a deed. No return favor necessary. This is the case in the extremely open ecosystem of Silicon Valley but, inside the startups too, it's the prevailing mentality. In 1994 – just two years before he returned to Apple – Steve Jobs perfectly described this reflex to the Santa Clara Valley Historical Association: "I've never found anyone who's said no or hung up the phone when I called – I just asked. And when people ask me, I try to be as responsive, to pay that debt of gratitude back. Most people never pick up the phone and call, most people never ask. And that's what separates, sometimes, the people that do things from the people that just dream about them. You gotta act."[19]

In the plantation however, the rule is "Return favors". I will scratch your back if you scratch mine. This is the rise of corporate politics, which are prevalent in the structures of the plantation. This is not how you grow small concepts and ideas into big ones. On the contrary. This is how you smother them into oblivion.

I think it would be very wise for plantation owners to closely look at the fundamentally different rules, different atmospheres and different cultures between themselves and the very fertile rainforest. Though they are excellent at scale, profitability and productivity, they could stand to learn from the rainforest when it comes to diversity, density, richness to foster creative dreaming, a culture of experimentation and failing forward into disruption in nonlinear ways. The plantation has been stripped of all of this messy complexity, but it has also been stripped of the rich, cultural diversity.

You need both. Or maybe even more than that.

THE TRIPLE POINT

Wouldn't it be great if your company would be 'bi-modal'? That it could behave as a plantation when you want to focus on growth and scale, and that it could behave as a rainforest when you need the serendipity and moonshot thinking to come up with 'Day After Tomorrow' concepts and ideas?

In my previous book, I introduced the concept of 'Business Thermodynamics'. Thermodynamics is probably one of my favorite areas of physics, a wonderful field that explains why – depending on pressure and temperature – water can be ice that you skate on, a liquid that you drink or vapor that you can inhale. It's the exact same molecule: H_2O but, depending on the temperature and pressure, it can behave in a totally different manner.

My favorite aspect of the thermodynamics of water is the 'triple point'[20]. It is that magical combination of pressure and temperature where *all* three of the phases can co-exist at the same time. You can have ice, water and vapor all at the exact same moment.[20]

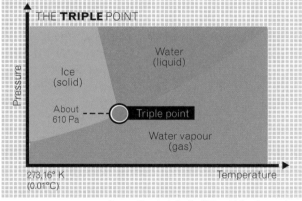

Source: Standards for the SI Base Units - Temperature

It's amazing to see that the underlying equations that govern the field of thermodynamics are essentially exactly the same mathematical constructs that govern the world of economics. And I believe you can apply this to the world of startups, scale-ups and corporates as well.

Startups are super-fluid structures that can shape-shift overnight to address a new market opportunity. As they grow and mature, they try to remain as fluid as possible. But, at one specific point, they find a revenue model that really works and 'freeze' it accordingly so they can keep optimizing it. What happens in parallel is that they often 'freeze' the organizational structures that help realize the growth of this plantation.

I used to refer to the 'solid' part of the cycle as 'frozen', but I've adapted this as the latter tends to have a negative connotation for most people (unless you are a Disney fan with young daughters). I use the word 'solid' now instead. Because there is nothing wrong with the stable and *solid* part of an organization that churns out those bananas and makes the revenue and the profit. It only gets dangerous if an organization *only* has solid parts and nothing remains fluid, let alone superfluid. The magic of the Triple Point is that they could all coexist. There is this magical composition where all three states can perfectly complement one another: superfluid, fluid and solid.

I love how Google is able to find balance at this triple point. It reorganized itself in a significant manner into its parent company Alphabet in 2015. This had very little to do with cosmetic branding reasons, and everything with restructuring itself as a portfolio of innovation. The core Google business of 'search' is the 'solid' part that brings in the lion's share of USD 90 billion in revenue. At the other end of the Alphabet spectrum is the very visible and superfluid X labs (previously known as Google X), where the rainforest magic runs wild and churns out crazy ideas like 'Stratospheric Balloons' and 'Diabetes Contact Lenses'. And in between – once the 'crazy' technologies start to grow and mature – you'll find the 'fluid' scale-ups. Alphabet, for instance, took the learnings from its driverless cars out of the X labs, and has now scaled this into Waymo: though still quite 'young', the company is now given the freedom to grow into a 'solid' plantation; one that could be the next big revenue driver for Alphabet.

Google has found that unique combination where the various cultures of the superfluid, fluid and solid co-exist in a productive manner. Though its sub-parts have completely different skills, sub-cultures, incentives and management techniques, everyone in Alphabet has that exact same purpose, passion, ambition and vision. They are all about the same long-term view, empowerment and transparency. They are all about big solutions, and about trying to improve the lives of as many people as they can. That's the glue that keeps them together, even if they do very different things, in very different ways. But I'm running ahead of myself here. I'll go deeper into Alphabet's secret sauce in chapter 6.

50 SHADES OF GREY

Peter Drucker once said: "The greatest danger in times of turbulence is not the turbulence— It is to act with yesterday's logic."[21]

Form or Function. It's an age-old discussion in architecture that will probably never be truly settled. And it probably shouldn't be. Today's modernist architects truly believe that 'form follows function'. They feel that the shape of a building, or of an object, should primarily be based on its intended function and purpose.

In the discussion of organizations about the 'Day After Tomorrow', I would argue that 'structure follows culture'. I believe that the cultural dimension is the very foundation of surviving these fast-flowing times. That's the true beating heart of a company: its people and how they 'infect' one another with ideas and thoughts, how they interact with customers, how they react to their environment, how they communicate, exchange information, even how they fight. Get that right first and then, only then, develop the structural mechanisms to support that.

Unfortunately, most companies have it completely backwards. They have been building, testing and trying 50-Shades-of-Grey variations on the classic hierarchical command and control model, hoping that one variation might be the silver bullet org chart that might allow them to prevail.

CULTURE BEFORE STRUCTURE

In my opinion, if you want to build organizations that are ready to tackle the 'Day After Tomorrow', you should build the cultural foundations first. You find the right people, unite them in a shared sense of purpose and empower them to make their own decisions (yes, even their own mistakes, because there will be mistakes). A command and control culture suffocates innovation, and will end up suffocating your company.

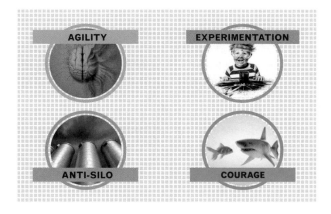

Devise an organization that has mental agility built in. One that allows people to break the shackles of silo-thinking. Dream up a company that fosters a culture of experimentation, and gives people the courage to question, to try new things and to engage in constructive dialogue.

There is a rainbow of ideas with which to paint. Let go of the Shades-of-Grey variations on the imperial command and control model. Perhaps 'Teal' is a color that is too off-beat for your spectrum. Maybe Holacracy may not work for your organization. But there are so many great innovators out there, as we'll see in chapter 6: each and every one of them with a strong culture. Let yourself be inspired by them, and then make their learnings your own.

The most fundamental aspect of the Google Alphabet experiment is that they have broken the 'one size-fits-all' approach of building organizations. In a truly unique manner, they're trying to find the 'triple point', where multiple culture and organizational forms can co-exist. They can be plantation and rainforest at the same time, and even some wonderfully colorful configurations in between.

So, my advice is: dare to paint a canvas of organizations that is not a one-size-fits-all solution. Have the courage to experiment with the enormous variation in colors of organizational cultures that you have at your disposal. But take it seriously. Focus your best talent on your 'people'. In many companies today, the composition of Human Resources is seriously anemic: they have too few people who are willing to take risks, who dare to be creative or show entrepreneurship in the thinking of the organizations for the 'Day After Tomorrow'. In my opinion, many HR departments have all too often become plantation-thinkers, while theirs is one of the departments that could stand to gain the most from the 'rainforest magic'.

THE LITTLE RED BOOK – PART II

I began this chapter with a reference to Facebook's little red book.

It is still one of my favorite reads. I often take it from the shelf and leaf through it when I need inspiration about how companies focus on culture first and on management structure second.

It's a wonderful document that describes the deeply rooted cultural values of Facebook. It's labeled the 'Hacker Way'. In their words:

"The Hacker Way is about pushing boundaries. About testing limits. Doing stuff people didn't realize could be done. Figuring out how to do more with less – sometimes with nothing. McGyver, not Bond. It's function over form and survival of the fittest. Effectiveness over elegance. It's the unshakable belief that there is always a way."

The Facebook culture is a combination of experimentation (the hacking way), of scale (change the world) and of speed. It is about inspiring their employees to go the extra mile. Because they believe they are building much more than a company, they are building a platform for the world. And for that, they must radically focus on the right culture; and on the right fit with new employees and their partners in the ecosystem.

They also believe that at the stage that Facebook is in now, they will have to work incredibly hard to realize their purpose. As the little red book puts it: "This isn't a fun place to work because it's easy. We make things that touch millions of people. We don't expect it to be easy. We expect you to change the world."

Of course, Facebook has management structures. And departments. And teams. And bosses. And governance. But in this company that is aiming for the 'Day After Tomorrow', "structure follows culture".

The philosophy of their 'Day After Tomorrow' is one of the most passionate I've ever seen, I was deeply touched by it. It gave me the inspiration to write this book and urge other companies to get in touch with their 'Day After Tomorrow'.

This is how it's written in the 'little red book':

6 months or 30 years

There is no point in having a 5-year plan in this industry.
With each step forward, the landscape you're walking on changes.
So we have a pretty good idea of where we want to be in six months, and where we want to be in 30 years.
And every six months, we'll take another look at where we want to be in 30 years to plan out the next 6 months.
Any other approach guarantees everything you release is already obsolete.

The question is: how would your culture read? Is your company one you would want to work for if you were fresh out of school and full of hopes and ambitions? Is it a company that aims big at changing the world? One in which each and every department and employee shares the very same goal, even if their approaches are different? One in which the 'Day After Tomorrow' is a priority, not something you could maybe tackle when things are a bit calmer which never happens?

Is it? It should be.

To paraphrase Peter Thiel: don't fuck up your culture.

'DAY AFTER TOMORROW' CULTURES: WHAT YOU NEED TO REMEMBER

Designing Company Cultures for Speed

When organizations grow, they are in danger of slowing down and growing stale. Culture is the one thing that can stop companies from losing their agility, speed, soul and ability to handle radical change. That's why the biggest challenge of today is to re-design our companies in terms of culture. Because our traditional command and control visions will not withstand the radical evolution of this 'age of networks'. If you want to build organizations that are ready to tackle the 'Day After Tomorrow', you should build the cultural foundations first, and only then cast it in the right structures.

Don't Copy & Paste

Culture is not something you can copy paste from another company. The right approach has to do with what kind of customers you have, which services or products you offer, where you are based, which types of profiles you are hiring and every last little bit that makes up the DNA of your company. Holacracy might not be for you. Teal may not be your color. Visa's chaordic organizing might drive you nuts. Eckart Wintzen's cell division and friendly competition could mess up your company. And becoming a pure rainforest might not be right for you. But a combination of these approaches might.

A Common Denominator

What's important is, in fact, not how others did it, but what the shared values of most of these extreme-culture companies are, and how you need to integrate them in some form or other to gain the agility and speed you need in the 'Day After Tomorrow':

- Transparency
- Connectedness & collaboration
- Empowerment & trust
- Decentralization
- Embracing chaos
- A risk-embracing pioneering spirit of experimentation

Triple Point

A large international organization cannot be as fast and as open as a startup, at least not in every way. The trick is to find that unique combination, that 'triple point', where various sub-cultures – superfluid, fluid or solid, depending on the sub-part of the company – can co-exist in a productive manner. A great example is Alphabet, where everyone has that exact same purpose, passion, ambition and vision. That's the glue that keeps them together, even if they do very different things, in very different ways, with different cultures. It's important that you set realistic goals if you're a large company: not every part can be a superfluid rainforest.

6

INGREDIENTS, BUT NO SURE-FIRE RECIPE

How Successful Companies are Preparing for the 'Day After Tomorrow'

> *"If you want to make an apple pie from scratch, you must first create the universe."*
>
> **CARL SAGAN**

THE FRANKFURT ROOM

You can certainly invent your 'Day After Tomorrow' with nothing but sheer ambition and pure willpower. But that is extremely rare. Some do succeed, though. My absolute favorite story of such a tremendous and super-human, single-minded resolve to invent the future is the story of how Samsung transformed itself.

In 1993, the chairman of Samsung Lee Kun Hee, went on a world tour to the branches of his company to check up on how everyone was performing. When he landed in Germany in June of that year, he checked into the Falkenstein Grand Kempinski Hotel in Frankfurt. He was extremely unhappy.

Lee Kun Hee had been running Samsung for six years at that time, having taken over the helm from his father who had founded the company back in 1938. Lee Kun Hee had been very successful up till now. Samsung had grown by two and a half times. Not bad. But the chairman was not content. Not even close.

During his epic world tour to understand his company better, he had traveled through Asia, then to the United States and, finally, to Europe. He had studied how electronics were marketed and purchased, how consumers used them, and how the Samsung brand was perceived around the globe. He liked to walk incognito into retail stores and check how his products were displayed, sold and purchased.

But he didn't like at all what he was seeing. While he was in a store in southern California, Lee Kun Hee almost threw a fit when he saw that his precious Samsung televisions were at the back of the electronics store gathering dust, while brands like Philips, Sony or Panasonic were prominently on display at the front.

By the time the chairman had landed in Frankfurt, he had basically had enough. He was utterly dismayed about the position of his company, so he sent an irate email to the top executives at Samsung with one message: get your ass to Frankfurt in the next 24 hours to shape the future of Samsung.

When the chairman summons you to the Falkenstein Grand Kempinski Hotel in Frankfurt, that's what you do. More than 200 of the company's top executives showed up at the modest hotel within 24 hours, and what happened next is the stuff of legend at Samsung.

For the next three days, the chairman berated the executives on the deplorable state of the Samsung brand. He fulminated about how they only had a mediocre brand while they deserved a much better spot in the world of electronics. He laid out a vision of a better way forward, and showed the executives a 'path to greatness'.

CHANGE EVERYTHING BUT YOUR WIFE AND CHILDREN

The 'Day After Tomorrow' for Samsung would be the transition from a second-tier manufacturer to the biggest, most innovative TV and smartphone maker in the world. The epic three-day speech became known inside the company as the 'Frankfurt Declaration of 1993'[1]: a grueling exercise for the executives with the chairman hardly allowing the team to take any breaks in the evening for some short periods of sleep.

The most famous quote to come out of the 'Frankfurt Declaration' was the call to arms from the chairman: "Change everything but your wife and children." It ushered Samsung into a frenzy of activity, and set the company on the path to become the most innovative electronics company by the year 2000.

The 'Frankfurt Declaration' was transcribed and even turned into a special illustrated version, like a comic book[2], that was delivered to every employee of Samsung. Overnight, the Samsung workforce became the builders of the 'new' Samsung. Together, they all worked towards realizing a 'Day After Tomorrow' quantum leap for the entire organization.

The speech was so influential, pivotal and important to Samsung that the company acquired all the furniture and decorations, down to the notepads and pencils, from that German conference room: they shipped them to Samsung's Korean headquarters and recreated the entire conference room inside Samsung. This 'Frankfurt room' is where the top executives gather every year to remind them of their mission to transform the company.

HAMMERTIME!

Chairman Lee reminds his people constantly that they can never rest. In his words: "Business is perpetual crisis. Pioneers meet every crisis head-on, and they triumph over it. Again and again."

'Quality first' was not a hollow slogan in the 'new' Samsung. In 1995, when the bigger-than-life chairman was unsatisfied with the quality of a new set of cellphone products, he ordered them to be stacked high in front of the factory in Gumi, Korea. "Build a bonfire", was his request. The entire stock of mobile phones was piled outside of the factory: a towering heap of 150,000 phones.

It was quite a drama. All 2,000 plant workers were gathered around the pile when the chairman and his board started demolishing the low-quality products with a set of sledgehammers. The workers kept watching as the pile was set on fire, burning the phones to ash. In a theatrical climax, bulldozers crushed the charred remains. Onlookers actually cried.

More than USD 50 million worth of goods was demolished and burned on that day, just to prove a point. That's a lot of dough to show how serious you are about the march towards world domination in electronics.

By the beginning of the 21st century, Samsung had done exactly what had been planned in that conference room of the Falkenstein Grand Kempinski Hotel. They had become the largest, the most innovative, and the most respected electronics company in the world. They had given the market leader in TVs, the Japanese Sony, a run for their money. Their smartphones were beginning to challenge the market pioneer Apple by constantly releasing phones that had many more features and functionalities than those of the Cupertino giant.

In 1993, Samsung had USD 10,77 billion in sales, with 123,000 employees. By the year 2012, the company had USD 187.8 billion in sales, with more than 236,000 employees. It had become the absolute world leader in their field. And it had all started with one meeting in the sausage capital of the world.[3]

THE ULTIMATE RECIPE

Impressive. But let's face it: not every company is capable of just taking the 'Frankfurt recipe' as a mechanism to reinvent itself for their 'Day After Tomorrow'.

In fact, please don't try to look for a ready-made 'how-to' manual. There isn't one. There is no 'silver bullet', or some 'magical *Harvard Business Review* case' that you can take, and make it all better. I wish there was.

It reminds me of when I was a kid. My favorite TV-show was 'Cosmos' presented by the amazing Carl Sagan. I loved that series, where the soft-spoken genius and science popularizer Sagan would explain the mysteries of the Universe, seasoned with a wonderful sense of humor.

One of the episodes that I will never forget, was where he pondered on how we as humans actually developed at all. How the very essence of life is not just about mixing all the ingredients together. Sagan said: "The beauty of a living thing is not the atoms that go into it, but the way those atoms are put together". I still vividly see him visualizing this standing behind a big black cauldron and putting in all the ingredients of a human being: "Start with 35 kilograms of oxygen. Enough to fill a freight container. Then add 6.4 kilograms of hydrogen. Enough to fill more than 4,700 party balloons. Then add in 17.5 kilograms of carbon, enough to load up a water softener in most houses. Then throw in some calcium, phosphorus, and potassium. Sprinkle in some copper, iodine and chromium. And add 2.5 grams of iron: enough to make one nail."

In case you were wondering, here's the full recipe of all the parts that make up a human being of 62 kilograms[4]:

35 kg Oxygen	18 g Silicon
6.4 kg Hydrogen	2.5 g Iron
17.5 kg Carbon	2.4 g Zinc
1.5 kg Nitrogen	83 mg Copper
1.0 kg Calcium	31 mg Iodine
0.54 kg Phosphorus	12 mg Manganese
110 g Sulfur	4.2 mg Fluorine
72 g Sodium	6.2 mg Chromium
120 g Potassium	5.4 mg Selenium
76 g Chlorine	4.9 mg Molybdenum
17 g Magnesium	1 mg Cobalt

But even if you would be able to put all of this together, you'll never be able to 'make' a human. As Carl Sagan pointed out, standing behind this cauldron: "Humans are, in fact, that list of atoms above. But humans are so much more, more than the dust of a dead star. Human atoms are the notes, their life the symphony."

The way to make a human is much more complicated than just throwing in the right amounts of atoms. Evolution is the 'magic' that takes this raw input, and turns it into the magic of humankind.

I'll have to disappoint you: in very much the same way, there is *no* ultimate recipe for the 'Day After Tomorrow'. It's not just a matter of putting the right ingredients together in the cauldron of a corporation so that it can 'reinvent' itself. No, it's not that simple. There will have to be some kind of 'magic' involved, often deeply engrained in the culture of the organization.

Sometimes a company will have to destroy a part of itself in order to live on. As a starfish-company, it might have to cut off one of its tentacles in order to regenerate new entities or organisms that can become the new lifeline. Sometimes you will have to destroy your old self, before the market does. Panta Rhei. Creative destruction. Whatever you lose in the fire, you will find back in the ashes.

PATTERNS OF THE 'DAY AFTER TOMORROW'

Over the past few years, I've had a very privileged view of radical innovation as I had the chance to follow some of the largest corporations in the world very closely: on their journey to re-invent, re-generate, re-boot, or re-think their very core existence. In the next few pages, I'll present the innovation approaches of some of the companies that stood out: those that have successfully tackled their 'Day After Tomorrow'.

Again, this is *not* by any means a cookbook with ready-to-follow recipes, but rather an inspiration smorgasbord. It's a set of patterns of the 'Day After Tomorrow' for you to compare and ingest to see if it could serve as stimulation for your organization, for your company, for your future.

So, once and for all, forget the silver bullet. There is no silver bullet when it comes to radical innovation.

The truth is that there are as many methods as there are companies. But if you look closely at some of the pioneers we describe in the following examples, patterns emerge. Clear patterns: the basic ingredients of corporate innovation. I'm not just talking about cultures or structures – which are obviously essential to the creative process – but about the methodologies behind some of the most radical business evolutions, responsible for new business models.

Let's get cracking.

PATTERN #1:
The Remote Silo

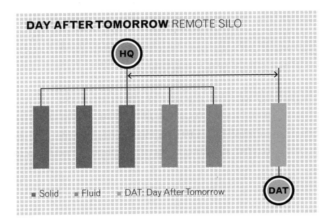

Many have tried to shield their 'Day After Tomorrow Magic' in a separate silo. They create a removed 'division' where they can – in splendid isolation – invent the future. Their 'Day After Tomorrow' team is neatly separated from the 'today' people, and the 'mess of yesterday'.

It's an incredibly alluring idea. But it proves incredibly difficult to pull off.

The most magnificent and inherently tragic example of this approach is that of Xerox PARC. Magnificent because it was the birthplace of some of the most leading-edge inventions in human history. Developments that have fundamentally changed the face of technology and how we use it: Ethernet, the Personal Computer, laser printing, the graphical user interface (GUI), object-oriented programming, ubiquitous computing - I could go on and on. Xerox PARC was the birthplace of modern computing as we know it.

Magnificent. But also inherently tragic. Xerox made one vital mistake. It isolated PARC way too much. It was too much of a 'silo'. Geographically, culturally and commercially. So much that it became disconnected from the mothership's core activities. And that is why Xerox never commercialized any of its brilliant and earth-shattering creations. Truly tragic. It took a genius like Steve Jobs to realize what PARC had been creating in Palo Alto. As part of a business deal, he got himself invited for three days on the premises to look at what its developers had concocted. He touched everything. Talked to everyone. And then hired 70% of the people of Xerox PARC who helped him make the Lisa and the Mac. The rest is history.

Xerox could be 'Apple *and* Google combined' today it if had succeeded in commercializing what had been developed in Xerox PARC. Instead, Xerox is a shadow of its former self, and a dim travesty of what it could have become. If you develop the 'Day After Tomorrow' and can never bring it into the spotlight, you run the risk of essentially destroying any fundamental value creation.

GOING THE DISTANCE

But if you do get it right, it could be a powerful weapon. One of my favorite examples of how to build this type of innovation potential is what is being developed and constructed at Johnson & Johnson. J&J is the world's largest healthcare product company, providing the world with everything from baby shampoo, to Band Aids and state-of-the-art pharmaceuticals to tackle schizophrenia.

Like Xerox, it is headquartered in the US, but on the east coast, in New Jersey. Its 'Day After Tomorrow' labs are not inside the mothership either. They are safely tucked away in other areas, in places like La Jolla, San Diego, where brilliant Head of Innovation Diego Miralles was, until recently (he became President of Adaptive Therapeutics), running a team of about 200 people whose sole purpose was (and still is) to focus on the 'Day After Tomorrow'.

Diego Miralles once jokingly told me that he would probably have been spending 95% of his time on corporate politics, had his team been located near the headquarters of his company. But he was lucky enough to be three time zones away; at a distance of a five-hour plane journey. This distance empowered him to focus exclusively on the 'Day After Tomorrow'. Instead of spending his time on corporate politics, battling with the 'today' and the 'tomorrow' people, he was able to dedicate 95% of his time on the 'Day After Tomorrow'.

He had all the benefits of the power and investments of the J&J brand, without the drawbacks of corporate and risk-averse meddling. It was what enabled his team to create things that were groundbreaking, radically pioneering and capable of really reinventing their organization and business model.

It's not as if this ultra-innovative approach was an option. The world of healthcare is going through a massive transformation. In the next 20 years, healthcare will be fundamentally transformed by technology. In 20 years' time, we will look back at today and think of our current healthcare system as 'medieval' by comparison. We are truly the last generation that knows so little about our bodies.

That's because today the world of healthcare is not about healthcare, it's about 'sick-care'. When we become ill, then we turn to the likes of J&J to help us and make us better. But in the future, healthcare and technology will allow us to live fuller, better and healthier lives. It will be proactive instead of reactive.

"Today, the number one type of customer of J&J is the hospital", Miralles told me. "When I ask the CEO of one of our largest hospital customers what their number one KPI is, it is the occupancy of their beds." Indeed, if the occupancy of hospital beds is above 90%, the hospital is making money. But if it drops below 80%, the hospital will be losing money. "But the 'Day After Tomorrow' of J&J is a world where we keep people healthy, and we don't need that many hospitals anymore." There's something fundamentally wrong with the fact that those who are supposed to heal us, only benefit from us being sick.

Imagine the corporate fight between a 'Day After Tomorrow' lab focused on healthcare and corporates focused on sick-care, on products that keep the CEOs of hospitals happy about bed occupation. And that's the exact reason why the 'J-Labs' were spread around the globe, to rethink the world of healthcare.

So, isolating your 'Day After Tomorrow' efforts in a separate unit inside your company is a good idea. But make sure you do not disconnect the entity. If it's too far removed – like PARC was from Xerox – it can backfire. The isolation of the remote silo can lead to frustration if the mothership doesn't pick up. It will be very difficult to cycle the innovation back into the mainstream of the corporate entity, as Xerox has shown. Perhaps it is the remoteness, perhaps the jealousy of the corporate body, or the lack of oversight and governance, or the combination of all of these. But, as J&J will show, there is an 'optimal distance' where the remote silo can indeed invent the 'Day After Tomorrow', and still infect the mothership to act on those insights.

PATTERN #2:
The Separate Entity

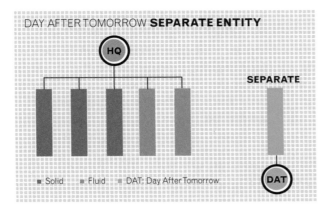

DAY AFTER TOMORROW **SEPARATE ENTITY**

HQ

SEPARATE

■ Solid   ■ Fluid   ■ DAT: Day After Tomorrow

DAT

"The test of a first-rate intelligence is the ability to hold two opposed ideas in the mind at the same time, and still retain the ability to function". I love that 1936 quote by author Scott Fitzgerald. It sums up *the* biggest challenges of large corporates: balance an existing business model with another one that operates on the flip side and might cannibalize the core business. They have to level out the solid (focused on exploiting) and fluid (focused on exploring) parts of their organization and keep both fully functional. Ambidextrous organizations – as the authors Michael Tushman and Charles A. O'Reilly III call them – solve this conundrum by separating the existing business from the emerging one. The reason is that the management structures, processes, mindsets and skills which are used to sustain the business tend to clash with those needed for radical innovation.[5]

The difficulty is to create a protective distance for your 'Day After Tomorrow' efforts – geographically and sometimes financially or hierarchically – without alienating your radical exploration from the core business. You need 'glue' to integrate both: a common sense of purpose, a shared company culture, strong leadership, etc. It's actually a Goldilocks situation: too much glue and chances are that the radical innovation is smothered by control. But not enough glue and management loses interest, like in the case of Xerox PARC described above. If a company has a severe integration problem with a radical 'Day After Tomorrow' silo, there is really only one solution: cut the umbilical cord.

A wonderful example of such a radical separation is that of CLAAS tractors – one of the top players in the EU market. In the US, the preferred tractor would be a John Deere. In Europe, the preferred tractor is a CLAAS. I live in a rural area, where most of my neighbors are farmers. Owning a CLAAS tractor is right at the top of their bucket list. That's how big that company is in Europe.

When I heard the story behind this family-owned business, I was really fascinated by the capability of this organization to keep reinventing itself. Today, the company founded in 1913 by her grandfather, is owned and run by Cathrina Claas-Mühlhäuser. She was only 35 when she was handed the reins of a thriving EUR 4 billion business with more than 11,000 employees.[6]

AGRICULTURE AS A SERVICE

The machines that CLAAS builds are incredibly intelligent: the pinnacle of 'precision agriculture' where big data meets self-driving. They make the Google cars pale by comparison in their autonomous capabilities. The farmers are only required to take the vehicles from one field to another. That's it. The tractors can do all the rest pretty much by themselves.

But Claas-Mühlhäuser didn't stop here. She dared to ask the courageous question: "Is the future of agriculture less about selling tractors than it is about providing agriculture as a service?" If the answer were 'yes', it would kill her existing business model in the long run.

Today the business of CLAAS consists of building complex machines and selling them to farmers. The future of agriculture, however, is more than likely about fleets of self-driving tractors and harvesters. The latter would allow CLAAS to play a whole new role in the agricultural value chain, to radically rethink their business model.

Therefore, they conceived a company called '365farmnet' which allows farmers to completely manage their farming and agricultural activities in a cloud-based solution. All kinds of sensors gather information about the farm in one single program: from cultivation planning to harvesting, from field to stable, from documentation to operating analysis. That's a radical move away from the tractor world of atoms and physical things to the world of bits and software. One that requires a very different set of capabilities, talents and processes.

It should not come as a surprise that the gap between the hundreds of tractor engineers and the much smaller team of software developers focusing on this radical 'Day After Tomorrow' farming service, was too big to be bridged. So, after a while it was decided to take 365FarmNet out of CLAAS and make it a subsidiary with a high level of independence. Today, 365FarmNet is located in

Berlin, surrounded by a great number of like-minded Internet of Things start-ups, where it is thriving and really making a dent.

Claas-Mühlhäuser realized that if she wanted to give her new 'agriculture-as-a-service' baby a real chance in life, she had to cut the umbilical cord with the mother company. It's similar to the Ori Brafman and Rod Beckstrom metaphor I wrote about earlier[7]: the CLAAS starfish severed an arm which, in turn, grew a separate 365FarmNet starfish. This approach gave the new intracompany startup the best autonomy and maximum speed and flexibility to grow.

Though not all of the most successful radical innovators out there use this method, separating their core business from their radical innovation efforts – inside (like J & J) or even outside (like CLAAS) your organization – it can be very effective. Just make sure it's a protected yet connected kind of isolation. Never lose touch with the outside world and – if we're talking about an in-company silo – not with management either. And that is the tricky part, which a lot of organizations get wrong.

PATTERN #3:
The 'Catapult'

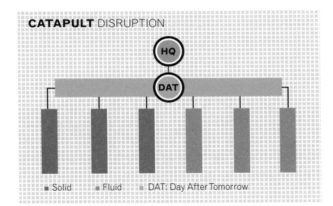

How do you get innovation to be really engrained in the organization? Especially when you have a large number of different silos within your company, and you want all of them to feel the heat of the 'Day After Tomorrow' initiative? How do you actively interweave innovation through all of the separate divisions in order to bring them closer together? How do you make sure that radical innovation is an integral part of the organization?

One of my favorite examples in the matter comes from the airline industry, where the International Airlines Group (IAG) – the parent company of Aer Lingus, British Airways, Iberia and Vueling – is performing a radical experiment in 'Day After Tomorrow' thinking. These innovation exercises – called 'catapults' – are headed by the brilliant Glenn Morgan, who used to be in charge of technology for British Airways before that.

I met Glenn years ago, as the then CIO of British Airways. When the airline merged to form IAG, he was given the opportunity to run the technology efforts for all four airlines. He chose to focus on building the disruptive 'Day After Tomorrow' future for the airline industry. Glenn is one of my favorite corporate innovators, one of the most daring and radical I know. He devised the concept of the 'disruptive catapult'.

During these catapults, eight senior executives – each from different business divisions – participate in an intense eight-week program. During that time, they are put in an innovation 'pressure cooker' scenario. They are literally bombarded with all kinds of eye-opening experiences and fed with all sorts of disruptive ideas, concepts, technologies and startups. The aim is that – using agile mechanisms – by the end of the experiment, they figure out one or more possible 'Day After Tomorrow' initiatives that are truly radical. They have to come up with projects that have the potential to change the course of their industry. Not just add-on innovations, but built-in innovations that have the potential to really become billion-dollar businesses. And then they have to present them to the board.

PRESSURIZING IT

Although the eight IAG executives are a permanent part of the existing business, they are separated from their own teams for these eight intense weeks. The reason is that they need to be able to fully concentrate on their 'Day After Tomorrow' thinking, steering clear of the 'mess of yesterday' that gets in the way of any kind of innovation endeavor.

Another crucial ingredient of these kinds of catapult approaches is time pressure. I think that the clear-cut timeframe of eight weeks is essential for providing a crystal-clear sense of purpose, keeping the passion and dedication alive and, at the same time, have the project evolve fast enough to keep it relevant. Decision inertia tends to be a major obstacle in siloed organizations and this catapult disruption is a very efficient manner to beat this challenge.

The best part of the catapult exercise has to do with ownership because, at the end of this exercise, one of the executives is actually going to have to lead the initiative. This intense catapult disruption is a brilliant way to cover all the different silos and to involve every single one of the different businesses.

Today, Glenn Morgan has even set up an innovation accelerator, called 'Hangar 51', right in the middle of the British Airways headquarters building. He firmly believes that innovation should be done integrated within the business, not in a separate remote environment. As he says: "It's just like with digital transformation. Too many 'digital' initiatives were just 'bolt-on' digital, but what you really have to do is embed that, so that it becomes 'built-in'. Our approach is focused on 'built-in', not on 'bolt-on'."

Catapults tend to work really well in large siloed organizations because they have the potential to close unhealthy gaps between certain teams and their endeavors. But they can only work if the innovation team has the right DNA, and if – regardless of their day-to-day work – they are unafraid to adopt radical decisions and if they are then truly empowered to test and implement the radical 'Day After Tomorrow' experiments they came up with. If these conditions are met, this type of method can truly work wonders.

PATTERN #4:
Customer Co-Creation

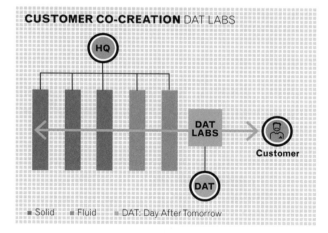

One of the most efficient ways to keep in touch with increasingly complex markets is to use co-creation with customers. It is a great way of looking ahead at a company's 'Day After Tomorrow' through the lens of their customers instead of through one's own lens. Ideas coming from outside the organization tend to meet with less resistance than when they are originated by employees with similar ideas. It's a strange form of bias, but it is the reason that valuable suggestions are too often ignored.

One of the best examples in co-creation comes from the international payment technology company, MasterCard, and its successful Innovation Labs which are run by Garry Lyons. I've discussed the credit card business before, and how Visa had used completely innovative organizational design principles to grow and scale. But its arch-rival MasterCard now has a killer way to put disruptive innovation into action, and Lyons is their absolute 'master of disruption'.

Garry is an entrepreneur who sold his company to MasterCard a few years ago. But instead of the traditional pattern, where the entrepreneur gets fed up with the bureaucracy, governance and hierarchy of the acquirer, and leaves in disgust, this story had a different twist. The CEO of MasterCard, Ajaypal Singh Banga, was able to perceive the talent in Garry Lyons, and made him an offer he could not refuse: run the digital innovation of all of MasterCard.

So, Lyons built MasterCard labs: originally only in Dublin, today, MasterCard has many of these Innovation Labs operating around the globe. The Master-Card labs run a pressure cooker process to come up with radical innovation. The concept starts with MasterCard working with their customers or partners to identify a well-defined problem. MasterCard then brings a multidisciplinary team of designers, developers and product experts from their Labs – augmented by subject-matter experts from the relevant part of MasterCard – to come up with a radical idea to solve the challenge in just one week. That's right: one week.

At the end of the week they have a working prototype, a video advertorial of the solution and a full-blown go-to-market plan. MasterCard runs these pressure cookers around the world on a weekly basis. I was part of one of those experiments and they are truly inspiring.

Many of the MasterCard customers that are involved in the Labs projects are obviously banks. But one of my favorite examples is the collaboration with Maytag. In the US, Maytag is the largest supplier of washing machines that are used in laundromats. The problem is that all these washing machines and dryers in laundromats typically operate on coins, quarters actually, a hopelessly outdated approach in a dematerializing world.

WATCHING CLOTHES SPIN

Maytag came into MasterCard Labs and in the course of just one week, they built a prototype of an app called 'Clothespin'. The app allows customers to use the laundromat 'coin-free', paying directly with their mobile phone. If they want, they can enjoy a beverage at the coffee bar next door while their laundry is being processed, because they are notified when the wash is done. I absolutely love the feature that for 50 cents extra, you can follow a webcam that is continuously showing your spinning clothes so that you are sure no one is stealing your socks.

You can imagine what kind of bonding this creates between MasterCard and their customers or partners when they jointly engage in such a program. That's why the salespeople at MasterCard love Garry Lyons. The sales teams know that if they bring a customer to the MasterCard labs, they are sealing a 'Day After Tomorrow' relationship that is going to last for a long time.

The most impressive part of MasterCard Labs is not just that they open a continual dialogue with their customers. It's also the speed at which the projects evolve. In just one week the project owners are able to evolve from idea to prototype, which can then be re-evaluated or actually scaled to a real-life product or service. There is no time for the projects to grow 'stale'. The innovation teams are empowered. Management is on board. And MasterCard's culture has a big part to play in that.

But co-creation is not just about keeping a close eye on a fast-evolving market. One of its lesser known characteristics in purely neuroscientific terms, as explained by Judith Glaser in *The Huffington Post*: listening to 'outsiders' – customers – without judgement and with a fresh perspective triggers our prefrontal cortex or executive brain to access higher-level capacities. This enables us to access new ways of thinking and to handle gaps between reality and aspirations. Without this part of the brain activated, Glaser warns that we tend to fall back into positional thinking and fight for our vested interests.[8]

In other words, co-creation stimulates us to focus on emerging business – on 'Day After Tomorrow' thinking – instead of obsessing about the status quo and company politics. Glaser continues by saying that as the co-creators develop a bonding experience (oxytocin rush), they start to open up new conversations about 'what ifs'. They imagine new possible collaborations, even fostering higher risk taking and openness. Co-creation opens the 'infinite space' where our minds need to be free to connect with others in new ways. It is not just about two different parties sharing ideas with each other that they would have

INGREDIENTS, BUT NO SURE-FIRE RECIPE

never thought of on their own. It is just as much about the individual parties being more open, alert and innovative themselves, because of the impact co-creation has on their brain.

I feel that the only drawback with this kind of co-creation labs is that they are sometimes not radical enough to survive the 'Day After Tomorrow' of an organization. They tend to be more about incremental innovation than about fundamental disruption. But when done right, they are a brilliant way to innovate and to instill a new form of thinking and perceiving at a company, through the lens of your customer.

PATTERN #5:
The Portfolio Organization

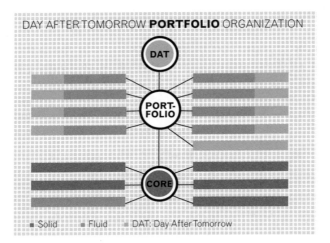

I've discussed the concept of 'corporate thermodynamics' before, where some companies have the possibility to combine superfluid, fluid and solid parts of the organization in pursuit of that fabled 'triple point' where all of these different states can coincide at the same time. One of the largest experiments in such a portfolio innovation strategy is how Google re-organized its entire corporate structure under the umbrella company Alphabet Inc., while keeping the engine revving.

The move from Google to Alphabet is anything but a simple cosmetic name change. It's a very clever portfolio exercise for the 'Day After Tomorrow', creating a new holding company that is composed of independent operating units, each with a separate and strong management. There has been a lot of speculation about Google's motives for this extreme move. Some say the new organizational structure was created to keep nurturing and attracting the best talent on the market. Others say that it had to do with providing clarity to investors. But I believe that the main reason is that even Google – by many perceived as the epitome of organizational agility – had to come to terms with the fact that it was not immune to the impact of its rapid growth. Or as Larry Page wrote in a memo explaining the move: "As you 'age' — even when you're still a teenager like Google — you have to work hard to stay innovative".[9]

Google realized that it had become too big to stay as fast, open and pioneering as ever. Like with any other large company, some parts had logically become 'solid'. So, it duly parked its older root businesses – search, advertising, Google Maps, YouTube, Chrome and Android – under Google Inc. These are all about optimizing operations, implementing lean strategies, consolidating structures or streamlining processes. About efficiency and revenue. Its advertising business, for instance, amounted to about USD 67 billion in 2015. This solidity is obviously needed to generate enough cash to invest in radical 'Day After Tomorrow' experiments. But other parts of the organization have to remain fluid and 'untouched' by the solid parts if a company is not to become rigid and die.

But the radically innovative and superfluid ventures are separated from Google Inc. and fall under the larger Alphabet umbrella: like X (the research and development facility) and DeepMind (the AI division). The X lab is, for instance, equipped to run radical tests and experiment on crazy ideas, and attracts brilliant researchers and entrepreneurs. When ideas are starting to scale, they 'graduate' from the X lab, and can be spun out. The same goes for the fluid parts, like Verily, or Google Ventures which is looking at the next new technologies on the horizon. Each part is managed quite similarly to how a venture capitalist would cope with a portfolio of investments.

ONE SIZE FITS NONE

What's fascinating is how Google realized that if it wanted to maintain the huge potential for the future, a 'one-size-fits-all approach' would not do. And that's why Alphabet was created: a portfolio of superfluid, fluid and solid parts of the organization that are kept at a safe distance from one another, because the capabilities, processes and structures needed by the (super)fluid and solid parts are so different that they would antagonize each other if they overlapped and intermixed.

To have this kind of restructuring and separation of the different parts of the organization work successfully, one critical component is absolutely essential:

culture. Everybody at Google and now Alphabet clearly feels the same engagement and purpose. They feel that they are part of the one company and share the same culture. These very powerful shared values are what allows far-reaching autonomy for the divisions without losing the interaction between the parts that are necessary for survival. Alphabet has successfully created this precarious balance between belonging and feeling that you are part of something but, at the same time, admitting that there are clear differences between the superfluid, fluid and solid parts of the organization.

Google is one of the first companies to leverage this kind of portfolio structure in such an extensive manner. But I'm sure that many companies – wanting to secure their 'Day After Tomorrow' ventures while, at the same time, leveraging their 'today' and 'tomorrow' revenue – are going to follow their example.

PATTERN #6:
The Accelerator

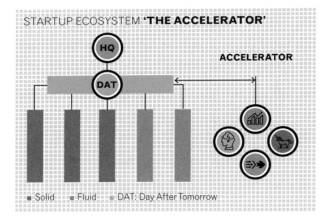

Many companies that are trying to tap into the fountain of eternal youth are setting up corporate 'accelerators'. In these accelerators, they are encouraging young (digital) startups to speed up their development by offering them mentoring, funding and access to corporate resources. The philosophy is that these young startups could be instigators for radical change in the mother company. The enthusiasm of these 'young guns' could inspire a cultural change in the mothership, and perhaps one of them could be the pot of gold to lead them to the 'Day After Tomorrow'.

When you visit the headquarters of Bayer – one of the largest chemical and pharmaceutical giants – the most unlikely figure you could meet is the person who runs their corporate accelerator: Jesus del Valle. His loud and colorful Hawaiian shirts stand out against the corporate grey and green interior of the German conglomerate. The way Jesus talks and walks the halls is in stark contrast with the classical German formality and demeanor. But Bayer is extremely happy to have Jesus on their side.

Bayer is Big. With more than 115,000 employees, and more than EUR 46 billion in revenue in 2016, and that is before they acquired Monsanto. Bayer is also old. They were founded in 1863, and one of the very first pharmaceutical giants. Bayer was the one to develop, and trademark 'Aspirin'. (Even today more than 40 thousand tons of Aspirin are produced each year.) Bayer also developed and trademarked 'heroin', which originally was marketed as a cough suppressant, but that quickly became a whole different story.

Bayer is Big and Old, but it keeps innovation at the core. The world of chemicals and pharmaceuticals is a world where you *have* to be able to look at the 'Day After Tomorrow'. The patent on a compound, a molecule, is usually 20 years. So, when a company like Bayer decides to try and build the new Aspirin, they are engaging billions of dollars on a 20-year journey in order to reap the rewards at the end.

JESUS IS A (CUBAN SCIENTIST) DJ

But even an innovative company like Bayer realizes that they need to look outside if they want to keep their edge. They realize that there could be players in the 'rainforest' that are dreaming up things that the scientists in the Bayer plantation could never cook up. Especially in the world of digital, which is likely to have a huge impact in the world of healthcare, and which is not the traditional habitat of Bayer folk.

So, they decided to set up a digital accelerator. And they chose the perfect person to run it: the Cuban Jesus. He was trained as a biological scientist, but kept his lifelong passion for music, and he's a pretty amazing DJ who loves parties and beer. A Cuban scientist DJ who can throw a mean party is obviously the perfect person to run the corporate accelerator for Bayer. In fact, every company should probably hire a Cuban scientist DJ called Jesus to keep their innovative edge. Maybe *that's* the silver bullet. (I'm only partially kidding.)

When I met him at the Berlin headquarters of Bayer HealthCare, he took me to the very heart of the accelerator in which stands a large ping-pong table.

Standard issue of course in any startup, but not quite at Bayer. "There is only one ping-pong table in the whole of Bayer", Jesus says, "And it took me an arm and a leg to get it here through Procurement."

The accelerator is called 'Grants4Apps': a three-month program where promising digital-health startups get 'accelerated'. The carefully selected chosen few receive EUR 50,000 in cash, and are located for three months on the Bayer campus. But the most important thing they get is not cash or housing. It's the mentorship. The selected startups get access to the top executives at Bayer who open up their network to 'accelerate' the growth of these fledgling companies. "That is incredibly valuable", says Jesus. The enthusiasm of the top Bayer executives is very high, and they see the startups for a half hour every week. "Many of my Bayer colleagues are very jealous", according to Jesus, "because they might see the top brass only once a year, while these startups get to walk into the offices of the top executives all the time."

Originally started in Berlin, the concept of 'Grants4Apps (G4A)', has spread around the world, and is now active in Singapore, Moscow, Tokyo, Barcelona, Shanghai… The reason Bayer runs this accelerator is not just to invest in these startups, but to learn to understand the 'Day After Tomorrow' and interact with new and radical business models.

The accelerator also contributes to the positive image of Bayer as an innovative company, even in the burgeoning digital health space. And, ultimately, it aims to build a more entrepreneurial startup spirit in the Bayer culture, so they can spread a little 'rainforest magic' inside the company. The top executives who mentor these young startups get excited, and feel the possibilities, which can trigger a tremendous top-down culture shift in the organization.

Companies that run this type of program need to really turn the mothership in a different direction and change the culture, slowly and steadily. If it's just a PR stunt, they'll never be able to leverage the output of the accelerator. They need to find themselves a Jesus. Jesus del Valle would have probably withered away in some lab in Leverkusen, but now he is riding high. He is the perfect bridge between the plantation and the rainforest. He is Bayer's very own 'culture DJ' of entrepreneurship and digital thinking.

PATTERN #7:
The Corporate Garage

STARTUP ECOSYSTEM 'THE GARAGE'

The problem with accelerators is their limited impact as the time during which they actively engage with the startups is very limited. In the case of Bayer, three months of a startup's life is often too short to have a lasting impact on the mothership.

In the Silicon Valley startup myth, the 'real' magic happens in a garage. Apple started life in a garage. Google started in a garage. Hewlett Packard started in the original mother of all garages. Basically, if you're a young entrepreneur and you or your parents don't have a garage, you're screwed.

So, shouldn't a corporate organization need a garage as well? Glenn Morgan built 'Hangar 51' inside the British Airway headquarters. Many corporates are building 'corporate garages' where startups can be hatched. And these often have more impact, greater influence and a longer effect than the standard 'short-lived' accelerators.

Deutsche Telekom's 'hub:raum' in Berlin is a good example of this kind of approach. It's a huge company, with more than EUR 73 billion in revenue in 2016, whose origins lie in the federal German post office. When it started to evolve into telecoms, the company grew spectacularly both in revenue and geography. Today it boasts a global business ranging from mobile telephony like T-mobile, and IT integration like T-systems, with about 220,000 employees worldwide.

The word 'hub:raum' in German means the 'cylinder capacity' of an engine. It's a measure for the true power of an engine, when the explosions inside the cylinders of a gasoline engine drive the pistons to create power. That's in fact the whole idea behind the 'hub:raum': to create an environment where startups can grow explosively and help drive the Deutsche Telekom dynamo.

hub:raum was first created in Berlin and today they are also active in Poland and Israel. The aim was to attract startups that have the potential to fundamentally transform major markets for Deutsche Telekom. When startups join hub:raum, they get the standard offering: financing to help grow the business and prove market traction, a co-working space in the heart of Berlin, and mentoring to help the startup grow and mature. So far, nothing spectacular, but the beauty is in the last offering: leverage.

The startups that join hub:raum are carefully selected to be able to leverage the Deutsche Telekom operating environment. There are specific areas that Deutsche Telekom wants to expand, and in which to branch out. The Internet of Things for example could make Deutsche Telekom a player in the world of trillions. When the selected startups start to develop their product and service offering, they get access to the Deutsche Telekom network.

This is a huge advantage, as the technology startups could only have dreamt of using the vast technical platforms, systems and networks of Deutsche Telekom to build their offering, had they been on their own. It gets even better: when the startup's products are commercially ready to scale, they can rely on the Deutsche Telekom salesforce to help them contact and convince their own customers.

It's a win-win-win. The startup wins because the technical and commercial benefits are massive. Deutsche Telekom wins because they can showcase innovative products and ideas faster, and remain on the cutting edge of innovation. And the final winner is the customer: they get early access to disruptive services and offerings.

If done right, the hub:raum could work wonders for Deutsche Telekom. It could develop their service offerings, help them keep their innovative edge, entice their customers and receive some great financial returns from their investments in those startups that become successful. But the right mix of skills to run this is essential. You need Venture Capital skills to invest in the right startups, you need mentoring skills to coach the startups, and you need the right manpower inside Deutsche Telekom to activate the internal organization and salesforce. If you are unable to fulfil one or more of these conditions, a concept like hub:raum will never become more than just a very expensive PR facade.

Deutsche Telekom also extends this 'garage' approach to internal employees in a corporate intrapreneurship program that is called UQBATE. The company fully understands that it would be a mistake to think that only the outside world is capable of starting a company. You need to nurture that kind of entrepreneurship inside your company as well with internal talent accelerators. That's because many employees are faced with so much pressure on the 'today' and 'tomorrow' focus, that it's very difficult to have them focus on the 'Day After Tomorrow'. As Seth Godin once put it so well: "So busy doing my job, I can't get any work done". That's why programs like UQBATE are essential to help corporates like Deutsche Telekom tap the potential of their own existing team.

PATTERN #8:
The Network Organization

One of my favorite 'Day After Tomorrow' approaches is Haier's quite extreme networked model. It is one of the most inspiring cases of audacious strategic thinking that I've ever come across in my life. It completely challenges the hierarchical command and control strategic thinking and, instead, radically empowers employees to take risks and seed out the future.

Haier's innovation story proves that the typically 'Move fast and break things' Silicon Valley startup approach can be successfully translated to a large corporate in the completely different Chinese culture and in one of the most traditional sectors out there.

And it all started with Zhang Ruimin. He grew up during the Chinese Cultural Revolution, and - like many - joined the Red Guards to help spread the communist philosophy. Not having been able to attend university, he began his career at a state-run construction company in Qingdao in 1968, where he slowly but steadily climbed the ranks. In 1984, he was eventually sent to the Qingdao Refrigerator Plant which, at the time, had the reputation of being one of the worst run factories in the entire Chinese economy. It was no gift.

The young Zhang found a company in ruins. But he was determined to completely transform the dying fridge factory into one of the world's biggest white goods companies. Today, Haier has 73,000 employees and generates USD 30 billion in revenue (2015)[10]. It is considered to be one of the most innovative, leading quality players in the field of appliances ranging from washing machines, microwave ovens and refrigerators. Ruimin is still the CEO.

The transformation was massive, and should earn Zhang Ruimin a Nobel prize for corporate turnarounds if there was ever such a thing. The quality of the products that the then dying company was churning out was so incredibly bad that when Ruimin took over the factory in 1984, he performed a legendary demonstration that made a very strong statement.

A dissatisfied customer had brought a faulty refrigerator back to the factory and showed it to Ruimin. Ruimin and the customer then went through his entire inventory of more than 400 refrigerators on the production line, looking for a replacement. In doing so, he discovered that there was a 20 percent failure rate in all of the merchandise of the factory.

HAMMERTIME 2.0

Furious, Ruimin ordered 76 faulty refrigerators to be lined up on the central hallway of the factory floor. He also issued sledgehammers to his employees and ordered them to destroy all of the refrigerators. At first the workers didn't dare touch the machines. The cost of one such refrigerator was almost two years' worth of their wages. But Ruimin told them "Destroy them! If we pass these 76 refrigerators for sale, we'll be continuing a mistake that has all but bankrupted our company." After he himself gave the example, all 76 machines were smashed to pieces in the end. One of the hammers is still on display at company headquarters as a reminder to posterity.[11]

The rest is history. With an almost obsessive focus on quality, Zhang Ruimin was able to completely overhaul the company. It started to produce quality products, grow extremely quickly, and to expand geographically. Soon, Haier was giving companies, like Whirlpool and GE, a run for their money.

By 2015, Haier was one of the largest companies in the world, and Ruimin was recognized by the *Financial Times* as one of the "50 most respected business leaders in the world."[12]

But he was not satisfied. He wanted, yet again, to take it one step further. Over the years, he had studied every management technique and operational improvement approach known to man. But to really take his Haier to the 'Day After Tomorrow', he wanted to go where no CEO had gone before.

He wanted to engender a culture of entrepreneurship inside his company by copying and transferring the rules of the outside market *inside* his company. The result was a highly competitive, even uncomfortable and chaotic environment, but one that yielded tangible results.

THE UNSTEADY CREW

One of the first measures Ruimin took was to eliminate middle management and chop his 73,000-employee workforce into hundreds of internal micro-companies with their own profit and loss account. He transformed his company into a fast flowing and competitive network with hardly any hierarchy. Employees were empowered to propose new ideas, which were then put to the vote. The winner would then become the project leader and could 'recruit' employees for his venture (who were free to join or leave at any time). In other words, these micro-companies functioned just like in actual startups.

Zhang Ruimin also introduced 'catfish' to keep everybody on their toes: shadow managers who follow the micro-entrepreneurs and ruthlessly report on missed targets and lost opportunities. Now, these are anything but traditional command and control managers. Haier's system is a lot cleverer than this: the catfish is the person who had a rival idea that came second in the voting, after the intrapreneur he's supposed to help *and* carefully watch.

The 'catfish management' metaphor actually comes from the fishing industry. Fresh sardine is delicious and succulent. But it loses its taste if you transport it in a tank. Unless you put its natural enemy the catfish, in the tank as well so that the latter can keep the sardine sharp, alert and ultimately very tasty.[13]

Zhang Ruimin cleverly used this 'catfish management' technique to counterbalance the natural chaos created by his micro-enterprise network philosophy.

One of my favorite parts of the Haier approach is its 'zero distance to customers' rule. Everything begins and ends with the end-user. They are the 'bosses' of their micro-entrepreneurs. In fact, Haier employees do not receive a fixed salary: it's the customers who 'decide' upon their remuneration. Again, this works just like in a real market, where entrepreneurs are completely at the mercy of the customer for their income.

When asked how he managed to strike the right balance between the chaotic entrepreneurial energy within his company and the need for corporate control at the top, Zhang's answer was simply: "We don't need to balance! An unsteady and dynamic environment is the best way to keep everyone flexible."[14]

Let me be clear, I'm not saying that this highly competitive approach will work for every company. I'll keep repeating it *ad nauseam*: there is no silver bullet when it comes to innovating for the 'Day After Tomorrow'. What works for one company, might destroy another. But I do believe that radical innovation needs an environment that's a little off, that seems a little dangerous, even. It needs a little pressure. The beauty of Haier's competitive and networked innovation approach is that only a certain type of 'gutsy' and entrepreneurial type of employee will be drawn to the company, which will reinforce its innovation culture. It's a perfect circle.

But perhaps the best result of the Haier culture is how its employees are used to continual change, which reduces the usual fear that is associated with it in most companies. If companies want to stay alive and even thrive in an accelerating market, they have to embrace continuous evolution and innovation, and one of the biggest obstacles to that is 'fear of change'. But Haier's culture is organized in such a manner that people always expect change. And that's a big enabler for 'Day After Tomorrow' thinking.

PATTERN #9:
The Integral Disruption

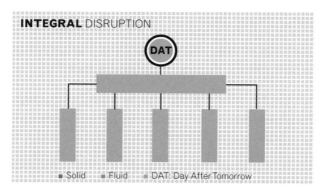

From time to time, I have the extreme privilege to observe a company that has 100% pure undiluted 'Day After Tomorrow' DNA. SpaceX is a perfect example of such an enterprise.

Unless you have been living under a (Martian) rock for the past few years, you'll know a thing or two about Elon Musk. As a young man, he amassed his fortune by successfully selling PayPal to eBay for USD 1.5 billion. But instead of retiring to the Bahamas, he wanted to reach higher. Much higher. With USD 100 million of his early fortune, Musk founded 'Space Exploration Technologies', or SpaceX, in May 2002.

He did not set out to make rockets at first. He 'just' wanted to land a miniature experimental greenhouse on Mars, a project he called 'Mars Oasis'. Now, that would obviously entail rockets in order to send materials and supplies into space. He contacted the European Space Agency, which turned him down. Then he flew to Russia to meet with companies such as the International Space Company 'Kosmotras', which offered him one rocket for USD 8 million. Musk was so appalled at the price that he stormed out of the meeting room.

On the flight back from Moscow, Musk decided to start a new company that would build him the rockets he needed. He came up with a revolutionary plan to completely change the cost equation of rockets. Instead of burning up the rocket in the atmosphere – which is how it had been done up till then – he wanted them to land vertically so he could recover them. That approach would cut the launch price by a factor of ten and allow Musk to enjoy a 70% gross margin.

How's that for a radical 'moonshot' (what Google X calls its radical solution projects)? Better yet: a Mars shot.

When you visit SpaceX just outside the LAX airport in Los Angeles, the first thing you see is a sign that reads: "Gravity is a Bitch". You know exactly what they are fighting against. The progress of the company is phenomenal, though. They launched their first rocket, the Falcon 1 in 2008. Only four years later they were the first commercial company to send a spacecraft into space that successfully docked with the International Space Station (ISS). This got the company the lucrative NASA contract to fly supplies to the ISS, which had been done by very expensive Russian carriers since NASA had abandoned its own Space Shuttle project.

OCCUPY MARS

When you walk around SpaceX, and talk about the NASA contract, you will hear: "Ah, that's just to pay the bills. What we really want to do is colonize Mars." The first time I heard that I thought they were nuts. But then you look around and everything in the company just shouts out this massive ambition. The coffee mugs in the cafeteria carry a slogan "Occupy Mars", the workers in the factory wear T-shirts with "Occupy Mars" printed on them, the doormat on which you wipe your feet reads "Occupy Mars".

Musk revealed his plans to start flying missions to Mars in 2016. It seemed strange, weird and just plain unrealistic. It still does. But then again, his idea of landing rockets vertically to recover the cost of the spaceships seemed strange, weird and unrealistic in 2002. Today, SpaceX has done what no other organization in the space industry has done before: launch a rocket and let it land again. The result is that he can launch rockets 90% cheaper than anyone else before him. Yes, there have been (major) failures, among which the explosion of the Falcon 9 rocket during a propellant fill operation. Yes, he was almost bankrupt a few times. Yes, Musk has been ridiculed a lot for his extreme ideas. But he carried on. He believed. And, in the end, he succeeded.

If any company can make it to Mars, it will probably be SpaceX. Such a burning, wildly ambitious dream as a company mission, is the hallmark of truly disruptive, 100% pure 'Day After Tomorrow' companies.

In 1976, when Microsoft was incorporated by Bill Gates and Paul Allen in Albuquerque, New Mexico, its mission statement was: "A computer on every desk and in every home". That was a true Mars shot statement as well. In those days, computers were the size of an 18-wheeler truck, and could only be afforded by big banks, insurance companies or governments. To claim that you would put a computer on every desk and in every home sounded ludicrous back then.

But they did. It was a radical 'Day After Tomorrow' dream, that allowed the early developers of Microsoft to build software that would fundamentally change our world. You probably remember the first computer that entered your house. Now when I ask you how many you own today, you'll probably need to think that through for a while, especially if you have kids. You are surrounded by computers in the form of tablets, smartphones and intelligent wearables.

Microsoft is an interesting case: the moment that their 'Mars shot' mission statement was realized, they became stale, and unimaginative. The company basically missed out on the mobile revolution and will have to work really hard to be a player in the Artificial Intelligence arena. The challenge of the new CEO of Microsoft, Satya Nadella, is not technology. It is about finding its new 'Day After Tomorrow' mission that everyone in the company can rally around.

Pure 'Day After Tomorrow' companies are rare, but they exist. Elon Musk has created an environment where his burning ambitions are being realized. He once said in an interview: "I want to die on Mars". When we visited SpaceX, his collaborators told us that the full quote sounded a bit different: "I want to die on Mars, but not on impact." It's people like that – with ambitions so big that they'll sound crazy to most of us – who will eventually end up changing the world. They are the ones who *will* solve the Huge Problems we're struggling with. Wouldn't you like people to say that about you?

PATTERN #10:
The Pollutants Strategy

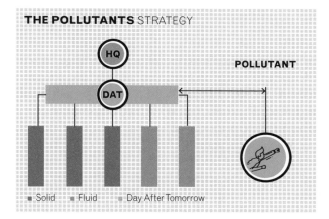

I already wrote about design thinker Mickey McManus. Mickey's brilliant. I especially love how he keeps pushing Autodesk towards the 'Day After Tomorrow' with the wonderfully extreme 'Pier 9' research lab. Now, when we hear 'Autodesk' most people think of the number one software product for architects: AutoCAD. It's true, the rise of the company Autodesk had a lot to do with the stellar growth of this particular software. More than 90% of *all* buildings in the world are designed with it. And more than 90% of *all* automobiles are designed with the same AutoCAD. It's the *de-facto* tool for designing products.

But a couple of years ago, the company felt that it had achieved pretty much everything it set out to be. Monopoly tends to breed complacency and Autodesk realized it was perhaps getting a little stale. The engine was revving, but not much truly disruptive innovation was in the pipeline. The company was desperate for a radically new approach to re-invent itself.

McManus's challenge was not to make AutoCAD a just little better. Or to make AutoDesk, the parent company, a little more efficient. Or a little faster. Nope. The challenge laid out for McManus was to help this company rekindle the innovative power they had unleashed back in 1982 when their original approach disrupted the way we think about drawing and designing. He saw that he would not be able to do that if he were to just extrapolate the past. In the 'Day After Tomorrow' philosophy, 'tomorrow' is often the 10% better than 'today', but if you want to shape the 'Day After Tomorrow' – the 10x disruptions – McManus knew he had to follow the outliers, or the 'pollutants' as he calls them: those users who are trying to do things radically different. The ones who are trying to accomplish 'crazy' things that have never been done before. These 'pollutants' will look absolutely 'nuts' to 99.99% of normal users. But they are essential to understand radical change.

Like James Cameron.

Cameron is one of the most influential filmmakers of our day and age. Movies like *The Terminator*, *Titanic* and *Avatar* have changed the way films are made as well as altered the entire industry. Not just in their storytelling and visualization, but also in their use of technology. Few know that he is also one of the 'pollutants' of AutoDesk: a radical crazy outlier who has helped AutoDesk to become smarter, better and more disruptive.

One of his biggest and most extreme accomplishments was the 2009 movie 'Avatar'. Cameron had been dreaming about making it for a very long time – since 1994, actually – but the timing just never seemed to be right. The technology to create an entirely new world from scratch – with breathtaking virtual landscapes consisting of hundreds of imaginary species of flora and fauna – was far out of reach for an extremely long time.

From start to finish, software from Autodesk played a pivotal role in helping Cameron pioneer new methods of virtual moviemaking for Avatar. A 'SWAT-team' of Autodesk software engineers built completely new systems just for Cameron and his crew because they knew that he was the outlier that would show them the 'Day After Tomorrow' of their company and thus transform their industry.

Together, they literally changed the way movies are made by using digital technology in a way that was impossible just a few years before that. Avatar came out in 2009 and, when it did, it finally beat Titanic (also by Cameron, of course) as the highest grossing movie with a box office of USD 2.8 billion.

As McManus says: "James Cameron helped us shine a light in an area of the 'Day After Tomorrow' that we wouldn't have looked into otherwise. What we learn from these encounters is massive. It's up to us to translate what these pollutants want into our 'Day After Tomorrow'."

I'LL GIVE YOU ANOTHER TEN, IF YOU WANT.

So, that's it? That's the whole list? A meagre ten approaches?

Hell, no! There are many more ways companies can accelerate and boost their innovation ventures in order to thrive in their 'Day After Tomorrow'. The success of each approach will always depend upon its match with the size, culture or structure of the organization.

Some will seclude their innovation teams to protect them from corporate suffocation. Others use short but highly inclusive sprints to make sure that the entire organization is involved. Some will co-create with customers, some will seek pollutants, and some will submerge the entire organization into the Kool-Aid of the 'Day After Tomorrow'.

But there are as many ways to find the 'Day After Tomorrow' as there are companies. I'm really sorry to disappoint you if you were looking for a ready-to-follow recipe. Just as life is an emergent property of all the atoms in our body, so is radical innovation an emergent quality of all the ingredients in your company. So, no. No sure-fire recipe. But there are ingredients that can stimulate this emergence, provided you respect the DNA of your company *and* dare to experiment with things that may even seem 'unnatural' to your industry.

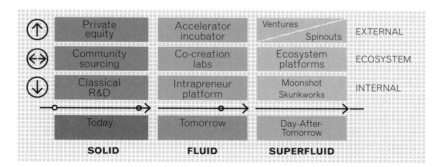

I've tried to paint a canvas of how different initiatives could play out in becoming 'Today', 'Tomorrow' or 'Day After Tomorrow' driven (on the horizontal axis). The more to the left, the more they will lean towards 'solid' approaches, the more to the right, the more 'fluid' they will prove to be.

The vertical axis separates between 'internal' initiatives, within the company, and 'external' initiatives outside of the organization. In between, you'll find the concept of an 'ecosystem' of innovation.

Today

When companies innovate with a 'today' lens, internally they will tend to focus on a 'research & development' activity. They might also reach out to the community around them by, for example, outsourcing activities or sourcing innovations from the community. On the outside, they will likely have an investment arm that, for example, will provide capital for private equity transactions.

Tomorrow

When we start to move up to the 'tomorrow' lens, in a more fluid setup, companies will set up intrapreneurial activities and platforms to stimulate internal ventures. Like the UQBATE example of Deutsche Telekom. Many of the co-creation labs, like the MasterCard Labs case, are good examples of fluid companies trying to reach out – in this case to customers – to invent the future. As we discussed earlier, many of those initiatives might not be utterly disruptive. They will rather tend to be incremental fluid innovation. And, on the outside, they could set up accelerators and incubators, like the Bayer Grants4Apps or the Deutsche Telekom hub:raum.

Day After Tomorrow

When we move to the 'Day After Tomorrow' lens, we see the truly disruptive labs inside companies. Setups like Google X, or JLabs in Johnson & Johnson. These are the places where the future is being made today. They tend to reside inside the bosom of the mothership, but remain far removed from corporate politics and guidelines.

Other companies are trying to invent the same 'Day After Tomorrow' philosophy by building completely new ecosystems. General Electric, for instance, is reinventing itself for the age of 'The Internet of Things'. It believes that the machines they produce today, from gas turbines to jet engines, will wake up, become smart and start to communicate. So, they came up with Predix, the software platform for building and managing industrial IoT apps, for both GE and non-GE assets. In doing so, they are creating an ecosystem where others can build new business models on information for the age of trillions.

And finally, there are the companies that are radically trying to invent the 'Day After Tomorrow' on the outside. Brilliant examples are investment vehicles like the Google Ventures and CLAAS, which has spun out its farming concept into 365FarmNet.

I believe that you don't have to choose just one spot on this 'Day After Tomorrow' canvas in which to be active. Many large companies, will have multiple initiatives spread over this canvas in order to maximize their chances for the 'Day After Tomorrow'. I'd advise not to put all of your talent and money in just one 'Day After Tomorrow' moonshot, because this kind of radical far-ahead thinking is always an experiment and never a sure thing.

I hope these examples and this canvas will give you inspiration to start acting on your 'Day After Tomorrow'. To help you gear up your company and engender your culture for radical innovation.

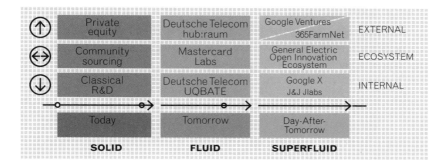

PREPARING FOR THE 'DAY AFTER TOMORROW'
WHAT YOU NEED TO REMEMBER:

There are as many ways to find the 'Day After Tomorrow' as there are companies. Just as life is an emergent property of all the atoms in our body, so is radical innovation an emergent quality of all the ingredients in an organization. There is no one-size-fits-all success formula, but there are ingredients that can stimulate the emergence of radical innovation, provided you respect the DNA of your company *and* dare to experiment with things that may even seem 'unnatural' to your industry.

My advice: keep your eyes open – trigger your brain with as many radical innovation cases as you can and find out which ingredients they are using – talk with as many pollutants as you can and just start experimenting. Maybe a radical internal lab is something for you. But you might also be better off with co-creation with your customers. Or you could thrive the most with a hub:raum-like ecosystem. Who knows, you might even need sledgehammers, like Samsung or Haier, to prove a point. (Though, that is *really* extreme.)

Just start trying. I wish you Godspeed.

7

A TALE OF TWO FUTURES

The Shadow of the 'Day After Tomorrow'

> *"One should... be able to see that things are hopeless and yet be determined to make them otherwise."*

F. SCOTT FITZGERALD

THE WORST OF TIMES

When I'm interviewed by the press, I am sometimes confronted with the extremely awkward question whether I'm not "Exaggerating this evolution of technologies just to scare people and sell more books". First of all, I'm quite sure that over-positive and simplifying books (that will have people believe that they can control everything if they "just put their minds to it") sell a lot better than mine. A lot of people don't like being confronted with the harsh truth so they will happily forego reading what I have to say.

If I wanted to sell more books, I would have to tell a "Don't worry, everything will be just fine, if you do X" story. But I won't. Yes, as a technologist I'm genuinely excited about the fundamental changes in the world of technology. But I'm not blind to the enormous social and economic consequences these might have on our companies and our personal lives. They could trigger dystopian outcomes for our society. I'm also utterly convinced that we're only getting started. That we are standing on a gentle slope that is about to become an exponential mountain and we are absolutely unprepared for what's coming.

We are at that stage in the evolution of mankind that is brilliantly summed up by the famous opening lines in Charles Dickens' masterpiece *A Tale of Two Cities*[1]: "It was the best of times, it was the worst of times". At this point in civilization, there is a huge potential in how technology could help better ourselves, our companies and our society. But it's also the worst of times, and we've never been closer to a total collapse of the world as we know it.

When writing this book, I realized that I spend 99% of my time interacting with large global corporations but rarely do I have the opportunity to discuss the 'Day After Tomorrow' with government officials, politicians and policymakers. And when I do, I often return home feeling extremely uneasy and worried about the future.

That's why it felt important to me to discuss the *downside* of the 'Day After Tomorrow' as well in this book. That's why this chapter is about the grim reality of how the bigger part of the current political leadership of our planet does not address the 'Day After Tomorrow' in any significant way. About how they are jeopardizing the future of our children and grandchildren in the most grotesque way possible. And why that concerns me. A lot.

WHY NATIONS REALLY FAIL

The book *Why Nations Fail*[2] was written by Turkish-American economist Daron Acemoglu, and the British political scientist James Robinson in 2012. Their main thesis is that economic prosperity in a country depends primarily on the 'inclusiveness' of economic and political institutions. Institutions are 'inclusive' when many people have a say in the political decision-making, as opposed to cases where a small group of people control political institutions and are unwilling to change. They take the well-documented example of Korea, a nation that was brutally divided into North Korea and South Korea after the 1953 war. The economies of both countries diverged in completely different directions with South Korea becoming one of the richest countries in Asia, while North Korea remains among the poorest.

According to Acemoglu and Robinson, non-inclusive rulers like in North Korea, have ruling elites that are terrified of 'creative destruction', as this would allow new groups to gain power, challenge their authority and capitalize their exclusive access to a country's economic and financial resources.

The book is an enjoyable and anecdotal historical, economic and political overview, but, for me, has absolutely no message going forward. I actually believe quite the opposite: our prevailing current political systems of 'inclusion' spawned a Political Myopia that's even worse than the Corporate Myopia that we discussed earlier. *That's* why nations will fail in the 'Day After Tomorrow'.

Most of today's political reality is centered around finding support in the electorate. To survive the next elections and make it through the next four to six years, politicians tend to use the rhetoric and knowledge of today, because "that's what keeps people busy". Very few of them dare to address a 'Day After Tomorrow' that is coming to us faster than ever before. We are being guided by a political ruling class that is almost completely blind to the world beyond the horizon of the next elections.

Worse still, when they try to make predictions for the future, they use 'Mess of Yesterday' economic and social paradigms that are totally obsolete. For instance, in most Western countries, politicians are still calculating 'pensions', government debts and budgets with economic models that stem from more than twenty years ago, from an analogue time when laws of change operated under very different circumstances.

Our 'inclusive' political leaders are not doing us a favor by only tackling those concerns that *can* be solved in periods that are no longer than their election term. Quite the opposite in fact, they are slowly plunging us into the abyss of an economic dystopia where the ignorance of technology, and the election cycle-induced myopia are the true reason why many nations will fail.

THE MOST DANGEROUS TIME

Perhaps you feel that I'm exaggerating. That I'm being too pessimistic.

Well, don't just take my word for it. Take the word of Stephen Hawking. The esteemed theoretical physicist, cosmologist, author and scholar wrote a remarkable opinion piece in *The Guardian* at the end of 2016. This was at that strange time when Donald Trump had been elected. The world seemed gloomy and dark by any standard. It still does.[3]

In his column, Hawking stated that: "This is the most dangerous time for our planet."

He outlined the economic consequences of globalization and accelerating technological change. In his words: "The automation of factories has already decimated jobs in traditional manufacturing, and the rise of AI is likely to extend this job destruction deep into the middle classes. This, in turn, will accelerate the already widening economic inequality around the world. The internet and the platforms allow very small groups of individuals to make enormous profits while employing very few people."

As he clearly stated, this was inevitable, it was part of the progress of the world of technology. So, there was no point in fighting it. But he also claimed these changes had the potential to be socially enormously destructive. And that the nature of these growing global inequalities would be far more visible than they had ever been because of the global spread of the internet and social media.

He outlined the huge challenges our planet was facing: not just the rise of machines, the impact of AI decimating work as we know it, but also the huge challenges for our planet as a whole: climate change, food production, over-population, epidemic disease, acidification of the oceans...

His conclusion was that we are at the most dangerous moment in the development of humanity. We humans have developed the technology to destroy our planet but we have not yet found a way to escape it. With not only jobs, but now entire industries disappearing, we must also figure out a way for humankind to retrain for a new world.

Hawking said that in order to survive as humanity, this was the time "to break down, not build up, barriers within and between nations."

Richard Florida, urban studies theorist and scholar at the University of Toronto, said something very similar in an interview with *Medium* at the end of 2016.[4] He claimed that the current clustering of knowledge about physical labor is among the most disruptive in recorded human history.

He describes the situation in the US, where the economy is rapidly shifting from an economy powered by natural resources and physical labor to one in which knowledge and the mind have become the dominant means of production. This shift has advantaged roughly a third of the population and workforce, while the other 66% have fallen further behind.

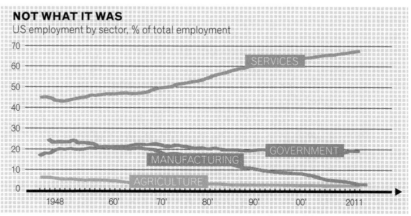

NOT WHAT IT WAS
US employment by sector, % of total employment

Source: US Bureau of Labour Statistics

The second big shift he sees is towards the urban clustering as the source of innovation and economic advantage. This evolution massively concentrates talent and economic assets in a handful of superstar cities and knowledge-tech hubs.

This graph, based on data by the US Bureau of Labour Statistics, shows the enormous flux in employment in the US since the Second World War. Just like jobs in agriculture dropped like a brick during the industrial revolution, the jobs in manufacturing have dropped spectacularly over the past few decades. Jobs in the 'services' sector, on the other hand, have risen spectacularly, up to 70% of total employment today.

We have truly transformed into a knowledge society, in which the services sector is the predominant way to employ the population. The big question is: what will happen when mass disruption by automation and AI starts impacting jobs in the service industry as well in a significant manner?

According to Richard Florida, this could give rise to several simultaneous nested transformations that could cause incredible disruptions of the economic, social and political order. That is why he claims we need a new 'social compact' for our urbanized knowledge economy. We need a new 'deal', a new vision of how the 70 million members of the low-wage service class in the US could prosper.

In his words: "It is now clear today, that our economy and our politics are completely out of sync."

A CONVERSATION WE NEED TO HAVE

At the end of his presidency, Barack Obama gave an intensely candid and intimate interview to *Wired* magazine, which revealed him as a geek with fond memories of watching *Star Trek* and a man with a fascination for the 'Day After Tomorrow' future.[5] It was framed as a conversation between the President and Joi Ito, the director of the MIT Media Lab. They mostly discussed AI, and the impact it could have on the world, on jobs, on the economy and on the United States in particular.

President Obama acknowledged that AI had the potential to reshape our world more than any other technology in the next fifty years. That it could impact every aspect of our lives: from medicine, transportation, education and accounting to electricity distribution. That it held an amazing promise to create a vastly more productive and efficient economy.

As Obama said: "If properly harnessed, AI can generate enormous prosperity and opportunity. But it also has some downsides that we're gonna have to figure out in terms of not eliminating jobs. It could increase inequality. It could suppress wages."

He is an optimist, that much is sure. He is optimistic in the sense that humankind has a great history of absorbing new technologies: as we figure out how to create an entirely new set of jobs, the standards of living generally go up.

But he is also realistic. In his words: "I do think that we may be in a slightly different period now, simply because of the pervasive applicability of AI. High-skill folks do very well in these systems. They can leverage their talents, they can interface with machines to extend their reach, their sales, their products and services. But low-wage, low-skill individuals become more and more redundant, and their jobs may not be replaced, but wages are suppressed. And if we are going to successfully manage this transition, we are going to have a societal conversation about how we manage this."

I would go further than that. It will most likely not just be the low-skill, low-wage earners that will be displaced by AI. A lot of high-skill, high-wage jobs – like those of certain doctors, lawyers, financial analysts, journalists, bankers and insurers to name but a few – will also be done by computers, algorithms and robots, and at a much lower cost point.

It's worth reading the interview. It was one of those rare moments when a politician drops his mask, and addresses the real issues at hand. This was not the President talking, or the politician, but rather the concerned citizen, and father. Someone who had to think about the next 25 years, not just about the next four years.

It's a shame that President Obama could only address these 'Day After Tomorrow' situations when he was on his way out. He had served his country for eight years, in the most esteemed way, but unfortunately, during his term, he mostly looked at the future with the knowledge of 'today'. In this rare interview, he had a different lens, a different perspective. He was looking at the future with the lens of the 'Day After Tomorrow'.

At the end of the interview, Barack Obama also mentioned the need for a serious conversation about 'Universal Basic Income'.

OTHER PEOPLE'S MONEY

UBI - Universal Basic Income - seems to be the absolute hype of the day. Everyone is talking about it: from the political left to the extreme right. Even the unions are buzzing about it.

Andy Stern is one of those who has a clear opinion on the matter. He is the former president of the Service Employees International Union (SEIU)[6], which represents two million workers in the United States and in Canada. After being a leader in the trade union movement for a long time, he decided to pursue a substituting different path in 2010. He wrote a book on the future of work – *Raising the Floor*[7] – and gave an unreserved interview to *Vox* with the ominous title: *Why we need to plan for a future without jobs.*[8]

Stern was a trade union veteran who saw the labor movement membership drop from one in three workers when he started, to one in sixteen when he left. He also felt the pain of society: "Fifty per cent of Americans say they don't believe in the American dream anymore, and they're justified in believing that. People with college degrees are not making anywhere near the kind of progress that their parents made, and that's not their fault."

The future of work in America is totally uncertain today. The only thing we *do* know is that things are going to change. Big time. Technology will destroy countless careers. Workers across numerous fields will be displaced. And it's not even entirely clear how many jobs will be replaced.

One of the great examples is the stupendously fast arrival of the autonomous driving world. What seemed like just science fiction a few years ago, is rapidly becoming reality. Today, in the US alone, there are three and a half million people who operate trucks and five million more who support them in various ways. Truck driving is the most important job in no fewer than 29 states. Driverless technology does not mean that the profession of truck driving will disappear overnight. But there will be many casualties. Of that, there is no doubt.

Financial services firm Morgan Stanley has calculated that the advent of autonomous technology will save the freight industry USD 168 billion annually, nearly half of which will come from staff reductions alone.

What is true of the transportation industry could be true of many other sectors. We could enter "an era of technological unemployment," says Stern, "in which machines render human labor useless and inefficient."

Stern is one of those who believe that a Universal Basic Income (UBI) is the best response to the social and economic disruption caused by technological change. According to Stern: "A significant number of tasks now performed by humans will be performed by machines and AI. We could very well see five million jobs eliminated by the end of the decade because of technology."

A UBI would essentially consist of giving every single working-age American a check every month, much like we do with social security for elderly people. It would be an unconditional wage from the government.

Stern believes that if we don't implement something like the UBI, the future could look bleak: "It would look like the Hunger Games. An enclave of extremely successful people at the center and then everyone else on the margins. There will be fewer opportunities in a hollowed out and increasingly zero-sum economy." A 2013 report from the Oxford Martin School looked at the effect of new technologies on the structure of the labor market. It predicted that, over two decades, 47% of all jobs in the United States were at risk of replacement.[9]

I honestly believe that most discussions on the UBI are incredibly naive. When we see how difficult it is to build reliable and affordable social security systems, healthcare systems or unemployment support systems – while the majority of the population are still working and paying taxes – won't it be incredibly difficult to implement UBI for an entire nation? The money to supply the UBI has to come from somewhere, it won't just magically fall from the sky.

Somewhere in this rhetoric I hear a magnification of the famous words of Margaret Thatcher when she described her disdain for leftist politics: "The problem with socialism is that, eventually, you run out of other people's money".

Bill Gates recently suggested that robots that take your job should pay taxes. "If a human worker does USD 50,000 of work in a factory, that income is taxed," said Gates. "If a robot comes in to do the same thing, why don't we tax the robot at a similar level?" He also added that robots should be denied access to the sort of accountants who know how to follow a tax-avoidance strategy.[10]

It does seem clear that we are facing fundamental debates about the future of work and living. And we must brace ourselves for a world where people who supply 'labor' will become less and less necessary in society. One where the people who supply the 'capital' for the AI-society will keep getting wealthier and wealthier.

Is this what AI and software are doing: substituting capital for labor?

The current impact of network effects on labor and society seem to support this basic theory. Thor Berger and Carl Benedikt Frey's report *Industrial Renewal in the 21st Century: Evidence from US cities*[11] investigated how tech companies like Facebook and Uber affect the wider economy of the United States. It showed that their effect on job creation is extremely small. Worse still, they seem to increase disparities in wealth.

It's quite clear we are witnessing the merger of the very ingredients of a massive revolution.

Douglas Rushkoff wrote the elegantly titled book *Throwing Rocks at the Google Bus* in 2016 to illustrate this growing unrest in society. It asks the question why the explosive growth of companies like Facebook, Google and Uber does not deliver more prosperity for everyone? Instead the first two give their billions of users 'free' services and applications that are highly addictive and, in return, these users pay for these 'free' services with their privacy. Instead, the players in the New Roman Empire are getting incredibly wealthy. Instead, the age-old, systemic problem of the rich against the poor is growing, and becoming more visible. And the polemic between the technologists and everybody else is growing.

In the new digital economy, where new collaborative models are prevalent, we can all easily get excited about the ease and comfort of using Airbnb or Uber. But this 'gig' economy has a dark side too. Most workers in this 'sharing' economy have no minimum wage, no unemployment benefits, no paid sick days, no pensions, and even no maximum or minimum working hours. They live at the whim of the platforms they've chosen to affiliate themselves with.

Rushkoff believes that the true conflict of our age is not between the unemployed and the digital elite, or even the 99% and the 1%. Rather, he believes that the tornado of technological improvements has spun our economic fabric out of control, and the whole of humanity is trapped by the consequences. According to Rushkoff: "It's time to optimize our economy for the human beings it's supposed to be serving."

Wait. Wasn't that supposed to be the task of our governments? Wasn't this the very task that we entrusted to our elected officials? No wonder that a whole global generation has lost faith in our political leadership and democracy.

Yasha Mounck, a Harvard University researcher, and Roberto Stefan Foa, a political scientist at the University of Melbourne, have extensively analyzed historical data on attitudes toward governments over various generations. They discovered that citizens of stable liberal democracies have grown jaded about their government. According to Mounck: "They have become more cynical about the value of democracy as a political system, less hopeful that anything they do might influence public policy." And it's among millennials that this "crisis of democratic legitimacy" is starkest.[13]

So much for 'inclusiveness'.

A whole generation of millennials no longer believe that their political leadership is capable of effectively leading them into the 'Day After Tomorrow'. This is the generation that will be faced with the most disruptive transformation in the history of humankind, the most radical rethinking of the global, social and economic system. How will we take care of the most vulnerable nodes in a runaway network economy where the rich only get richer, and the politicians are blind to the 'Day After Tomorrow'? How will we manage countries when capital is fundamentally and irrevocably substituting labor?

Oh, if only Karl Marx were alive today.

DAS POST-KAPITAL

Paul Mason is one of my favorite journalists. He 'groks' the new world of the 'Day After Tomorrow', and is also the author of the concept of 'PostCapitalism'.

He believes that the end of capitalism as we know it, has begun. As he says: "Without us noticing, we are entering the postcapitalist era. At the heart of further change to come is information technology (IT), new ways of working and the sharing economy. The old ways will take a long while to disappear, but it's time to be utopian."[14]

He describes the three fundamental changes that IT and the age of networks has brought us in the past 25 years. First, it has fundamentally reduced the need for work. Tech is blurring the edges between work and free time and is loosening the relationship between work and wages. Mason argues: "The coming wave of automation, currently stalled because our social infrastructure cannot bear the consequences, will hugely diminish the amount of work needed – not just to subsist but to provide a decent life for all."

The second element of this massive transformation is the corrosion of the ability of the market to set prices correctly. Almost all of today's economic market models are based on the concept of scarcity, a remnant of the industrial revolution. But that is about to change, because the new economic models are based on networks where information is abundant. He claims: "The system's defense mechanism is to form monopolies – the giant tech companies – on a scale not seen in the past 200 years, yet they cannot last. By building business models and share valuations based on the capture and privatization of all socially produced information, such firms are constructing a fragile corporate edifice at odds with the most basic need of humanity, which is to use ideas freely."

Lastly, he sees the spontaneous rise of collaborative production: some goods, services and organizations no longer respond to the dictates of the market and the classical hierarchies. The biggest information product in the world – Wikipedia – is made by volunteers for free, abolishing the encyclopedia business and depriving the advertising industry of an estimated USD 3 billion a year in revenue.

Paul Mason is, like me, fascinated by history. He loves finding hooks in the past and connecting those to today and the future ahead of us. And he found a brilliant hook in a publication by Karl Marx - *The Fragment on Machine*s – which was not published until the mid-20th century.[15]

In this manuscript, Marx describes an economy in which the main role of machines is to produce, and the main role of people is to supervise them. Marx was very unambiguous about how, in such an economy, the main productive force would be information. Organization and knowledge, in other words, made a bigger contribution to productive power than the work of making and running the machines.

Marx, ever the socialist, wrote that in an economy where machines do most of the work, the nature of the knowledge locked inside the machines must be 'social'. He even imagined the creation of an 'ideal machine', an end point of his revolutionary ideas where information would be stored and shared in something called a 'general intellect', which is the mind of everybody on Earth connected by social knowledge.

In his treatise, Marx had imagined something extremely close to the information economy in which we live. And, he wrote in conclusion, its very existence would "blow capitalism sky high".

I would have loved to see Karl Marx use Google and Facebook today. I'd 'friend' him in a heartbeat.

Things could easily go totally wrong with such a 'general intellect' that understands and controls all our social knowledge. Plenty of dystopian novels have been written about governments that use this to control their citizens. George Orwell's *Nineteen Eighty-Four* is generally seen as the poster-child of such a dystopian future, although I personally prefer the Russian Novel *We*, by Yevgeny Zamyatin, from which Orwell got his inspiration. 'We' describes a world of total harmony and conformity within a united totalitarian state, run by an 'ideal machine'.[16]

Paul Mason goes back to the beginning of the industrial revolution, more than 200 years ago, when the political voices trying to maintain the status-quo were warning of the harmful side-effects of the industrial age, claiming that 'factories' were a new and dangerous form of democracy: "Every large workshop and manufactory is a sort of political society, which no act of parliament can silence, and no magistrate disperse."

In today's network economy, Mason argues that the whole of society is a 'factory'. He says: "Today it is the network" – like the workshop 200 years ago – that they "cannot silence or disperse".

Mason has a bold vision of PostCapitalism: "It will replace the current form of capitalism that is quickly becoming corroded by information. Most laws concerning information today define the right of corporations to hoard it and the right of states to access it, irrespective of the human rights of citizens." Mason thinks this is a fundamental element to reset if we want achieve the utopia of the information society. He claims: "The equivalent of the printing press and the scientific method is IT and its spillover into all other technologies, from genetics to healthcare to agriculture to everything we know in society."

SUSPENSION OF DISBELIEF

He is not alone. Today we see a rising group of economists who claim that we have to completely re-boot the field of economics. They too claim that our current models are no longer in tune with the new information network intelligence-based reality.

Samuel Taylor Coleridge was the 19th century poet and philosopher who coined the term "willing suspension of disbelief"[17]. It describes the capability of a great writer to draw their reader so intensely into a story, that the reader would suspend judgement concerning the implausibility of the narrative. 'Suspension of disbelief' is the very essence of storytelling. It is an essential element for a 'magic' circus act because the audience is not expected to actually believe that a woman is cut in half in order to enjoy the experience. The entire Hollywood industry is built on the suspension of disbelief, and although *Mad Max*, *The*

Return of The Jedi or *The Muppets* have nothing to do with reality, we still enjoy them.

Paul Romer might very well be the intellectual leader of a growing group of scholars calling for a complete overhaul of the study of economics. This Chief Economist and Senior Vice-President of the World Bank (currently on leave from the Stern School of Business at New York University) is convinced that the way we are conducting economics today is a true 'suspension of disbelief'.

In a 2016 paper called *The Trouble With Macroeconomics*, Romer states: "For more than three decades, macroeconomics has gone backwards." "Macroeconomics," he argues," is like a science that has not only stalled for three decades, but has actually gone backwards in its ability to be in touch with and understand reality."[18]

Romer says that if we want to make sense of the economies for the 'Day After Tomorrow', we have to understand how IT and network effects are fundamentally changing our world: how they are moving the focus of economics away from land, labor and capital towards "people, ideas and things".

He claims that elitist economic circles have lost touch with reality. Macroeconomist equations assume that only unpredictable shocks from the outside can disturb economic equilibriums. He claims our economic thinking has become over-reliant on these kinds of super-abstract mathematical models. In *The Trouble With Macroeconomics*, Romer mocks these imaginary disruptions. He compares the results to a kind of physics that only works if there are "trolls, gremlins and aether".

Instead of reducing reality to a few variables in some abstract mathematical model, he proposes the concept of the 'agent-based model'. The model tries to replicate reality – and its randomness – in detail, by using the network and the power of information, to 'simulate' the evolution of markets, consumers and players. Only that way can we understand real behavior of real consumers, real citizens and entrepreneurs. Only that way can we grasp the true economic consequences of different scenarios. Paul Mason compared Romer's vision to a global professional version of the open-ended city-building computer game series *SimCity*, which would use the age of networks as input for a 'general intellect' so that we can turn economics into a simulation game.

Karl Marx would have loved it.

Google would be a really good substrate for that kind of global statistical and economic simulator. Facebook would as well. How long will it take before these kinds of global network giants know much better than governments what the economic propensity of a region is?

Google already knows a lot more than the city of Los Angeles about what goes on in the streets of LA, with the input from Google Maps and Waze. Facebook knows much more about what people think about news articles on CNN than CNN.com itself. Amazon knows much more about what people are willing to buy – and at which price – than any 'bureau of statistics' or 'economic ministry' in the world could ever comprehend.

Paul Romer believes we have to re-start the science of economics. Or that we need to at least upgrade it to the era of IT and global networks. Paul Mason, for his part, is a true techno-optimist and utopian believer in a wonderful 'Day After Tomorrow' of 'Post Capitalism'.

My biggest fear is that in all of these discussions, our political systems have become the slowest moving part in society. Worse, we 'regulate' many industries with insights, models and mechanisms of the past, instead of looking to the future.

Take healthcare for example.

I follow this field very closely. We are the last generation that knows so little about our bodies. What we know about our health will change spectacularly. The cost of genomic sequencing has dropped sensationally over the last few years. Faster than Moore's law. Craig Venture decoded the very first human genome in 2001 at a cost of more than USD 100 million. Yes, 100,000,000 dollars. Just 16 years later, there are commercial end-user products on the market for less than USD 1,000. In about a decade from now, the cost will be so low that every child will have their complete genetic profile at hand from the moment they are born. Or even before that.

The combination of sensors, wearables, devices and chips will allow us to move from 'sick care' - where we make drugs against diseases – to 'healthcare'. And *if* we do still become ill, we will be able to build personalized medicines, based on our genetic information and bodily state. Healthcare will become an ultra-customized 'market of one', focusing on the personal needs of individuals, not just on 'average patients'.

That's great, right? Yes, yes it is.

But think about how this will affect how we live. How better healthcare will allow people to live longer and healthier lives … in a world where there will be less and less work.

And think about how healthcare 2.0 will affect how we work. How our hospitals will function in a completely new way. How pharmaceutical companies will have to reinvent themselves. How we will need to completely reinvent the world of healthcare.

The regulator will have to move as well. In the US, all healthcare products have to be approved by the FDA, the Food and Drug Administration. I was privileged to observe how this established institution is re-inventing itself for the world of precision medicine. President Obama, in one of his last acts as president, approved the funding to focus on the new healthcare market of 'one'. It gives me energy to see such an entrenched establishment repositioning itself for the 'Day After Tomorrow': how the big oil-tanker of the Food and Drug Administration is putting a tiny little tug boat out there to experiment with a personalized 'Day After Tomorrow' medicine. But I also see how slow this progress can be, and how easily the rope between the oil-tanker and the tugboat could snap.

The World Economic Forum labelled most current systems of public policy and decision-making as 'Second Industrial Revolution': these models come from a time when decision-makers had the time to study a specific issue and develop the necessary response or appropriate regulatory framework in a linear way. But today, with the Fourth Industrial Revolution's rapid pace of change and broad impacts, legislators and regulators are being challenged to an unprecedented degree. And most have shown themselves unable to cope.

I think we need to introduce this 'Day After Tomorrow' thinking in every market where there is government oversight. True, we have to stay realistic about the pace of society, but if we keep being reactive about the future and not proactive, we're always going to be lagging behind.

THE RED QUEEN'S RACE

One of my favorite scenes in *Through the Looking-Glass* by Lewis Carroll is the Red Queen's race. In this scene, Alice is running like a madman and making no progress whatsoever. She remains firmly in the exact same spot.[19]

When she confronts the Red Queen with her peculiar situation, this is the conversation that ensues:

"Well, in our country," said Alice, still panting a little, *"you'd generally get to somewhere else—if you run very fast for a long time, as we've been doing."*

"A slow sort of country!" said the Queen. *"Now, here, you see, it takes all the running you can do, to keep in the same place. If you want to get somewhere else, you must run at least twice as fast as that!"*

I love this story. And think about that: are you living in a 'slow sort of country', or is it running twice as fast to keep up with the advent of the 'Day After Tomorrow'?

Imagine everything we talked about in this book. The advent of radically new 'Day After Tomorrow' technologies. The explosive rise in machine learning and AI. The rethinking of our industrial fabric with 3D printing, robotics and the Internet of Things. The creation of entirely new networked business models based on blockchain technologies. The radical rethinking of customer interactions with technologies like augmented reality.

All of this will change business models, markets and how we engage with consumers. It will completely transform our concept of organizations. Yet, our governments are not running twice as fast. Worse, they are not even running fast enough just to keep up. No wonder the next generation has disconnected.

Futurologist Mark Stevenson puts it like this: "Politicians have not been able to achieve any major innovation in how democracy works in nearly 200 years.

Scientists innovate, artists innovate, corporations innovate, but politicians are clinging to the same system of government, parliaments, ministries and political parties, with the most painfully slow progress possible for mankind."[20]

In the 1980s, the term 'Atari Democrats' was used to refer to a group of young Democratic legislators in the US who suggested that the support and development of hi-tech and related businesses would stimulate the economy and create jobs. Al Gore was linked to these 'Atari Democrats'. His passion for technology, biomedical research, genetic engineering *and* his insights about the environmental impact of such evolutions is well known. But the world seems to have an 'Al Gore' deficiency.

It is high time today to upgrade our institutions, our laws, our policies and our entire system of politics ready for this age of disruption and the 'Day After Tomorrow'.

Political Myopia about the 'Day After Tomorrow' is a hell of a lot more difficult to solve than the Corporate Myopia in large organizations, and *that* is already such a big challenge. But that doesn't mean we shouldn't try.

When I do have the rare occasion to engage with people in political positions, the number one response I get is "Yes. We know. We should. But it's really hard you know. It's really difficult to get anything done around here. We really can't change things. It's out of our control." It must be horrible to think that. The notion that comes to mind is the concept of 'learned helplessness'.[21]

This idea was researched in the field of psychology during the 1970s with a horrible experiment. Researchers put two dogs in two cages and submitted them to severe and frequent electrical shocks. Both dogs got exactly the same shocks, exactly the same dosage, with the same levels of pain for the animals.

But one of the dogs had a button in its cage. It could stop the electrical shocks by pressing the button, and the shocks would stop, for both dogs simultaneously and instantly. The dog in the cage with the button would learn very quickly that when the shocks came, it could press the button and make the torture stop.

The other dog – who could *not* control his destiny – was suffering from a rapidly deteriorating mental health. After periods of intense, and painful electrical shocks the dog that could control his destiny, the one that could make the shocks stop, still kept its mental strength and capability to learn. The other dog, who had suffered *exactly* the same set of shocks, but had no control over its destiny, had completely lost the capability and will to learn anything new.

This concept of 'learned helplessness' is something that is common in the world of psychology. When people are mentally abused, treated cruelly or severely mistreated, without any chance of changing their outcome, they fall into a state of lethargy and lifelessness.

I believe that in many of our political institutions and administrations, we have a great deal of this kind of 'learned helplessness'. It is so incredibly difficult to change things, and progress is so excruciatingly slow, that people lose the belief that their deed could have a real effect.

"It's really difficult to get anything done around here. We really can't change things." Let's move beyond that, shall we. Before it's too late?

But it's not just the responsibility of governments to wake up to the 'Day After Tomorrow'.

CARGO-CULTS

We have to rethink our role as citizens as well: as inhabitants of a region, as entrepreneurs in an economy, as citizens of the Earth. Are we actively contributing to making things better? Or are we mainly complaining about the learned helplessness of our pathetic overlords?

Are we expecting that everything will just fall out of the sky, and roasted chickens will fly into our mouths?

I learned of the wonderful story of the cargo-cults while researching the life of Richard Feynman, the Nobel prize-winner and inventor of the field of Quantum-Electro-Dynamics. He opened a congress at Caltech with a story about the creation of a new set of religions right after World War II in remote areas in Polynesia, Micronesia and Papua New Guinea. These regions were populated with primitive tribes and cultures, who suddenly became the central theatre-of-war during the naval warfare between the US and Japan. In that period, US troops would use these remote islands as command posts and had to be supplied with goods and food. All sorts of cargoes were dropped from the sky onto these unspoiled islands.

When Japan capitulated, and the American troops withdrew, the airdrops of cargoes came to an end. But the indigenous tribes of these idyllic remote islands – who had no idea of the major geo-political events that had been happening – were completely taken off guard. All of a sudden, the extremely handy 'cargo-from-the-sky' phenomenon had stopped.

The result was fascinating. When anthropologists visited these far-away regions a few years later, they found what they labeled 'cargo-cult' religions: the native inhabitants of the islands had done everything they could think of to please the Gods so that the cargo would start raining from the sky again. They had built 'mock-airplanes' out of bamboo and then had sacrificed gifts to them. They had recreated 'landing-strips' out of rocks, branches and twigs. Some cargo-cults even constructed 'command towers' where priests with hand-carved wooden headphones were trying to lure the 'silver giant birds' back to their region, to parachute their cargo onto the shores.

You might laugh when you read this, but there is a lot of 'cargo-cult' thinking going on in today's society.

True, the pace of our government institutions is by far not what we would expect in a Red Queen's race. But, at the same time, we also see that many Western societies are crippled by expectations from the side of labor unions who are still expecting the cargo to fall from the sky, in increasing amounts, more and more.

It is time to realize that we have to accelerate. That we have to work at both ends of the spectrum: government and society, politics and business, establishment and unions.

Klaus Schwab, the founder and CEO of the World Economic Forum, made such a call to action at the 2016 Davos meeting. He said that as the physical, digital and biological worlds continue to converge, new technologies and platforms will increasingly enable citizens to engage with governments, voice their opinions and coordinate their efforts. At the same time, governments will gain new technological powers to increase their control over populations, based on pervasive surveillance systems and the ability to control digital infrastructure.

In the words of Schwab: "Governments will increasingly face pressure to change their current approach to public engagement and policymaking, as their central role of conducting policy diminishes owing to the redistribution and decentralization of power that new technologies make possible."[22]

But he wasn't sure they would be able to reinvent themselves: "Ultimately, the ability of government systems and public authorities to adapt will determine their survival. If they prove capable of embracing a world of disruptive change, they will endure. If they cannot evolve, they will face increasing trouble."

NATIONS, CORPORATIONS AND NETWORKS

Two hundred years ago, nations were the undisputed realms of power. Countries would go to war to fight boundaries, secure trading rights and defend lucrative markets. Regions would be colonized by nations. Empires rose and fell.

In the past 100 years, we've seen the rise of corporations as the true embodiment of power. My father worked for Exxon his entire career. If you ask me who has more real power worldwide – my home country Belgium, or a corporation like Exxon – the answer is very simple. In the last 50 years of globalization especially, corporations have taken over control. World players like Nestlé, Exxon, General Electric or Monsanto have become global powerhouses of influence and authority.

Today we see the rise of the global networks: giant companies like Facebook, Google, Amazon, Alibaba, Baidu and TenCent. These new global networks grow even faster than corporations. They are more connected to their users *and* know everything about them. That's because they have access to the oil of the 21st century: information.

Where the battle of the 20th century was about the power balance between nations and corporations, the 21st century has added an exciting new player into the mix: the global information networks. They are moving faster, with more impact and with a clear desire to dominate the world of Post-Capitalism.

The irony in the world of nations is that instead of focusing on economies of scale, the world of nations seems to be crumbling. Even when we construct the concept of a European Union, the British vote to opt out with Brexit. The Catalans and the Basques want to leave their Spanish motherland. From Scots voting for independence to jihadi declaring a new state in the Middle East, the concept of nations is crumbling, while the concept of networks is growing like wildfire.

Debora MacKenzie wrote a brilliant piece on the 'End of Nations' in the *New Scientist*. She clearly stated that there is a growing feeling among economists, political scientists and even national governments that the nation state might not necessarily be the best scale on which to run our affairs. But it's all we've got at the moment.[23]

She sees a possible future where hierarchies could give way to global networks of experts and bureaucrats from nation states. Today, governments already work with these kinds of flexible networks such as the G7 (or G20) to manage global problems, often more and better than with the UN hierarchy.

"Networked problems require a networked response." Today we are seeing problems that are emerging from the global interrelatedness, such as economic instability, pandemics, climate change or cybersecurity, that can only be solved with networks. It's Stanley McChrystal's "It Takes a Network to Defeat a Network".[24]

THE LITTLE RED DOT[25]

But are there no examples of nations, where politicians *are* looking at the 'Day After Tomorrow'?

Of course, there are. Not many, but the way they do it could be a shining example for many.

My top favorite example is the Republic of Singapore. The legendary Lee Kuan Yew became Prime Minister, and with his vision, leadership and guidance, he moved the fledgling country from a Third World economy to First World affluence in just one single generation. Today, Singapore is a global commerce, finance and transportation hub and one of the pivots of the Southeast Asia economy. The World Economic Forum has named Singapore the most 'technology-ready' nation on the planet.

The tiny sovereign city-state of Singapore has a population under 6 million inhabitants. But today it is at the forefront of how technology is shaping society as it has actively been trying to understand the future, and implement and build that future.

In my opinion, this is the most perfect example of how a 'Day After Tomorrow' strategy should be implemented. Singapore has been able to attract the best and the brightest talent of their population to work in the government. And the best and brightest in the world of technology are working in the Infocomm Development Authority, which leads the 'Smart Nation' initiative. This initiative played a big role in the evolution and innovation of Singapore in areas such as healthcare, education, transportation, mobility, housing, etc.

This group set out a vision, wanting to make Singapore an entirely smart city-state, that would be truly citizen-centric and business-centric. They looked at all possible technologies and concepts that would impact society over the coming years, and then figured out how these could impact and improve the lives of their citizens and businesses. And then, working backwards, they defined the architecture, infrastructure, applications and data that would be necessary to enable the Smart Nation to become a reality.

This Smart Nation is a close collaboration between government, businesses and citizens. Crucial herein is a willingness to collaborate, and a common trust and openness. "A Smart Nation is built not by Government, but by all of us – citizens, companies, agencies", as stated on their website.

And the essence of such a truly Smart Nation is information. In the words of Jacqueline Poh, founding CEO of the Government Technology Agency of Singapore and one of the leading roles in the Smart Nation initiative: "We found, for example, that citizens are actually willing to give up quite a bit of privacy, completely depending on how useful they find the applications. If they're getting something useful in return, they will share data with us, that only makes the Smart Nation even smarter."[26]

Critics will say that Singapore is small, and therefore more agile than Big Nations. It's easier to change on a scale of 6 million citizens than trying to transform the US or even Europe. Critics will also point out that Singapore isn't the most democratic system in the world. True, but Singapore is a country that is run like a corporation. And, honestly, if this allows a region to focus on the 'Day After Tomorrow', and build a future where its citizens and businesses can thrive, I wish there were more countries run like corporations. It would make me feel much safer than hoping that the 'cargo will keep falling from the sky'.

THE 'DAY AFTER TOMORROW' FOR OUR GRANDCHILDREN

> "The biggest problem is not to let people accept new ideas, but to let them forget the old ones."
> **JOHN MAYNARD KEYNES**

John Maynard Keynes was perhaps the most influential economist of the 20th century. He's known as the father of modern macroeconomics. His ideas shifted the emphasis from the economic behavior of individuals and companies (microeconomics) to the behavior of the economy as a whole (macroeconomics). *Time* magazine included him in its list of 'Most Important People of the 20th Century', because he laid the foundations for a new school of economic thinking (known as Keynesian economics).[27]

The Wall Street Crash of 1929, known as 'Black Tuesday', was the most devastating stock market crash in the history of the United States, and it signaled the beginning of the 10-year 'Great Depression' that affected all Western industrialized countries. Keynes was 46 years old when Black Tuesday happened.

He was a strong advocate of increased government expenditures and lower taxes to stimulate demand and pull the global economy out of the Depression. *Time* said: "His radical idea that governments should spend money they don't have, may have actually saved capitalism." In the economic philosophy of Keynes, state intervention was vital to moderate 'boom and bust' cycles of economic activity.

During his life, and long thereafter, he was heavily contested. His ideas have often been challenged, notably by the American economist Milton Friedman, who took the opposite view: supporting free markets and a reduction in the size of government. That fundamental debate remains very much alive in the economic policy discussion of today.

Keynes published a remarkable essay in 1930, while the world was still reeling from the impact of the Wall Street crash. It was called *The Economic Possibilities for Our Grandchildren* in which he imagined a world where all of mankind's economic problems had been solved.[28]

He envisioned what the world would be like, 100 years later, in 2030. Even in that dark moment of the Great Depression, he proved to be an absolute optimist. He imagined that, by 2030, the standard of living would be dramatically higher. He projected that people, liberated from want (and without the desire to consume for the sake of consumption), would work no more than fifteen hours a week, devoting the rest of their time to leisure and culture. It was a high-energy pep talk for a truly depressing time, when people wondered if the great waves of progress of the nineteenth century had come to a crashing end.

Harry Truman once said: "It's a recession when your neighbor loses his job; it's a depression when you lose your own."[29]

Keynes was right about many things. Our standard of living has skyrocketed all over the world. Since *The Economic Possibilities for Our Grandchildren* was published, the US gross domestic product has grown, in real terms, by a factor of sixteen, and the GDP per capita by a factor of six. What holds for the United States goes for most of the rest of the world as well: in the past eighty years, the global economy has grown at a similar rate.

In his essay, he chronicles that the nineteenth century had unleashed such a torrent of technological innovation: "electricity, petrol, steel, rubber, cotton, the chemical industries, automatic machinery and the methods of mass production, but predicted that this would not stop. In his article, Keynes speaks of 'technological unemployment' driven by the emergence of new technologies that displace human labor through more efficient modalities.[30]

But a number of other things he got fundamentally wrong. In his essay, Keynes believed that this rise of technology, and our consequent elevated standard of living, would allow us to work less. Much less. He believed that technological progress would end the laborious struggle for survival that has characterized mankind's history.

In his words: "Thus for the first time since his creation, man will be faced with his real, his permanent problem — how to use his freedom from pressing economic cares, how to occupy the leisure, which science and compound interest will have won for him, to live wisely and agreeably and well."

Rebecca Rosen mused on this in an article in *The Atlantic* entitled *Why Do Americans Work So Much?*.[31] Keynes predicted that the advent of prosperity and technology would allow us to work much less, and that our most important query in life would be "How will we all keep busy when we only have to work 15 hours a week?". For a while, it looked like Keynes was right: in the 1930s the average workweek was 47 hours. By 1970 it had fallen to slightly less than 39. But then it went flat: instead of continuing to decline, the average workweek hovered just below 40 hours for nearly five decades.

In his closing remarks, the understatement of Keynes was that he noted: "There will be no harm in making mild preparations for our destiny."

Almost 100 years after *The Economic Possibilities for Our Grandchildren*, we're in dire need of a new reflection – and action – for the 'Day After Tomorrow'. We owe it to our own grandchildren. And, for that, we can all learn a lot from the tiny little city-state of Singapore.

With the advent of 'Day After Tomorrow' technologies, radically new business models, fundamental changes in the rise of networks and information, enormous systemic shifts in employment, and the totally different economics of capital and labor, we will undoubtedly have an amazing piece of history in front of us for the next 100 years.

If you were to try and map out the 'Day After Tomorrow', and then work your way back to 'tomorrow', the latter would look totally different than if you were to just extrapolate 'today'. It won't be easy to imagine, and yes, there will be a lot of 'wild' guesswork, but if we don't reflect on that 'Day After Tomorrow', and start to 'make preparations for our destiny', we're essentially flying blind.

The Economist's article *The onrushing wave* – about the advent of new technologies and the future of employment – concluded: "Even if the long-term outlook is rosy, with the potential for greater wealth and lots of new jobs, it does not mean that policymakers should simply sit on their hands in the meantime".[32]

Now is the time to act. Not 'tomorrow', and certainly not in the 'Day After Tomorrow'. Now.

I believe that if you take the best economists, politicians and sociologists to 'calculate backwards' from the 'Day After Tomorrow', that our budgets, plans and economic policy for our nations, regions and governments would look quite different. 'Quite' being the understatement of the century.

To me, this is the shadow side of the 'Day After Tomorrow'. Never before in history has the future been so volatile, uncertain, complex and ambiguous (VUCA). Yet never before in history have we underutilized our enormous mental capacity to think ahead. Instead we seem to be plunging ever deeper into short-term political focus. We look no further than 'today' and, even then, our minds our muddled with the 'Mess of Yesterday'. This *must* change.

We *have* to think about our 'Day After Tomorrow'.

Every last one of us.

Educators. Scientists. Artists. Farmers. Statisticians. Politicians. Doctors. Company directors. Urban planners. Astronomers. Ethics specialists. Philosophers. Engineers. And everyone else on the entire planet, … and beyond (not to discriminate against the good people of the International Space Station for instance).

This is a challenge that is much too big to solve on our own. We can only accomplish it by "running twice as fast" together.

THE SHADOW OF THE 'DAY AFTER TOMORROW': WHAT YOU NEED TO REMEMBER

Political Myopia is even worse than Corporate Myopia, because it involves the entire planet. In a world that's hurtling at us at an exponential speed, it's insane to focus on the things that are 'bothering' us today.

It's insane to wait until automation eats up 45% of all jobs.
It's insane to leave education models unchanged since the 19th century.
It's insane to issue economic predictions with 100-year-old, super-abstract mathematical models.
It's insane to try to solve the ageing population problem with a system that dates from the 20th century.
It's insane to leave major automation ethics challenges unsolved.
It's insane to stand by while global warming will cause oceans to rise.
It's insane that – knowing what they know – most governments look no further than four to six years ahead.

In fact: forget everything that I wrote above. Just remember this one thing: start thinking *now* about the 'Day After Tomorrow' of your company, your country, your planet and your loved ones, and start acting on it.

Oh, and do yourself a favor: please don't vote for short-termist politicians with populist solutions that will only leave us with an enormous pile of 'Mess of Yesterday' when their term of office is over.

You are the difference between the world as it was and the better place it will become. [33]

8

CONCLUSION

GRAPHENE AND FROGS

When I was part of a team at British Airways working on disruptive new ideas a few years ago, I had the chance to meet Soviet-born Dutch-British physicist Andre Geim, from the University of Manchester. He is the only person in the world to have won both the Nobel prize for physics in 2010, and the Ig Nobel Prize in 2000.[2]

Everyone knows the Nobel prize, the most prestigious scientific honor you can receive as a scientific researcher. But not many people know the 'Ig Nobel' prizes. Since 1991, the magazine *Annals of Improbable Research* has been giving out 10 prizes a year to honor scientists for experiments so outlandish that they "first make people laugh, and then make them think."[3]

Geim won the Ig Nobel in physics in 2000 for levitating a live frog with magnets. He ran the advanced physics lab at the University of Manchester and held regular Friday night sessions there, blowing off steam after a long week of 'traditional' physics classes. These late-night physics jam-sessions – labelled Friday Night Experiments (FNEs) – involved beer, as well as the really cool and fancy equipment in the lab. During one of those alcohol-induced FNE sessions, there was an argument about the magnetic properties of water, about how its properties would not be strong enough to counter gravity. Geim argued that it would, and put his theory to the test: he threw a live frog, on 'loan' from the biology lab, into a huge super electro-magnet, turned up to full blast. The frog just 'floated' in the electromagnetic field, and defied gravity.

The image of the flying frog went around the world like wildfire. Geim received a serious reprimand from the University, but he carried on with the Friday Night

Experiments. In his words: "It is better to be wrong than be boring." He's not just a provocateur, he sees these as experiments in divergent thinking: "These sessions allow us to question things people who work in that area never bother to ask. The biggest adventure is to move into an area in which you are not an expert." It got him the Ig Nobel prize in 2000, which he accepted.

In 2010, Geim, together with Konstantin Novoselov, won the Nobel prize for the discovery of Graphene. This is the 'magical material of the future'. It's just an extremely thin layer of pure carbon: just one atom thick, with the atoms arranged in a honeycomb-shaped lattice. The material has amazing properties: it is about 200 times stronger than the strongest steel, it is one of the lightest materials known to man, and also the best conductor of electricity known in the universe. It is predicted that Graphene could replace silicon and transform the electronics industry as we know it.

And it was discovered by Geim in another one of those Friday Night Experiments. Graphene had been talked about since the 1960s, but it seemed elusive to isolate at scale. Until Geim one Friday night used an ordinary pencil (the core lead of the pencil is carbon, actually graphite), and a piece of Scotch sticky-tape. By stroking a pencil over the Scotch tape, Geim and his students were able to produce large flakes of Graphene. It might seem playful but, in Geim's words, that is deliberate: "Playfulness lets us withstand enormous uncertainty." He prefers the term 'curiosity-driven research'. The title of his Nobel Prize lecture acceptance speech was titled a 'Random Walk to Graphene'.

Meeting Andre Geim had a profound impact on how I came to see the world.

So many corporate enterprises have truly amazing research facilities and wonderful R&D activities. Yet many of them will probably only turn out 'extrapolations' of what they already know to be true. They have brilliant processes, people and institutions taking them to 'tomorrow'. But I fundamentally believe that you need to include the messiness of 'playful' experiments, the 'curiosity-driven' research, and perhaps the informal nature of the equivalent of Friday Night Experiments to take your innovation endeavors to the level of the 'Day After Tomorrow'.

FOUNTAIN OF YOUTH

Today, corporate growth is no longer the primary fascination of large organizations, even though it was their center of attention throughout the last century. Today, large corporations are mesmerized by 'rejuvenation', by the possibility to re-generate themselves. That's why so many corporations are spellbound by the shiny power of startups.

The quest for the 'fountain of youth' has inspired literature for centuries. It appeared in writings by Herodotus (5th century BC), the Alexander romance (3rd century AD), and the stories of Prester John (early Crusades, 11th/12th centuries). Stories of similar waters were also found among the indigenous peoples of the Caribbean during the Age of Exploration (early 16th century), who spoke of the restorative powers of the water in the mythical land of Bimini.[4] Today, busloads of corporate executives jet around the world in search of this 'fountain of youth'. They fly down to Silicon Valley in California, or to Silicon Roundabout in London. They travel to Tel Aviv, Berlin and Shanghai in order to find the 'magic' to make them young again. They want that secret ingredient that will make them innovative, agile and lean again.

To be left behind by the changing times is *the* biggest corporate anxiety of the 21st century. To have a wonderful machine that was built for the past, not for the future. To suffer in a world that is accelerating through disruptive changes, and feel that you can't attract the bright and willing like you did in the past.

Today, ambitious young talent doesn't want to work for the establishment anymore. The prodigious poster boy of the new ambition is Mark Zuckerberg. He's who they want to be, not some boring corporate slave driver who looks like an undertaker and lives like a monk. Their bucket list reads: drop out of Harvard before you graduate, build a billion dollar business by the time you're 22 and shine on the cover of *Time* magazine as 'Person of the Year' by your 26th birthday. Afterwards, donate USD 45 billion to 'advance human potential' when you have your first baby. Easy peasy.[5]

This is not so much youthful arrogance as it is about belief. The belief that you *can* make a difference as a startup. That it's possible to escape the drudgery and bureaucracy of large organizations. That you can make a dent in the universe. That's exactly what this next generation is seeking. In 2016, *The Economist* tried to understand the motives of the upcoming Millennial generation of business leaders, and how they see the world differently. They found out that this next generation is so engrained with advancements in technology, that the world seems to be at their fingertips. They see their success in life not measured by mere financial performance. They are motivated by impact. By the chance to do something useful, awesome and inspiring.[6]

This is the generation that will find the transition to startup-life quite simple. Where the previous generations preferred the 'easy' road to a bank, an oil company or an insurance firm, this next generation now feels the lure of the 'rainforest'. Brilliant talent that would once have worked on Wall Street, or for companies like P&G or Exxon, now try their luck in the startup-life. In fact, this has become the new MBA.

If you run a startup, and succeed, then you will have achieved much more than by climbing the org-chart at some multinational. If you don't succeed, you will have learned so much in such a very short time, that this will trump any business school's teachings.

It would be foolish to underestimate the power of these startups, of these humble beginnings. Look at Apple, and how fragile and brittle it was in the beginning, and how it became the most valuable company in the world.

You really need the crazy ones, the troublemakers, the rebels to think radically and drive disruption. You need the ones who see things differently, the round pegs in the square holes. Every corporation needs an Andre Geim throwing frogs into a super magnet. Or a Cuban scientist DJ called Jesus.

WE CAN'T AFFORD NOT TO MAKE MISTAKES

My 'Today, Tomorrow and The Day After Tomorrow' model is so simple that it will prove to be practically useful.

Now that we're almost ready to part, let me repeat what for me is the essence of this model, and even of this entire book: if you look at tomorrow, with what you know today, and extrapolate that, you might miss out on some fundamental changes. But if you try to imagine the 'Day After Tomorrow', with all possible scenarios of fundamental change, and work your way back from there, you might end up with a different kind of tomorrow.

I have come to believe that you can apply this to your company's strategy. But also to your brand, your organization, your roadmap. You can apply this to your team, your division, your people. You can apply it to your country, your schools and your government. You can also apply this to yourself. What are *you* going to do differently when you look at the 'Day After Tomorrow'?

We all know that there is a huge gap between 'knowing' and 'doing'. Even if you were to imagine a 'different tomorrow', how can you move yourself, your team and your entire organization in that direction?

I said it and will keep on repeating it: you need a *bold* culture. One that is not afraid to take risks. That is the true differentiator between the corporate and the startup, between the plantation and the rainforest. The startup has a 95% chance of *not* making it. It *has* to take risks. In a startup, risk-taking and failure is the norm, because it is the only way to survive, and even grow.

Nelson Mandela once said "I never fail. I either win, or learn".[7] Large organizations should adopt this as their corporate mantra. They should 'learn' to adopt a culture where failure is seen as a learning mechanism.

In 2015, Francesca Gino and Bradley Staats wrote an excellent article in the *HBR* called *Why Organizations Don't Learn*.[8] They described a number of 'biases' that are impeding organizations from truly transforming themselves. In their paper, they argued that although business leaders across different organizations may *say* that learning comes from failure, their actions mostly show a preoccupation with success.

This 'Bias Toward Success' manifests itself in four fundamental challenges they set out for organizations:

Challenge #1:
Overcome the 'fear of failure'

In many organizations we have, unconsciously, institutionalized a 'fear of failure'. We structure projects so that no time or money is available for experimentation, and we award bonuses and promotions to those who deliver according to plan.

Challenge #2:
Overcome the 'fixed mindset'

A fixed mindset limits our ability to learn because it makes individuals focus too much on performing well. Failure is seen as something to be avoided, fearing it will make us seem incompetent.

Challenge #3:
Dismantle the over-reliance on past performance

Business leaders often put too much emphasis on performance and not enough on the potential to learn. We should stimulate the capability to acquire new skills and fuel the thirst for learning.

Challenge #4:
Overcome the attribution bias

Business leaders often ascribe their successes to hard work, brilliance and skill rather than luck; however, they blame their failures on ill fortune and bad luck. Unless people will recognize that failure resulted from their own actions, they will not learn from their mistakes.

I think this is the beginning of the recipe for Leadership in the 'Day After Tomorrow'. It means we'll have to re-program many of the business leaders who were trained in the teachings of the 20th century. We'll have to overcome these biases towards success, and allow business leaders to understand the power of experimentation and be agile in their quest for their new tomorrow.

I vividly remember taking a group of senior executives from a large European Telecom operator to visit the headquarters of Box on the outskirts of Silicon Valley. We had a chance to meet with Dan Levin, the COO of the company. He walked in wearing a T-shirt and jeans, staring at a room full of suits from the Old Continent.

He gave one of the best performances I've ever seen in my life. No slides, straight from the heart, about how they were doing things differently at Box, trying to compete with the HPs and Dells of this world in the space of cloud computing. He said: "The only thing you control is the employee's mindset." Being a manager, he reminded the group of executives, is all about the head, but being a true leader is all about the heart. He told the stunned group of European Executives, who had spent their careers climbing the corporate hier-archy: "You have all been trained not to make mistakes. That works great for you, in your job, your role. But that wouldn't work here for us. That would take too long. We can't afford not to make mistakes."

It's pretty ironic that those companies whose immense success we are trying to understand and copy, are telling us about learning to fail. That is the true learning of the rainforest. In the words of Franklin D. Roosevelt: "The country needs and, unless I mistake its temper, the country demands bold, persistent experimentation. It is common sense to take a method and try it: If it fails, admit it frankly and try another. But above all, try something."[9]

THE UNDERTOW OF THE INVISIBLE

Genrich Altshuller was a Soviet engineer, inventor and scientist. He created one of the most influential methods of categorizing innovation called 'TRIZ'. TRIZ is a Russian acronym which stands for: 'Teoriya Resheniya Izobretatelskikh Zadatch' (Try saying that 5 times in a row if you're not Russian). It's basically the holy grail of how to perform innovation, and it was almost lost on mankind.[10]

Altshuller was a clerk assigned to the 'Innovation Center' of the Russian Navy in 1946. His job was to screen possible patents, document them, and then prepare the paperwork to prepare applications for the patent office. He screened thousands of patents, and it lead him to realize that there were patterns to be found in their seeming chaos: patterns of innovation.

He realized that an innovative solution was needed whenever there is an unresolved 'contradiction', in the sense that improving one parameter impacts negatively on another. He later called these 'technical contradictions'. An example would be that if you needed to reduce the weight of an object, this would require a thinner material that could then no longer be stress-resistant. Here the 'weight' and the 'thickness' of the material are 'technical contradictions'.

He also found patterns that could serve as archetypical solutions to resolve these 'technical contradictions'. He organized these technical contradictions into a matrix, and mapped them onto 40 'principles of invention' that could solve these contradictions.

He then made the worst career mistake of his life. He wrote a letter to Joseph Stalin, the head of the Communist Party of the Soviet Union, and told him that the way the Russian military was organizing innovation was a disaster. He said that he knew how to revolutionize the innovation of the Soviet empire. Stalin was not particularly known for his welcoming attitude towards constructive criticism, and consequently sentenced Genrich Altshuller to 25 years in the Vorkuta Gulag forced-labor camp – just north of the Arctic Circle.

Amazingly, Altshuller, kept on perfecting his method. He left a revolutionary science behind: the 'Theory of Inventive Problem Solving' (TRIZ), where the ultimate goal is to optimize the contradictions in such a manner that innovation simply becomes 'invisible'.

In e-commerce, we all remember the days when buying something online was cumbersome, intense and difficult. And then Amazon revolutionized the world by introducing 'one-click' buying. Today it has moved on to Alexa: no more clicks necessary, just your voice, when you want to order something. Innovation fades away the concept of clicks. From 'three clicks', to one 'click' to 'no clicks'. In other words, invisible.

In the world of call centers, we were able to optimize the time with the customer and reduce the need for humans. Today, we have chat-bots and might finally arrive at excluding the human element. No more call center agents. No humans. Invisible.

In the taxi business, Uber revolutionized the customer experience by taking away the most cumbersome part of the taxi process, the payment at the end of a ride. You just step out of the car, and the payment is fulfilled automatically. Today, it goes one step further and its driverless fleet is taking the human driver out of the equation. Payments become invisible. Human drivers become invisible.

The most dangerous thing about invisible technologies is that we don't 'feel' them any longer. In the world of the 'Day After Tomorrow', in the world where things will wake up, we will see a surge in invisible technologies at work. Their impact will be huge. The undertow of these currents of invisible technologies could pull us away into the abyss of the ocean if we're not careful.

THE DISRUPTION COMMITTEE

When you scale companies, the only way to achieve operational excellence is to put irrefutable and waterproof governance systems in place. The epitome of these systems comes in the form of the audit committee, that is safely nested into the warm bosom of the board. It is there to oversee 'correct' usage of the rules, governance and operations of an organization. The way I see it, most audit committees excel at finding the most boring people on the planet and inviting them into their midst.

Don't get me wrong, you need them. Someone has to make sure that people follow the rules. Someone needs to keep organizations in line and have them play by the book. Right? This could get ugly otherwise. No CEO, director or chairman wants to go to jail because some employee overstepped their boundaries or possibly committed a crime.

The problem with audit committees is that they have a very strong voice in large organizations. Too strong. They are intensifying the 'Bias Toward Success' and can dangerously obstruct the 'experimentation' or 'risk-taking' culture that is essential to put some 'rainforest magic' into your plantation.

That's why I coined the idea of a disruption committee as a counterbalance to the audit committee. Large organizations need a group of people who are constantly thinking: "Why don't we color outside the lines?". They need a team that is persistently challenging the status quo: that is driving a company outside of its comfort zone, and tackling the challenges of the 'success bias'.

Audit committees are often made up of very similar profiles. People with an economic or financial background, with very similar training, very similar ideas, very similar perceptions. I would argue that the disruption committee should be exactly the opposite. Just as Frans Johansson argued in *The Medici Effect*, which he wrote in 2004: "Innovation comes from diverse industries, cultures and disciplines when they all intersect, bringing ideas from one field into another."[11] I think the ideal disruption committee should assemble widely diverse profiles of people. They should be passionate enough to collectively dream up the 'Day After Tomorrow' for your company.

If you look at the future, are you concerned about control or relevance? That's the question you should be asking yourself.

Audit committees focus on control. They give companies the comforting assurance that all is well and that they have control over their destiny. Disruption committees, on the other hand, are focused on relevance. They question everything, look at companies from different angles, rip them apart, put them back together in a different form, perform experiments with beer and frogs, have fun, challenge the status quo, laugh at management's rigid ideas and do the exact opposite of what you would want them to do. If they don't give you sweat stains on your otherwise spotless shirt, you have chosen the wrong people. If they do, if they're the reason that you can't fall asleep, then these are the people who will make sure you stay relevant in the 'Day After Tomorrow'. The round pegs in the square hole that your company still is today.

YOUR PERSONAL DAY AFTER TOMORROW

One last note to conclude this book. A personal final note.

I hope this book has given you the inspiration to act on the 'Day After Tomorrow' of your organization. But what about yourself? How will you personally sail the 'winds of change' going forward? How will you reinvent yourself?

Millennials entering the job market today can expect to have between 15 to 20 'jobs' in their lifetime. The half-life of knowledge and experience is falling rapidly, and we constantly have to keep up to make sure our expertise is actual and valuable. It's a never-ending rhythm of making sure you don't fall behind.

At the very same time, there is an enormous opportunity to rethink how we work *and* how we live. It will give us unprecedented possibilities to focus on those things in life that give true value, true impact and true rewards.

When Dee Hock – the visionary leader who transformed the mess of BankAmericard into the triumphant Visa network – retired, he gave an amazing farewell speech: "Through the years, I have greatly feared and sought to keep at bay the four beasts that inevitably devour their keeper — Ego, Envy, Avarice and Ambition. When I sever the connections with business for a life of isolation and anonymity, I am convinced I'm making a great bargain by trading money for time, position for liberty, and ego for contentment — that the beasts can be securely caged."[12]

When I personally bade the addictive startup-life farewell in 2010, I traded a life of chasing the 'next new thing' for a life of observation. It gave me the chance to see some of the most amazing companies in the world, and how they were preparing for the future. I sometimes feel like the Petrarch of the digital age, just as he was observing the transition from the 'Dark Ages' to the Renaissance, I feel just as privileged to observe the transition from the industrial age to the 'age of networks'.

I spend most of my days traveling around the world, talking to organizations, understanding how they think and work, and I love presenting on every possible stage in every corner of the globe about the challenges and the opportunities of the 'Day After Tomorrow'.

But I have also made personal choices on 'caging the beasts'. Since I left the startup scene, I've made it a personal rule that I don't work when my children have a school vacation. I take every possible minute of our precious time together to be a 'dad'. They don't care that I address 4,000 people on a stage in Las Vegas to talk about the 'future'. In those moments, I focus on the 'now'. (Yes, that *is* ironic when this entire book has been about looking forward, but it does not make it less true.) It's been the best investment I've ever made in my entire life.

But I'm curious about how you will determine and set your own personal goals for the 'Day After Tomorrow'. How will you avoid getting caught up in the rat-race of 'today' thinking, and cleaning up the mess of 'Yesterday'? How will you reinvent your personal balance for the future? How you will 'cage your beasts' of Ego, Envy, Avarice and Ambition? I can only hope that this book has given you some inspiration in the matter and that you've picked up some ideas and stories that will change your path.

We're almost there.

"It was the best of times, it was the worst of times": I like to open my speeches with these mesmerizing first lines of Charles Dickens' *A Tale of Two Cities*. They perfectly reflect how we live in the most amazing times of technological change *and* that there is a scary side to this whirlwind of massive disruption. But the full opening of this book is even more heartbreakingly beautiful.

I leave you with these fine words, and I wish you Godspeed in the 'Day After Tomorrow'.

It was the best of times, it was the worst of times,
It was the age of wisdom, it was the age of foolishness,
It was the epoch of belief, it was the season of light,
It was the spring of hope, it was the winter of despair,
we had everything before us, we had nothing before us …

THE END

NINE RULES FOR THRIVING IN THE 'DAY AFTER TOMORROW'

Before we part (Yes, this book *does* have multiple endings, much like the movie version of *The Return of The King),* I want to leave you with some basic guidelines to help you find your 'Day After Tomorrow'. They are not so much laws you should follow (see 'rule' number one), but rather inspiration for when you feel you're being swallowed by the 'Mess of Yesterday'.

1. BREAK THE RULES

If you're the rule-following type, you won't survive in the 'Day After Tomorrow'. Make your own rules. Then bend, break and renew them. Permanently. Disruptors are rule-breakers by definition, so even if you stick to tradition, they'll force you out of it eventually.

2. SPEND 10% ON BEING RADICAL

Spend about 10% of your time, budget and talent on radical experiments for your 'Day After Tomorrow'. That is how you will make a dent in the universe. If it's less, you won't make it in the long run. If it's more, your today and tomorrow 'machines' might grow weak and you need them to fund your 'Day After Tomorrow'.

3. TRAVEL BEYOND THE LIMITS

Fight the status quo. Flying used to be impossible. The idea of Skyping sounded preposterous 50 years ago. Growing new organs once seemed like science fiction. Until someone refused to be limited by 'reality'. Push the boundaries. Break down barriers. Aim farther than the moon. Aim for Mars. The impossible is just a possibility waiting to be born.

4. GROW A PAIR

Avoidance of risk is not 'safe'. It keeps you from evolving fast enough. Accept that innovation is messy. It's chaotic. It's a rainforest where anything might happen. It's about embracing what makes you scared. It's about trying, failing, learning and starting over. Remember, "Everything you want is on the other side of fear."[1]

5. CULTURE BEFORE STRUCTURE

Find leaders who don't want to lead. Find employees who do. Hire people who don't 'fit' in your company. Hire loners, connectors, watchers, thinkers, doers, makers, breakers, runners, questioners and answerers. Hire anyone, as long as they are passionate and committed to your customers. Your people are your culture, so choose them carefully.

6. THOU SHALT NOT MISTRUST

The age of disruption is about trust. Trust in the empowerment of your employees. Trust in your customers (so that small group of unreliable consumers won't mess up the experience for the others). Trust that someone staying in your apartment via Airbnb won't wreck it. Trust that when you share your ideas, they will grow bigger. Suspicious minds will miss 'The Day After Tomorrow'.

7. FOLLOW THE VEXERS

Listen to those troublesome, almost irritating customers that demand the impossible and will push your company beyond its limits. Those who will make you see the things you did not see before. Find your pollutants, as Mickey McManus would say.

8. MOVE FAST AND BREAK THINGS

Move *before* your company peaks. Move when the disruption of your industry is clear, but before it's a threat. Move before you think you should be moving. And keep moving. That is how you'll find and keep 'eternal youth' for your company.

9. UN-BECOME YOURSELF

This is the 'Wright Time' to reinvent yourself. There are so many tools, ideas, platforms and people just waiting to be connected. Keep your eyes open. Learn. Think. Un-think. Un-learn. Close your eyes. And then re-connect the dots. You'll see a completely different picture. *That* is your 'Day After Tomorrow'.

10

YOUR RULES
FOR THE
'DAY AFTER
TOMORROW'

> *"Some people never go crazy.*
> *What truly horrible lives they*
> *must live."*
>
> **CHARLES BUKOWSKI**

Now forget all about the page before this one. Use it as inspiration, and then move on.

It's your turn now: I want you to write your own rules for the 'Day After Tomorrow' on the following 2 pages.

Make them radical. Go nuts. Even one 'rule' will do. One word. A number. A dot. Anything. Just do *not* leave this page blank. Draw something. Tape a photograph of the last moment you felt ecstatic. Cut out a hole. Leave a print of your baby's foot. As long as it means something to you and your 'Day After Tomorrow'. (I even invite you to share it on social media as I'd love to see what you've created. Though I *would* understand if you wanted to keep it private.)

So, that's it. We've arrived at the actual ending. Thanks for sticking with me until now and may your 'Day After Tomorrow' be a glorious one!

ADDENDUM

CUSTOMERS IN THE 'DAY AFTER TOMORROW'

By Steven Van Belleghem
Partner at nexxworks and Snackbytes

My nexxworks business partner and friend Steven Van Belleghem has been my loyal companion for the past couple of years during our experiences and tours in Silicon Valley, Europe and Asia. I'm a technologist, looking at the 'Day After Tomorrow', and am trying to understand what it means for organizations and customers. But Steven looks at it from a different perspective: he's a marketing expert at heart, who has such a profound insight into the behavior of customers, as well as a deep understanding of how 'Day After Tomorrow' technologies can help us connect with them.

Steven is writing a book on this subject (which will be launched at the end of 2017), but I feel blessed to already share a sneak preview in this addendum chapter called 'Customers in the Day After Tomorrow'. Enjoy!

PETER HINSSEN

Over the past few years, Peter Hinssen and I have had the opportunity to visit hundreds of innovative firms. From Silicon Valley to New York, from Shanghai to Singapore, from Berlin to London. Each time we were able to see, from up close, what the future holds.

As you will have read in the previous chapters, Peter loves technology. Being so knowledgeable about emerging technology, he lucidly explains what the opportunities could be for large companies. It's a pleasure to observe his rationale and way of thinking.

I'm no technologist. I'm an economist with a deep passion for marketing and customers. Pairing a technologist with a customer service officer to visit such companies has paid dividends. We see the same things, but interpret them for the client-firms from quite different perspectives. My focus is chiefly on the impact for customers. It's a great honor for me to be asked to write a chapter for Peter's book on the impact of technology on the customer relationship.

Actually, in a few months from now, the roles will be reversed. Then I'll be writing a new book entitled *Customers in the Day After Tomorrow* and Peter will be writing a chapter for it. In the meantime, please enjoy a sneak preview in the coming pages.

Before we dive into the future, I would like to explain the history of 'customer experience' on the basis of three books.

The first book is *The Nordstrom Way* (1995).[1] Twenty years ago, retailer Nordstrom was one of the most innovative companies in the field of customer experience. The book told the market about their service philosophy. In a nutshell, this story was about optimized processes to make the customer's life as happy as possible. The first step to getting satisfied customers is to simply ensure that the transactions go smoothly. Disney, for example, is – just like Nordstrom – an icon in the field of perfect processes for their customers. Visit one of the Disney theme parks today and you'll see that their processes are incredibly well conceived.

The second book is entitled *The Ultimate Question* (Fred Reichheld, 2006).[2] This book introduced the 'Net Promoter Score'. In order to calculate the 'Net Promoter Score', you ask your customers, on a scale of 0 to 10, to what extent they would recommend the company to third parties. Whoever gives a score of a 9 or a 10, is a promoter. Those rating you with a 0 to 6 are detractors. The number of promoters minus the number of detractors is the 'Net Promoter Score'. The claim in the book is quite simple: measure the NPS and, on the basis of that one figure, you'll know whether your company is doing well or not. If the score is higher than zero, then you will enter a growth environment. Score below zero … and you've got problems. The main impact of the NPS is felt in the boardroom. Many top executives suddenly had a customers' KPI that was dead easy to measure and interpret. There are proponents and opponents of the NPS, but no one can deny its impact was huge. Customer experience evolved from something you had to 'believe in'… to something you could 'measure'.

The third book with a strong impact is *Delivering Happiness*, written by Tony Hsieh, the CEO of Zappos in 2010.[3] Zappos – one of the biggest online fashion retailers – is generally regarded as a company that leads the way in the 'customer experience' world. They became world-famous because of a few extreme decisions. Some examples. Suppose you want to buy a specific pair of shoes and you see them pictured on Zappos.com. If you ring the contact center of Zappos, they'll help you find them. They'll first check on Zappos.com. If the shoes aren't in stock there, they'll look up at least five competitors to somehow find your dream shoes. They once remained on the line with a customer for over ten hours. In most contact centers this case would go down in history as the biggest failure ever. At Zappos, they hastily distributed a press release: they had broken the world record for phoning with a customer, they wrote! 'Delivering Happiness' is a brilliant book. It might appear to be about the 'customer experience' but, actually, it's about corporate culture. The 'Zappos-story' has been told and read so many times by managers all over the world that 'corporate culture – tailored to the customer' has been placed higher on the agenda than ever before.

Each of these stories adds a key component in the creation of a fantastic customer experience. A good process (1), measuring the right feedback (2) and a corporate culture tailored to the customer (3) are – all three of them – important building blocks towards achieving delighted customers.

CUSTOMER EXPERIENCE FOR **TODAY AND TOMORROW**

Process · Measurement · Culture

A NEW CUSTOMER JOURNEY: ALGORITHMS WILL BE KEY

We are now at the beginning of a new phase. Throughout his book, Peter outlines the evolution of Artificial Intelligence (AI). The spectacular events of last year - Google wins in Go, Uber uses driverless cars at customer locations… - are all signs of this new phase. Over the next few years, AI will hugely affect the customer relationship. The way in which consumers take decisions is about to change again. 'Gut feeling' will play less and less of a role, as will our own search engine process. Without us realizing it, the big tech companies have been molding and grooming us, for 20 years now, for this new phase. When, back in the nineties, you bought a book from Amazon.com, you received (yes, even back then) a recommendation; from Amazon, to buy another book. That was a new, spectacular twist back then. I, myself, have bought many books suggested to me by Amazon. In fact, at that moment, I was making a purchase decision based on… an algorithm. Similarly, when Netflix makes a suggestion for a new series, that too is an algorithm trying to influence me. This evolution will gain momentum in the years to come.

One of the key drivers of that change is, without a doubt, the emergence of virtual personal assistants. Amazon Echo is a big hit. About one in three users of Amazon Echo use the interface to buy products through Amazon. That is mighty impressive. You place, in other words, a kind of speaker in your home. You talk into that thing. You say: "Hi Alexa, can you buy me x". Provided you're an Amazon Prime Now member, that product is delivered to your door within two hours. You don't even need to press a button for that, just talk into the speaker.

For consumers, that's fantastic news. Ease of use is increasing again. But it's not so obvious for service providers. The customer journey is changing more radically than ever. When the internet and social media arrived on the scene, the channel where consumers got their info shifted. In the 'Day After Tomorrow', the consumer will outsource the 'search engine' part to a digital interface. Over the next few years, algorithms will become more determinant in the purchase cycle of products and services, at the expense of the classic method for searching data.

FROM MOBILE TO AI FIRST

If the customer journey changes course, there is no choice. Companies will have to adapt and follow. That shift can already be seen today among the big tech companies. The big tech companies have, in 2016, changed tack: 'AI first'. There are no exceptions. Trade and industry will follow suit in the years to come. The evolution from digital first, to mobile first to AI first is a foregone conclusion.

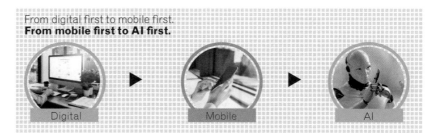

From digital first to mobile first.
From mobile first to AI first.

Digital   Mobile   AI

Simply put, Artificial Intelligence is all about the power of prediction. The better a computer can predict a situation, the greater the impact. If a customer needs an airline ticket, then a computer is able to use the data available (a business schedule, habits, a location) in order to predict when, exactly, that ticket should be purchased. If that prediction is done correctly, then you – as the customer – need do nothing and the correct ticket is purchased. Currently we get recommendations, but 'tomorrow' we'll get specific, personalized suggestions and, the 'Day After Tomorrow', those personalized purchases will be done for us.

As Artificial Intelligence makes its debut in the customer journey, then you just know that a lot of 'AI first' applications will appear in this area. For companies, the most relevant AI solutions will increase the level of staff engagement in the customer journey. Initially, the focus isn't on AI in the customer interface, but on IA (Intelligence Augmented) instead. By using smart technology, the suite of services provided by staff will be more personalized, faster and cheaper.

'Digital Genius' is a good example of this. This software builder produces software that automates the customer service back office. They use customer questions from the past two years as input. They 'translate' the words into mathematical expressions. As a result, their user interface is language independent.

When a customer asks a question, that question is fed into a mathematical model. The question is compared against past questions and then combined with real-time input. Based on that analysis, the software offers a suggestion for a potential answer to the question. The customer service agent sees the suggestion, is able to make some 'human' modifications and then transmits it to the customer. The software also gives an indication about the correctness and accuracy of the answer. You can even empower the system to answer the customer's question automatically provided the risk of a correct answer is higher than, for instance, 97%. The essence of the software consists in allowing staff at contact centers to work faster and in a more personalized way. 'Intelligence Augmented'.

FROM GUT FEELING TO CONSUMER SCIENCE

'Customer Experience Management' is evolving from a world built on gut feeling to a veritable science. When, in the past, firms wanted feedback from customers, it was gathered via questionnaires, for example. You were soon looking at six weeks to complete a run-of-the-mill market survey. In today's fast-moving world, six weeks is way too long. Besides, asking the customers loads of questions isn't the answer. What people say and what people do, are sometimes worlds apart.

In today's world, it's possible to collect a lot of information and customer viewpoints without questionnaires. What's more, that information is available in real time. The interpretation of behavior is one of the most powerful sources of customer feedback.

Netflix is, without a doubt, one of the leaders in this field. Their slogan "In God we trust, all others bring data", is omnipresent in their offices. When developing their first 'own-content', they made the most important choices on the basis of their existing streaming data. It was no coincidence that Kevin Spacey plays the main role in that series. It is based on behavioral data. They didn't ask their users who their favorite actor was; no, they looked for the actor with the highest 'streaming loyalty'. If asked to name their favorite actor, consumers would probably have answered "Tom Cruise". The nice memories of *Top Gun* being a likely reason. But, in reality, those same people, probably, barely watch anything these days with Tom Cruise in it. The question was answered, primarily, on nostalgia. There's nothing wrong with that, but Netflix is none the wiser for it. By focusing on behavioral data, the entire cast and screenwriters were chosen for *House of Cards*. And we all know the rest...

INVEST IN THE CUSTOMER FOR THE 'DAY AFTER TOMORROW'

If you consider the new technologies that Peter describes in this wonderful book, the impact on the customer will be significant. There's a whole lot of stuff coming our way. If you – as a consumer – like to be served quickly, with a minimum of effort on your part, and in person, then a wonderful world awaits. For companies who want to gear up for that world, it's crucial to make the transition to AI first with, all around it, a 'consumer science' mindset.

To serve the customer well in the 'Day After Tomorrow', four axes for investment may come in useful.
1. Convenience is the New Loyalty
2. Platform Strategy
3. Scalable Communication
4. Invisible Technology

In the rest of this chapter, I explain each of these four axes, in order to consider, with you, what's needed to satisfy the customer's expectations in the 'Day After Tomorrow'.

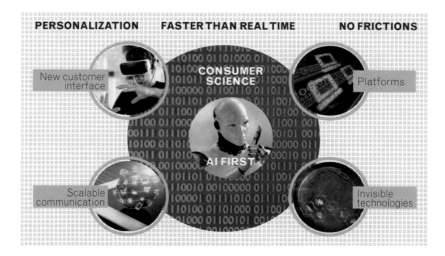

1. Convenience is the New Loyalty

Time for a small self-test.

Do you use Booking.com from time to time?

If so, name five positive things about Booking.com in the next 30 seconds?

Third question: are you also (secretly) a bit in love with the brand, Booking.com?

I have tried out this small experiment, these past 12 months, at many keynotes in pretty much every country of Europe. These are my findings (the target group is, of course, a business audience).

There is ca. 90% market penetration for Booking.com among business people. Users can usually reel off 10 plus-points about the site within 60 seconds: it's fast, individually tailored, the powerful app, easy to cancel a booking, no pre-payment needed, the visitor reviews, photos, cards, simple & easy to use, the points scheme and the huge range of accommodation on offer, are the most frequently cited advantages.

Incidentally, only 1% of customers are in love with the brand.

That last point is unbelievable, don't you think? Nearly everyone uses the platform, everyone is full of praise but … hardly anyone loves the brand. For classic marketing profiles, this is an incredible paradox. But, in the 'new world', this is the 'new normal'. People are not in love with a brand, but with the interface of the brand. You could probably make the same analysis for Uber.

The *Harvard Business Review* of April 2015 carried a brilliant article: *Why strong customer relations trump powerful brands*.[4] Christophe Binder and Dominique Hanssens conducted an impressive survey in order to identify the key value drivers for a company. They took the acquisition value of a hundred companies and, over a period of ten years, looked for the key building blocks of that value. Their study showed that, ten years ago, a 'brand' was the key value driver. Today, having a strong brand is still important, but only half as much as 10 years ago. No, the rising star in value creation is 'customer value'. They define this as 'the value of existing repeat customers that are known in person'. This driver has, in the past ten years, doubled in importance.

In order to be ready for the 'Day After Tomorrow', it will be interesting to see how budgets of companies keep up with these trends. Investing less in classic marketing and investing more in user interfaces is a key first step to acquiring the customer in the 'Day After Tomorrow'.

2. Platform Strategy

We find ourselves in 'winner takes all' markets. Amazon is the retail winner. Uber is the mobility winner. Facebook the communication winner. The second player is finding it tougher: Lyft is struggling and Twitter's engine is sputtering. We find ourselves in a world of super-apps like Facebook, Amazon and WeChat (China).

In every industry, platforms appear that accelerate the market dynamics and that increase the power of the leading players. These days, you have no choice but to join the platform economy.

There are two strategic options. The first option is to build a platform yourself. Philips is currently working on a healthcare platform. Consumers will be able to connect all their health-related devices to this platform. BMW, for its part, is building a platform for greater mobility. They want to make a fleet of BMWs available in big cities and to launch Uber-type ride-sharing services. Today, a BMW gets sold once for EUR 30,000. In the 'Day After Tomorrow', a BMW will be sold 1,000 times at 30 euros a time. BMW is evolving, therefore, from a car-maker to a mobility platform. There's also a possibility that several players in an industry build a platform together. Imagine the big banks cooperating to build a platform in order to contract loans, supported by blockchain technology. That would help the industry move forward. The strategic choice to make one's own platform, is very powerful. In reality, however, it's a very tough option. In view of 'the winner takes all' movement and the emergence of super-apps, bringing that choice to a successful conclusion is no picnic.

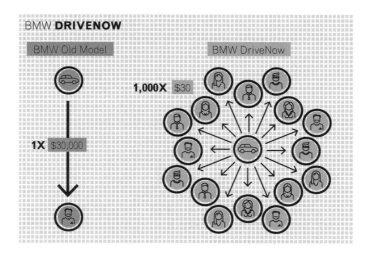

The second strategic option is to join an existing platform. For example, Walmart elected to use Uber's logistics network for e-commerce deliveries. Amazon, for its part, has developed a gigantic, in-house logistics system. For Walmart, it would take too long and cost too much to build something similar on its own. So, making use of existing platforms is a smart choice. For the vast majority of organizations, option two will be the only option.

3. Scalable Communication

If you're at an airport and you have a query about your flight, waiting an hour is just too long. Customer service in the 'Day After Tomorrow' is a real-time world. Thanks to AI-driven bots, it also becomes affordable.

The classic KPIs of a contact center are based, among other things, on call avoidance and handling per client. The cost per contact is high. Thanks to Artificial Intelligence, a large proportion of customer questions can be answered automatically. Bots are small, AI-driven programs that deal with customer service questions via Facebook Messenger, on a website, in an app, in WhatsApp, … As a customer, it's fantastic, because your question is answered straightaway. These days, the bots are a kind of optimization of a search key.

This summer I needed a new raincoat. During my search, I came across 'The North Face' website. A friendly bot helped me find what I needed. The conversation went like this:

Steven: I would like to buy a jacket.
Bot: OK, great. What would you like to do, when wearing the jacket?
Steven: Go hiking in Yosemite.
Bot: Cool, Yosemite. Which season are you going?
Steven: Summer.
Bot: Got it, what is the main function of this jacket, in your eyes?
Steven: It has to protect me from heavy rainfall.
Bot: OK, great. Are there any other specific aspects about the jacket that are important?
Steven: Yes, I'd like a blue one please.
Bot: Blue it is. That's my favorite color too. There you go!

As you can see, that was a fantastic conversation between the bot and me. We even have the same taste it seems. It was very user-friendly. It was in real time: both the conversation and the update of the product(s) on offer after each question. After each answer from me, the bot filtered out the right jackets for me. Great stuff. Compare this to buying a jacket from Zalando. There you'd get 'page 1 of the 48' as your 'unpersonalized' result.

The optimization of the search process is, in itself, a great feeling for the consumer. Over the next few years, bots will evolve, in record time, into a daily interlocutor for every consumer.

4. Invisible Technology

Look at the new technologies coming our way: the Internet of Things, Artificial Intelligence, data analysis, robots that work behind the scenes, ... All these technologies have one thing in common: they are invisible to the customer. If these technologies function well, then they ensure automation, hyper-personalization and faster than real-time customer service. In the 'Day After Tomorrow' we shall see an increasing use of invisible technology to give the customer a magical experience.

Perhaps the best example of invisible technology is the payment system at Uber. Upon arriving at your destination, you thank the driver. You alight. You close the door. Once the door has closed, you have in fact already paid. You don't know how you paid, but it feels neat and efficient. In chapter 3, Peter spoke about blockchain and smart contracts. Those, too, are fine examples of invisible technology that provide a new service for the customer.

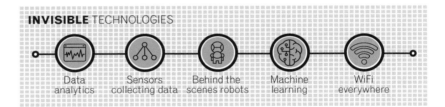

Conclusion: the Dawn of a 'New Age' for the Customer

A New Age is about to start for the customer. New interfaces will further simplify and automate our daily lives. As always happens, we will soon get used to these new tools and expectations will rise, once again, as regards customer service.

At the beginning of this book, Peter outlines the 'Day After Tomorrow' model. This model is an ideal leitmotif to hold a discussion, within your company, about the customer relationship in the 'Day After Tomorrow'. What level of resources is needed to serve today's customer? What is realistic 'tomorrow' and what would be absolutely wonderful in the 'Day After Tomorrow'? How can we work backwards from that perfect customer relationship, towards 'implementation'? How much capital can we raise and what business talent do we need to get this started? How can we organize our customer divisions like a network to make good speed, but with the right expertise? Important, fascinating and difficult questions, without exception. All of them essential in order to win the customer's heart and business in the 'Day After Tomorrow'. In a few months, the sequel to Peter's book will be available, 'Customers in The Day After Tomorrow', written by myself. This chapter gave you a taste of what to expect. To be continued.

ENDNOTES

CHAPTER 1
Introduction: Why I Wrote this Book

1. Alcatel would later merge with Bell Labs to become Alcatel-Lucent and, much later still, merged into the re-christened Nokia.

CHAPTER 2
Surviving Speed by Being Radical

1. Actually, there are quite a few concepts in life that we all acknowledge and appreciate, but that we haven't really gotten around to creating a word for. My favorite writer, Douglas Adams, picked up on this idea in a book he wrote in 1983 called The Meaning of Liff. The book is basically a 'dictionary of things that there aren't any words for yet', and the word I've frequently encountered while writing this book was: Farnham (n.): The feeling you get at about four o'clock in the afternoon when you haven't got enough done.
2. https://www.weforum.org/about/klaus-schwab and Gideon Rose, The Fourth Industrial Revolution, A Davos Reader, 2016
3. Robert Gordon, The Rise and Fall of American Growth: The U.S. Standard of Living Since the Civil War, Princeton University Press, 2016
4. https://singularityhub.com/2015/01/26/ray-kurzweils-mind-boggling-predictions-for-the-next-25-years/
5. Steven Kotler and Peter Diamandis, Abundance: The Future is Better Than You Think, 2014
6. Steven Kotler and Peter Diamandis, Bold: How to Go Big, Create Wealth and Impact the World, 2016
7. http://wadhwa.com/2015/01/21/book-review-peter-diamandiss-bold-a-reminder-of-how-entrepreneurs-will-control-the-worlds-fate/
8. Peter Hinssen, The New Normal: Explore the Limits of the Digital World, MachMedia, 2010
9. Joseph Schumpeter, Capitalism, Socialism and Democracy, 1942
10. Peter Diamandis, http://singularityhub.com/2016/06/27/why-the-world-is-better-than-you-think-in-10-powerful-charts/
11. Tim Urban, http://waitbutwhy.com/2015/01/artificial-intelligence-revolution-1.html
12. Ray Kurzweil, http://www.kurzweilai.net/the-law-of-accelerating-returns
13. Charles C. Kenney, Riding the Runaway Horse: The Rise and Decline of Wang Laboratories, Little, Brown, 1992
14. I just had to share this hilarious fact: in the 1970s a new policy was introduced of announcing the office name after the city of location, e.g. 'Wang London', 'Wang Paris'. But the German HQ was in Cologne, so that was quickly changed to 'Wang Germany'.
15. http://uk.businessinsider.com/chambers-40-of-companies-are-dying-2015-6
16. http://www.huffingtonpost.com/peter-diamandis/why-tech-is-accelerating_b_8951550.html
17. http://www.iftf.org/leadersmakethefuture/
18. Portio Research and Andreessen-Horowitz, The message is the medium, The Economist, March 26th 2015
19. Elisabeth Kübler-Ross, *On Death and Dying*, 1969
20. https://www.reddit.com/r/business/comments/4xya36/nokias_ceo_we_didnt_do_anything_wrong_but_somehow/
21. Chris Bradley and Clayton O'Toole, *An Incumbent's Guide to Digital Disruption*, McKinsey Quarterly May 2016
22. A short-sighted and inward looking approach to marketing that focuses on the needs of the company instead of defining the company and its products in terms of the customers' needs and wants. It results in the failure to see and adjust to the rapid changes in their markets: http://www.businessdictionary.com/definition/marketing-myopia.html

258

23. http://www.businessinsider.com/reed-hastings-netflix-qwikster-2011-9
24. https://www.chargify.com/blog/6-companies-that-succeeded-by-changing-their-business-model/
25. https://www.forbes.com/2010/07/07/ibm-transformation-lessons-leadership-managing-change.html
26. John Battelle, The Search: How Google and Its Rivals Rewrote the Rules of Business and Transformed Our Culture, 2006
27. https://www.gsb.stanford.edu/insights/mark-leslie-key-enduring-growth-strategic-transformation
28. https://www.linkedin.com/pulse/arc-life-mark-leslie

CHAPTER 3
The Engine of Our Future

1. https://en.wikipedia.org/wiki/Internet_of_things
2. https://en.wikipedia.org/wiki/Hydrodynamica
3. https://en.wikipedia.org/wiki/History_of_artificial_intelligence
4. Humans and other animals process information with neural networks. These are formed from trillions of neurons (nerve cells) exchanging brief electrical pulses called action potentials. Computer algorithms that mimic these biological structures are formally called artificial neural networks to distinguish them from the squishy things inside of animals. However, most scientists and engineers are not this formal and use the term neural network to include both biological and nonbiological systems. From: The Scientist and Engineer's Guide to Digital Signal Processing, by Steven W. Smith, Ph.D. (http://www.dspguide.com/ch26/2.htm)
5. https://www.theregister.co.uk/2017/03/21/ai_bots_can_invent_their_own_language/
6. https://www.bloomberg.com/news/articles/2017-02-28/jpmorgan-marshals-an-army-of-developers-to-automate-high-finance
7. http://news.stanford.edu/thedish/2017/03/14/andrew-ng-why-ai-is-the-new-electricity/
8. Peter Lucas, Joe Ballay, Mickey McManus, Trillions: Thriving in the Emerging Information Ecology, John Wiley & Sons, 2012
9. https://www.linkedin.com/pulse/nature-things-mickey-mcmanus
10. https://www.linkedin.com/pulse/blockchains-disruptive-short-mid-term-arno-laeven
11. William Mougayar and Vitalik Buterin, The Business Blockchain: Promise, Practice, and Application of the Next Internet Technology, 2016
12. http://www.economist.com/news/leaders/21677198-technology-behind-bitcoin-could-transform-how-economy-works-trust-machine
13. http://www.businessinsider.com/zuckerberg-why-facebook-bought-oculus-2014-3
14. In response to the ending of Moore's law, some have started to build computer chips in 3D, by stacking components and transistors on top of each other to boost the power of the chips, but the heat-problem there is even bigger, because of the increased surface area.
15. When the metal niobium is cooled down, it becomes what is known as a superconductor, and it starts to exhibit quantum mechanical effects. This in contrast to conventional transistors which are mostly made from silicon. Source: https://www.dwavesys.com/tutorials/background-reading-series/introduction-d-wave-quantum-hardware
16. http://whatis.techtarget.com/definition/quantum-computing

CHAPTER 4
Networks, Platforms & Bits

1. Andry Grove, Only the Paranoid Survive, 1996. It's one of my favorite management books of all time.
2. https://en.wikiquote.org/wiki/Ed_Colligan
3. https://www.cbinsights.com/blog/big-compay-ceos-execs-disruption-quotes/
4. http://uk.businessinsider.com/steve-ballmer-just-praised-apple-2016-11
5. https://hbr.org/2016/04/pipelines-platforms-and-the-new-rules-of-strategy
6. https://www.brainyquote.com/quotes/quotes/s/steveballm368841.html
7. If you're ever in the neighborhood, I really advise you to go to the 'Computer History Museum' in Mountain View. It's an amazing place if you want to understand the history of computing, and the raison d'être of Silicon Valley. You will see amazingly unique pieces that are almost impossible to see anywhere else, like the Alto – the breakthrough graphical PC developed by the Xerox guys in PARC. You will see the most brilliant collection of computers from virtually all of the Silicon Valley pioneering companies, but alas, almost nothing that comes from Apple itself. Apple Computer does not want to dwell on its history, it believes in looking forward instead of looking backwards.
8. http://www.computerhistory.org/collections/catalog/102712693

9. Jobs had created a 'pirate' team and moved them across the street of Apple's HQ to work on the Mac, because he thought that the team working on the Lisa computer would just end up with a slow and boring product. Unfortunately, both the Lisa *and* the Mac failed to sell and Jobs was fired from his own company as a result.

10. https://www.fastcompany.com/3042431/meme/the-biggest-business-comebacks-of-the-past-20-years

11. https://www.wsj.com/articles/SB10001424053111903480904576512250915629460 and http://a16z.com/2016/08/20/why-software-is-eating-the-world/

12. Grok is a term that was coined by science-fiction writer R.A. Heinlein, meaning 'to understand something thoroughly by having empathy with it'. In an interview he gave in 1996, Steve Jobs said: "Some people think design means how it looks. But, of course, if you dig deeper, it's really how it works. To design something really well, you have to 'get it.' You have to really grok what it's all about." https://www.wired.com/1996/02/jobs-2/

13. Back in 2005, Linus Torvalds, the creator and founder of Linux, created a piece of software called Git as a better way to keep improving on Linux. Git made it very easy for large groups of people to work on the same Linux code at the same time.
GitHub was then created as a website where any other software project could operate much like the Linux project, with the same philosophy, borrowed from the Git concept. Nowadays, pretty much everyone hosts their open source projects on GitHub. WiReD magazine called GitHub "a kind of bazaar that offers just about any piece of code you might want – and so much of it for free." https://www.wired.com/2015/03/github-conquered-google-microsoft-everyone-else/

14. http://tech.economictimes.indiatimes.com/news/internet/alibaba-founder-jack-mas-advice-for-the-future/57013902

15. http://a16z.com/2016/08/20/why-software-is-eating-the-world/ ; About Platforms eating the world: https://www.forbes.com/sites/gregsatell/2016/09/02/platforms-are-eating-the-world-3/#5f49d2074064

16. Geoffrey G. Parker, Marshall W. Van Alstyne, Sangeet Paul Choudary, *Platform Revolution: How Networked Markets Are Transforming the Economy – And How to Make Them Work for You*, 2016

17. https://hbr.org/2016/04/pipelines-platforms-and-the-new-rules-of-strategy

18. http://www.thedrum.com/opinion/2016/08/01/how-china-became-world-s-e-commerce-king

19. http://www.newsweek.com/2016/06/17/silicon-valley-takeover-468182.html

20. http://www.adweek.com/digital/google-now-controls-12-percent-all-global-media-spend-171701

21. Activate: Tech & Media Outlook 2017: https://www.slideshare.net/ActivateInc/think-again-tech-media-outlook-2017-67604099

22. The Luddites were a group of English textile workers and weavers in the 19th century who destroyed weaving machinery as a form of protest. Since then the term has come to mean one opposed to industrialisation, automation, computerisation or new technologies in general. https://en.wikipedia.org/wiki/Luddite

23. https://en.wikipedia.org/wiki/Frontier_Thesis

24. https://www.theguardian.com/culture/2016/aug/21/san-francisco-exhibition-victoria-albert-revolution-silicon-valley

25. https://www.ft.com/content/00585722-ef42-11e6-930f-061b01e23655

26. Clayton M. Christensen, *The Innovator's Dilemma*, 1997

27. https://hbr.org/2015/12/what-is-disruptive-innovation

28. http://www.insideredbox.com/blockbuster-ceo-redbox-netflix-not-on-radar-screen-as-competition/

29. https://techcrunch.com/2016/02/27/why-clayton-christensen-is-wrong-about-uber-and-disruptive-innovation/

30. http://www.web-strategist.com/blog/2013/11/

CHAPTER 5
It's a Culture Thing

1. https://medium.com/@bchesky/dont-fuck-up-the-culture-597cde9ee9d4

2. Frederick Winslow Taylor, *The Principles of Scientific Management*, 1923

3. https://en.wikipedia.org/wiki/Theory_X_and_Theory_Y

4. http://foreignpolicy.com/2011/02/21/it-takes-a-network/

5. http://uk.businessinsider.com/zappos-employee-sets-record-for-longest-customer-service-call-2016-7

6. Tony Hsieh, *Delivering Happiness. A Path to Profits, Passion and Purpose*, 2011

7. Grassroots movements and organizations utilize collective action from the local level to effect change at the local, regional, national, or international level. Grassroots movements are associated with bottom-up, rather than top-down decision making, and are sometimes considered more natural or spontaneous than more traditional power structures. Source: https://en.wikipedia.org/wiki/Grassroots.
8. http://community.cengage.com/GECResource2/info/b/management/
9. Frederic Laloux, *Reinventing Organizations. A Guide to Creating Organizations Inspired by the Next Stage of Human Consciousness*, 2014
10. http://www.holacracy.org/backstory?hilite=sociocracy and https://en.wikipedia.org/wiki/Holacracy
11. https://hbr.org/ideacast/2016/07/the-zappos-holacracy-experiment.html
12. https://en.wikipedia.org/wiki/The_Nature_of_the_Firm
13. BSO stood for 'Bureau voor Systeem-Ontwikkeling', or Agency for System Development. https://www.wired.com/1996/11/es-wintzen/
14. https://www.wired.com/1996/11/es-wintzen/
15. Dee Hock, One from Many: Visa and the Rise of Chaordic Organization, Berrett-Koehler Publishers, 2005
16. Ori Brafman and Rod A. Beckstrom, The Starfish and the Spider: The Unstoppable Power of Leaderless Organizations, 2008
17. Victor W. Hwang and Greg Horowitt, The Rainforest: The Secret to Building the Next Silicon Valley, Regenwald Publishing, 2012
18. Eric Ries, The Lean Startup. How Relentless Change Creates Radically Successful Businesses, 2011
19. http://stevejobsdailyquote.com/steve-jobs-quotes-about-life/page/3/
20. https://en.wikipedia.org/wiki/Triple_point
21. https://www.torbenrick.eu/blog/change-management/20-awesome-quotes-on-change-management/

CHAPTER 6
Ingredients, but No Sure-Fire Recipe

1. http://www.businessinsider.com/how-samsung-became-the-biggest-electronics-company-in-the-world-2013-3
2. https://032c.com/2014/samsung-uber-alles-artist-simon-denny-exhibits-the-electronic-companys-climb-to-global-dominance/
3. http://www.samsung.com/us/aboutsamsung/investor_relations/financial_information/annual_reports.html
4. https://blogs.scientificamerican.com/but-not-simpler/excerpts-from-the-mad-scientiste28099s-handbook-the-human-recipe/
5. https://www.forbes.com/sites/petercohan/2012/02/27/how-big-companies-can-exploit-and-explore/#6a0206206b3d ;
https://hbr.org/2004/04/the-ambidextrous-organization
6. http://www.mtu-report.com/Agriculture/Agriculture-is-high-tech
7. As a reminder: they claim that starfish represent decentralized organizations while spiders are like hierarchical command and control structures.
8. http://www.huffingtonpost.com/judith-e-glaser/self-expression-the-neuro_b_9221518.html
9. http://uk.businessinsider.com/ceo-larry-page-considers-google-a-teenager-2014-10
10. http://www.haier.net/en/about_haier/
11. Turns out that both Samsung's Lee Kun Hee and Haier's Zhang Ruimin had the same dramatic flair for delivering messages that stuck (and a predilection for sledgehammers).
12. http://www.haier.net/en/about_haier/ceo/introduction/
13. https://en.wikipedia.org/wiki/Catfish_effect
14. https://www.forbes.com/sites/peterhinssen/2017/03/02/innovating-on-the-edge-of-chaos-getting-to-haier-ground

CHAPTER 7
A Tale of Two Futures

1. Charles Dickens, *A Tale of Two Cities*, 1859
2. Daron Acemoglu and James Robinson, *Why Nations Fail: The Origins of Power, Prosperity, and Poverty*, 2012
3. https://www.theguardian.com/commentisfree/2016/dec/01/stephen-hawking-dangerous-time-planet-inequality
4. https://medium.com/@Richard_Florida/the-most-disruptive-transformation-in-history-80a50ef89b4d

5. https://www.wired.com/2016/10/president-obama-mit-joi-ito-interview/
6. http://www.seiu.org/about
7. Andy Stern, *Raising the Floor: How a Universal Basic Income Can Renew Our Economy and Rebuild the American Dream*, 2016
8. https://www.vox.com/conversations/2016/10/17/13245808/andy-stern-work-universal-basic-income-technology-artificial-intelligence-unions
9. https://www.technologyreview.com/s/519241/report-suggests-nearly-half-of-us-jobs-are-vulnerable-to-computerization/
10. http://www.marketwatch.com/story/bill-gates-says-robots-should-pay-taxes-if-they-take-your-job-2017-02-17
11. http://www.oxfordmartin.ox.ac.uk/publications/view/1849
12. Douglas Rushkoff, *Throwing Rocks at the Google Bus: How Growth Became the Enemy of Prosperity*, 2016.
    The book's title comes from an incident when incensed protesters against the gentrification of Silicon Valley and San Francisco had shattered the windows of a bus carrying Google employees to work.
13. https://qz.com/848031/harvard-research-suggests-that-an-entire-global-generation-has-lost-faith-in-democracy/
14. https://en.wikipedia.org/wiki/Paul_Mason_(journalist)
15. http://www.generation-online.org/p/fpvirno10.htm
16. https://en.wikipedia.org/wiki/Nineteen_Eighty-Four
17. https://en.wikipedia.org/wiki/Suspension_of_disbelief
18. https://paulromer.net/wp-content/uploads/2016/09/WP-Trouble.pdf
19. https://en.wikipedia.org/wiki/Red_Queen%27s_race
20. http://anoptimiststourofthefuture.com/?page_id=2
21. https://en.wikipedia.org/wiki/Learned_helplessness
22. https://www.weforum.org/agenda/2016/01/the-fourth-industrial-revolution-what-it-means-and-how-to-respond/
23. https://www.newscientist.com/article/mg22329850-600-end-of-nations-is-there-an-alternative-to-countries/
24. http://www.belfercenter.org/publication/it-takes-network-defeat-network
25. The Little Red Dot is the 'nickname' of Singapore.
26. https://www.smartnation.sg/
27. http://www.thefamouspeople.com/profiles/john-maynard-keynes-191.php
28. http://www.ippr.org/juncture/keynes-and-our-grandchildren-recapturing-an-alternative-vision-of-economic-progress
29. http://www.goodreads.com/quotes/17985-it-s-a-recession-when-your-neighbor-loses-his-job-it-s
30. http://www.newyorker.com/magazine/2014/05/26/no-time
31. https://www.theatlantic.com/business/archive/2016/01/inequality-work-hours/422775/
32. http://www.economist.com/news/briefing/21594264-previous-technological-innovation-has-always-delivered-more-long-run-employment-not-less
33. From the introductory video to the Apple Event keynote address of September 2014. https://en.wikiquote.org/wiki/Apple_Inc.

CHAPTER 8
Conclusion

1. https://en.wikiquote.org/wiki/Apple_Inc.
2. https://en.wikipedia.org/wiki/Andre_Geim
3. https://en.wikipedia.org/wiki/Ig_Nobel_Prize
4. https://en.wikipedia.org/wiki/Fountain_of_Youth
5. https://en.wikipedia.org/wiki/Mark_Zuckerberg
6. http://www.economist.com/news/special-report/21688591-millennials-are-brainiest-best-educated-generation-ever-yet-their-
   elders-often
7. https://www.inc.com/jim-schleckser/nelson-mandela-s-secret-to-winning.html
8. https://hbr.org/2015/11/why-organizations-dont-learn
9. https://en.wikipedia.org/wiki/Franklin_D._Roosevelt
10. https://www.triz.co.uk/what
11. https://www.fransjohansson.com/books-by-frans-johansson/
12. https://www.fastcompany.com/27333/trillion-dollar-vision-dee-hock

NINE RULES FOR THRIVING IN THE 'DAY AFTER TOMORROW'

1.   Quote by Jack Canfield. http://www.goodreads.com/quotes/495741-everything-you-want-is-on-the-other-side-of-fear

ADDENDUM
Customers in the 'Day After Tomorrow'
By Steven Van Belleghem

1.   Robert Spector and Patrick D. McCarthy, *The Nordstrom Way: The Inside Story of America's #1 Customer Service Company*, 1996
2.   Fred Reichheld, *The Ultimate Question: Driving Good Profits and True Growth*, 2006
3.   Tony Hsieh, *Delivering Happiness. A Path to Profits, Passion and Purpose*, 2011
4.   https://hbr.org/2015/04/why-strong-customer-relationships-trump-powerful-brands

PHOTO CREDITS

ABOUT PETER HINSSEN

Peter Hinssen is a serial entrepreneur, adviser and keynote speaker on the topics of radical innovation, leadership and the impact of all things digital on society and business.

ACCLAIMED AUTHOR

Peter is the author of three bestselling business books. *The Network Always Wins* (2014) explains how and why companies have no choice but to become a network when the outside world has evolved into one. In *The New Normal* (2010), he writes about how companies should explore the limits of the digital world, and what happens when technology just becomes 'normal'. *Business/IT Fusion* (2008) is a guide about how to solve the conflict between business and IT. Peter is frequently asked to contribute to (international) publications and is a Forbes contributor as well as a LinkedIn Influencer.

SOUGHT-AFTER KEYNOTE SPEAKER, BUSINESS SCHOOL LECTURER & BOARD MEMBER

Peter has given numerous keynote speeches around the world, among which those for Google Think Performance, Nimbus Ninety, Gartner, NEXT Berlin, Tedx, PayPal, MasterCard, Microsoft, CIO City, SAS, Accenture and Apple. He lectures at renowned business schools like the London Business School, the MIT Sloan School of Management and the Paul Merage School of Business at UC Irvine. He is also a multiple board advisor on subjects related to innovation and technology.

SERIAL ENTREPRENEUR

For more than fifteen years, Peter led a life of technology start-ups. His first company e-COM was acquired by Alcatel-Lucent, his second, Streamcase, by Belgacom, and Across Technology by Delaware Consulting. His third venture (Porthus) was quoted on the stock exchange in 2006 and acquired by Descartes. Between start-ups, he has been an Entrepreneur in Residence with McKinsey & Company, with a focus on digital and technology strategy. Peter's current company nexxworks helps organizations become fluid, innovate and thrive in The 'Day After Tomorrow'.

OTHER BOOKS BY PETER HINSSEN

THE NETWORK ALWAYS WINS (2014)

This powerful guide from serial entrepreneur and radical innovation though-leader Peter Hinssen shows you how to keep your company up to speed with your market, engage with customers at a time when loyalty keeps fading into the background, and transform your organization into a network in order to thrive in this era of digital disruption.

THE NEW NORMAL (2010)

In The New Normal, Peter Hinssen looks at the way companies have to adapt their information strategy, their technology strategy, their innovation strategy and the way they are organized internally. This book is an interesting read for any manager who is concerned with the future of his company as it is hit by the digital revolution.

BUSINESS/IT FUSION (2008)

It is time for a major transformation of IT. It is time for a quantum leap. For years, the way we have run IT, as a CIO, was to command an army of order-taking specialist workers, an underground army hidden away in the basement of our companies. These reactive armies of craftsmen are a thing of the past. In a Fusion concept, we need a new breed of professionals, with a new blend of capabilities. The challenge becomes how to crack the culture code in IT transformation.

LIFE PICTURE PUZZLE

WELCOME TO LIFE'S SIXTEENTH
PICTURE PUZZLE BOOK

Well, to paraphrase Ronald Reagan, here we go again.

We got into the Picture Puzzle game—actually, we invented it—way back in 2006. Others have leapt in, certainly, but we hope you would agree that nobody does it like LIFE. We've had No. 1 best-sellers in the puzzle category and we've received lots of letters from our fans (including a few complaining we were being too tough—sorry!). So here we go again with our 16th—can you believe it?—puzzle book. We're becoming downright venerable.

"Vacations," "Holidays," yada, yada—the themes were driving us mad. So that was it! Let's make the next book Picture Puzzle Madness. Let's let it all hang out. The most fun, the most colorful, the most wacky, the most *mad* pictures we can find, and then our Puzzle Master will work his magic and our loyal game-players will have a ball. A big, bouncy ball.

As ever, the book progresses from simple to not-so-simple to really hard to borderline impossible. Below and on the opposite page, any newcomers among you can see how to play the puzzles, and on the pages soon after these you can dive in. As always, in a special section that only LIFE can offer (accept no imitations!), we goof with some classic photographs from our storied archive. Nobody but nobody gets to toy with LIFE photography! Except us . . . and you.

So here we go again. Come along, for a fine bit of madness.

[OUR CUT-UP PUZZLES: EASY AS 1-2-3]

We snipped a photo into four or six pieces. Then we rearranged the pieces and numbered them.

Your mission: Beneath each cut-up puzzle, write the number of the piece in the box where it belongs.

Check the answer key at the back of the book to see what the reassembled image looks like.

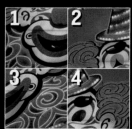

[HOW TO PLAY THE PUZZLES]

Cuppa Coffee?

Elephants also enjoy a well-brewed blend

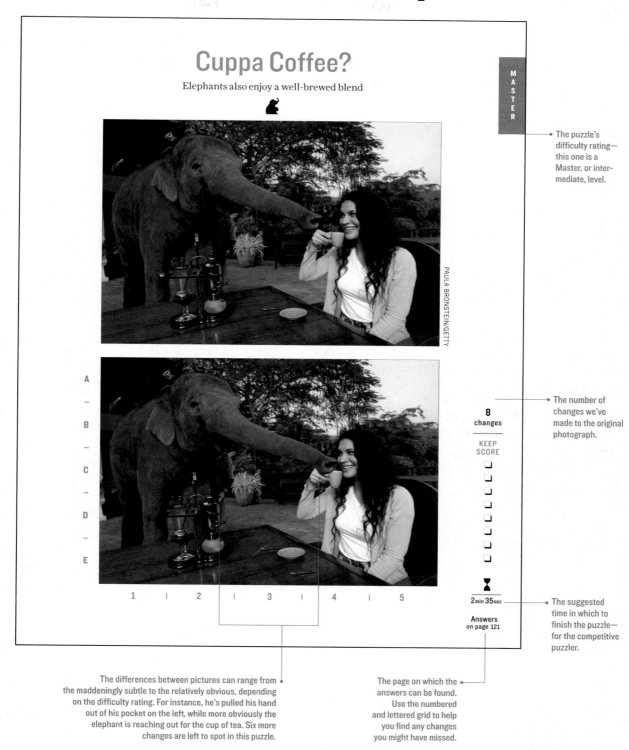

PAULA BRONSTEIN/GETTY

MASTER

The puzzle's difficulty rating—this one is a Master, or intermediate, level.

8 changes

KEEP SCORE

2min 35sec

Answers on page 121

The number of changes we've made to the original photograph.

The suggested time in which to finish the puzzle—for the competitive puzzler.

The differences between pictures can range from the maddeningly subtle to the relatively obvious, depending on the difficulty rating. For instance, he's pulled his hand out of his pocket on the left, while more obviously the elephant is reaching out for the cup of tea. Six more changes are left to spot in this puzzle.

The page on which the answers can be found. Use the numbered and lettered grid to help you find any changes you might have missed.

LIFE PICTURE PUZZLE

Puzzle Master Michael Roseman
Associate Puzzle Master Steve Walkowiak
Editor Robert Sullivan
Director of Photography Barbara Baker Burrows
Deputy Picture Editor Christina Lieberman
Writer/Reporter Marilyn Fu
Copy Editors Don Armstrong, Barbara Gogan, Parlan McGaw

Editorial Operations

Richard K. Prue (Director), Brian Fellows (Manager), Keith Aurelio, Charlotte Coco,
Tracey Eure, Kevin Hart, Mert Kerimoglu, Rosalie Khan, Patricia Koh, Marco Lau,
Brian Mai, Po Fung Ng, Rudi Papiri, Robert Pizaro, Barry Pribula, Clara Renauro,
Katy Saunders, Hia Tan, Vaune Trachtman

Time Home Entertainment

Publisher Jim Childs
Vice President, Business Development & Strategy Steven Sandonato
Executive Director, Marketing Services Carol Pittard
Executive Director, Retail & Special Sales Tom Mifsud
Executive Publishing Director Joy Butts
Director, Bookazine Development & Marketing Laura Adam
Finance Director Glenn Buonocore
Associate Publishing Director Megan Pearlman
Assistant General Counsel Helen Wan
Assistant Director, Special Sales Ilene Schreider
Book Production Manager Suzanne Janso
Design & Prepress Manager Anne-Michelle Gallero
Brand Manager Roshni Patel
Associate Prepress Manager Alex Voznesenskiy
Assistant Brand Manager Stephanie Braga

Editorial Director Stephen Koepp
Editorial Operations Director Michael Q. Bullerdick

Special thanks to Katherine Barnet, Jeremy Biloon, Susan Chodakiewicz, Rose Cirrincione,
Lauren Hall Clark, Jacqueline Fitzgerald, Christine Font, Jenna Goldberg, Hillary Hirsch,
David Kahn, Amy Mangus, Robert Marasco, Kimberly Marshall, Amy Migliaccio, Nina Mistry,
Dave Rozzelle, Ricardo Santiago, Adriana Tierno, Vanessa Wu

PUBLISHED BY

LIFE Books

an imprint of Time Home Entertainment Inc.

Copyright © 2013
Time Home Entertainment Inc.
135 West 50th Street
New York, NY 10020

ISBN 10: 1-60320-961-1
ISBN 13: 978-1-60320-961-8

We welcome your comments and suggestions about LIFE Books. Please write to us at:
LIFE Books
Attention: Book Editors
PO Box 11016
Des Moines, IA 50336-1016

If you would like to order any of our hardcover Collector's Edition books, please call us at 1-800-
327-6388 (Monday through Friday, 7 a.m. to 8 p.m., or Saturday, 7 a.m. to 6 p.m. Central Time).

COVER PHOTO: LONELY PLANET IMAGES/GET

READY, SET, GO!

NOVICE

[
These puzzles are for everyone:
rookies and veterans,
young and old. Start here, and
sharpen your skills.
]

Cranky Kitty

Be careful. This is one fed-up cat.

NEILSON BARNARD/GETTY

A
—
B
—
C
—
D
—
E

1   2   3   4   5

7
changes

KEEP
SCORE

❏
❏
❏
❏
❏
❏
❏

⧗

2min 10sec

Answers
on page 121

High-Wire Act

He may not have a chariot, but she's still swinging low

9
changes

KEEP
SCORE

❏
❏
❏
❏
❏
❏
❏
❏
❏

⧗

2min 45sec

Answers
on page 121

No Mere Munchkin

But don't take a bite. It's a bit stale.

7
changes

⧗

2min 20sec

Answers
on page 121

KEEP SCORE ★ ❑ ❑ ❑ ❑ ❑ ❑ ❑

Spin Cycle

Let's hope he didn't have a big lunch

A
—
B
—
C
—
D
—
E

1   2   3   4   5

9
changes

2min 45sec

Answers
on page 121

KEEP SCORE ★ ❏ ❏ ❏ ❏ ❏ ❏ ❏ ❏ ❏

Walk This Way

They're playing follow-the-leader

A
B
C
D
E

1   2   3   4   5

10
changes

3min 35sec

KEEP SCORE ★ ❏ ❏ ❏ ❏ ❏ ❏ ❏ ❏ ❏ ❏

Answers
on page 121

An Electric Personality

He gets turned on with the flip of a switch

A
—
B
—
C
—
D
—
E

1   2   3   4   5

9
changes

⧗
2min 45sec

Answers
on page 121

KEEP SCORE ★ ❏ ❏ ❏ ❏ ❏ ❏ ❏ ❏ ❏

Come Fly with Me

However, you'll have to get your own jet pack

KEVORK DJANSEZIAN/GETTY

A

B

C

D

E

1　　2　　3　　4　　5

10
changes

KEEP
SCORE

❏
❏
❏
❏
❏
❏
❏
❏
❏
❏

⏳
2min 35sec

Answers
on page 121

One Big Step for a Man

And one step's different from the others

1

2

3

4

5

6

0min 55sec

Answer
on page 121

AFP/GETTY

Shake, Rattle, and Roll

If you know which photo is different, just scream

1

2

3

4

5

JOHANNES SIMON/GETTY

6

0min 45sec

Answer
on page 121

The House Began to Pitch

Don't blame the Wicked Witch for this tourist attraction

A
—
B
—
C
—
D
—
E

1   2   3   4   5

11
changes

⏳
3min 55sec

Answers
on page 121

KEEP SCORE ★ ❏ ❏ ❏ ❏ ❏ ❏ ❏ ❏ ❏ ❏ ❏

A Real Cowboy

But he better hang on tight

JOHANNES SIMON/GETTY

7
changes

KEEP
SCORE

❏
❏
❏
❏
❏
❏
❏

⌛

2min 35sec

Answers
on page 122

A
—
B
—
C
—
D
—
E

1 | 2 | 3 | 4 | 5

Hailing a Cab

Just whistle and say, "Here, Fido!"

ROBERT NICKELSBERG/GETTY

A
—
B
—
C
—
D
—
E

1   2   3   4   5

9
changes

KEEP
SCORE

☐
☐
☐
☐
☐
☐
☐
☐
☐

⌛
4min 5sec

Answers
on page 122

Please Feed the Animals

Wanna snack, Mr. Giraffe?

TPG/GETTY

A
—
B
—
C
—
D
—
E

1 | 2 | 3 | 4 | 5

9
changes

⌛
3min 50sec

Answers
on page 122

KEEP SCORE ★ ❏ ❏ ❏ ❏ ❏ ❏ ❏ ❏ ❏

Bargain Bazaar

Prices are always in flux

10
changes

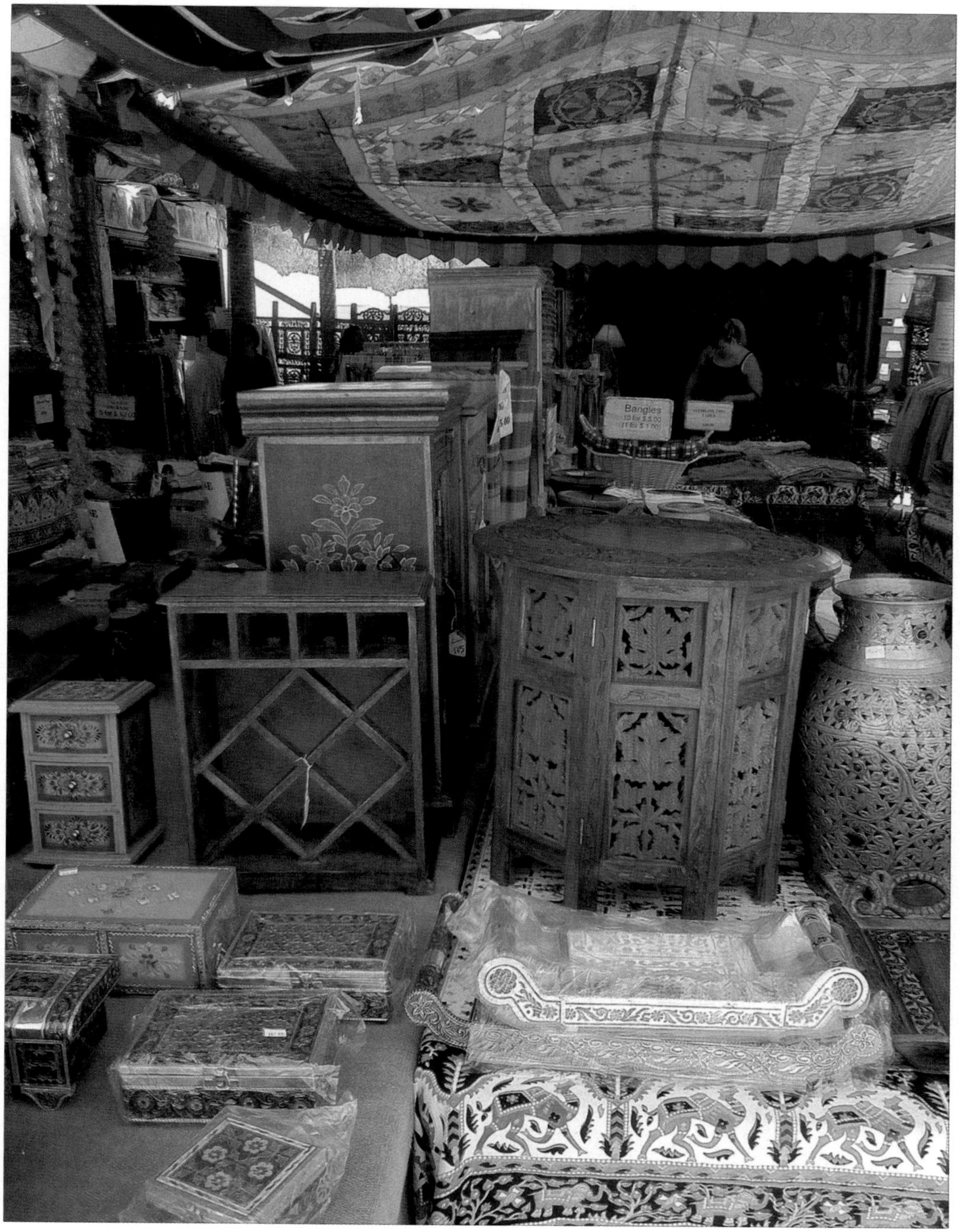

KEEP
SCORE

❏
❏
❏
❏
❏
❏
❏
❏
❏
❏

⏳

3min 10sec

Answers
on page 122

Rainy Day Games

These guys won't let the weather
dampen their enthusiasm

A
—
B
—
C
—
D
—
E

1 | 2 | 3 | 4 | 5

9
changes

⧗

3min 35sec

Answers
on page 122

KEEP SCORE ★ ❑ ❑ ❑ ❑ ❑ ❑ ❑ ❑ ❑

Speak of the Devil!

Do manta rays celebrate Halloween?

JOHANNES EISELE/AFP/GETTY

A

B

C

D

E

1   2   3   4   5

8
changes

KEEP
SCORE

❏
❏
❏
❏
❏
❏
❏
❏

⧗

2min 45sec

Answers
on page 122

Two Pretty Misses

Hi ho, hi ho, it's off to school we go

A
B
C
D
E

1   2   3   4   5

9
changes

⏳
3min 15sec

Answers
on page 122

KEEP SCORE ★ ❏ ❏ ❏ ❏ ❏ ❏ ❏ ❏ ❏

Let the Games Begin

Let's bring some order to this situation

BEN STANSALL/AFP/GETTY

0min 30sec

Answer
on page 122

KEEP SCORE

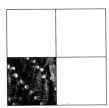

A Purr-fect Christmas

Rearrange this picture to let the sleeping cat lie

JOE BOMBA

KEEP SCORE

⧖

0min 25sec

Answer
on page 122

Striking a Pose

Venice is quite a *dandy* city

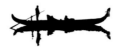

A

B

C

D

E

1   2   3   4   5

10
changes

KEEP
SCORE

3min 25sec

Answers
on page 122

Twilight Zone

She's masking her fear

CARLOS TISCHLER/LATINCONTENT/GETTY

5

4

3

2

1

A — | — B — | — C — | — D — | — E

11
changes

KEEP
SCORE

☐ ☐ ☐ ☐ ☐ ☐ ☐ ☐ ☐ ☐ ☐

⏳
4min 15sec

Answers
on page 122

MASTER

[Here, puzzles get
a little harder. You'll
need to raise
your game a level.]

Headwind

His umbrella may have flipped out,
but at least he still has his hat

SHELLY PERRY/GETTY

A
—
B
—
C
—
D
—
E

1   2   3   4   5

9
changes

KEEP
SCORE

4min 15sec

Answer
on page 122

Horsing Around

Someone needs a lesson on how to ride

A

—

B

—

C

—

D

—

E

1   2   3   4   5

9
changes

3min 35sec

KEEP SCORE ★ ❏ ❏ ❏ ❏ ❏ ❏ ❏ ❏ ❏

Answers
on page 123

Lots to Juggle

They really look like clowns out there

10
changes

KEEP
SCORE

2min 55sec

Answers
on page 123

Send for Mary Poppins

She'd know what to do about flyaway bumbershoots

A
B
C
D
E

1 2 3 4 5

8
changes

⏳
3min 55sec

KEEP SCORE ★ ❏ ❏ ❏ ❏ ❏ ❏ ❏ ❏

Answers
on page 123

No Monkey Business

Who's the genius behind this experiment?

A
—
B
—
C
—
D
—
E

1 | 2 | 3 | 4 | 5

11
changes

⧗
3min 35sec

Answers
on page 123

KEEP SCORE ★ ❏ ❏ ❏ ❏ ❏ ❏ ❏ ❏ ❏ ❏ ❏

A Day at the Races

But remember, kids: There's no gambling at this track

A
—
B
—
C
—
D
—
E

1 | 2 | 3 | 4 | 5

10
changes

⏳
3min 45sec

KEEP SCORE ★ ❏ ❏ ❏ ❏ ❏ ❏ ❏ ❏ ❏ ❏

Answers
on page 123

Fishing for Dummies

It's no big deal if he doesn't catch anything,
as long as he can just chill out

NICK DOLDING/GETTY

A
—
B
—
C
—
D
—
E

1   2   3   4   5

11
changes

⌛
3min 55sec

KEEP SCORE ★ ❏ ❏ ❏ ❏ ❏ ❏ ❏ ❏ ❏ ❏ ❏

Answers
on page 123

Street Art?

One man's Picasso is another man's Velvet Elvis

EMILY PRESCOTT

14
changes

KEEP
SCORE

❏
❏
❏
❏
❏
❏
❏
❏
❏
❏
❏
❏
❏
❏

⌛

4min 15sec

Answers
on page 123

Door-to-Door Service

He always rolls up the same way. Almost always.

1

2

3

4

5

6

1min 5sec

Answer
on page 123

OLI SCARFF/AFP/GETTY

Feel the Spirit

¡Que vivan los Negros y que vivan los Blancos!

1

2

3

4

5

6

LUIS ROBAYO/AFP/GETTY

0min 30sec

Answer
on page 123

Dwarfed by History

These two don't seem to go in for art appreciation

A

B

C

D

E

1   2   3   4   5

9
changes

⏳
3min 20sec

KEEP SCORE ★ ❏ ❏ ❏ ❏ ❏ ❏ ❏ ❏ ❏

Answers
on page 123

Changing Stations

It's just about time for the doors to open and the fun to begin

A
–
B
–
C
–
D
–
E

1 | 2 | 3 | 4 | 5

9
changes

⏳
4min 15sec

Answers
on page 124

KEEP SCORE ★ ❏ ❏ ❏ ❏ ❏ ❏ ❏ ❏ ❏

Smile for the Camera

Then concentrate again on the parachute

A

—

B

—

C

—

D

—

E

1 | 2 | 3 | 4 | 5

9
changes

KEEP
SCORE

☐ ☐
☐ ☐
☐ ☐
☐ ☐
☐ ☐
☐ ☐
☐ ☐
☐ ☐
☐

⌛
3min 25sec

Answers
on page 124

Let There Be Lights

If you're as bright as these pictures, you'll find the one that's different

1

2

3

4

5

6

1min 5sec

Answer
on page 124

MATT CARDY/GETTY

Shuttle Diplomacy

NASA's making changes

1

2

3

4

5

MICHAEL NAGLE/GETTY

6

1min 15sec

Answer
on page 124

A Visit to Oz

They're getting the condensed Aussie experience

BRENDON THORNE/BLOOMBERG/GETTY

11
changes

KEEP
SCORE

⏳
4min 50sec

Answers
on page 124

Linemen

Do you have enough power to put
the grid back on line?

1min 25sec

**Answer
on page 124**

KEEP SCORE

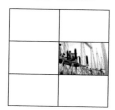

Floral Frenzy

Pretty as a picture if order can be restored

KEEP SCORE

1min 30sec

Answer
on page 124

Step Right Up!

It's time to play the game

A
—
B
—
C
—
D
—
E

1   2   3   4   5

11
changes

4min 5sec

Answers
on page 124

KEEP SCORE ★ ❏ ❏ ❏ ❏ ❏ ❏ ❏ ❏ ❏ ❏ ❏

Her Kind of Town

She's all in pieces over having to leave

SCOTT OLSON/GETTY

12
changes

KEEP
SCORE

❏
❏
❏
❏
❏
❏
❏
❏
❏
❏
❏
❏

⌛
5min 15sec

Answers
on page 124

EXPERT

[

Only serious puzzlers
dare to tread past this point.
Who's in?

]

Table Manners

Please help set the place settings by rearranging the feast

TANG CHHIN SOTHY/AFP/GETTY

KEEP SCORE

⏳
4min 15sec

Answer
on page 124

Striking Poses

One of these harlequins is an impostor. Which?

1

2

3

4

5

6

FRANÇOIS LE DIASCORN/GAMMA-RAPHO/GETTY

2min 25sec

Answer
on page 124

Big Drummer Boys

They always stand on ceremony

1

2

3

4

5

6

JOE KLAMAR/AFP/GETTY

1min 55sec

Answer
on page 124

The House That Fish Built

It may not be a palace, but it's home. Or a tourist trap.

SARAH CATES

A

B

C

D

E

1   2   3   4   5

14
changes

KEEP
SCORE

❑
❑
❑
❑
❑
❑
❑
❑
❑
❑
❑
❑
❑
❑

⧖

4min 35sec

Answers
on page 125

My Precious

What has it got in its puzzleses, eh?

HAGEN HOPKINS/GETTY

5 | 4 | 3 | 2 | 1

A | B | C | D | E

12
changes

KEEP
SCORE

☐ ☐ ☐ ☐ ☐ ☐ ☐ ☐ ☐ ☐ ☐ ☐

⌛
5 min 5 sec

Answers
on page 125

PICTURE PUZZLE **LIFE** | 83

Crossing Guard with Attitude

But he's polite to a fault

PAUL WHITE/AP

5

4

3

2

1

A

B

C

D

E

14
changes

KEEP
SCORE

⊔ ⊔ ⊔ ⊔ ⊔ ⊔ ⊔ ⊔ ⊔ ⊔ ⊔ ⊔ ⊔ ⊔

⏳

5min 15sec

Answers
on page 125

Handy Man

I touch, therefore I know

5

4

3

2

1

A

B

C

D

E

14
changes

KEEP
SCORE

❏
❏
❏
❏
❏
❏
❏
❏
❏
❏
❏
❏
❏
❏

4min 20sec

Answers
on page 125

Hidden Treasures

Each one of these dolls has layers upon layers inside

1

2

3

4

5

6

MISHA JAPARIDZE/AP

⧖
2min 45sec

Answer
on page 125

Clear Sailing

And a good time was had by all

1

2

3

4

5

ROBERT GOTHARD

6

2min 55sec

Answer
on page 125

All Bottled Up

Even at this size, how do they get it in?

DAN KITWOOD/GETTY

11
changes

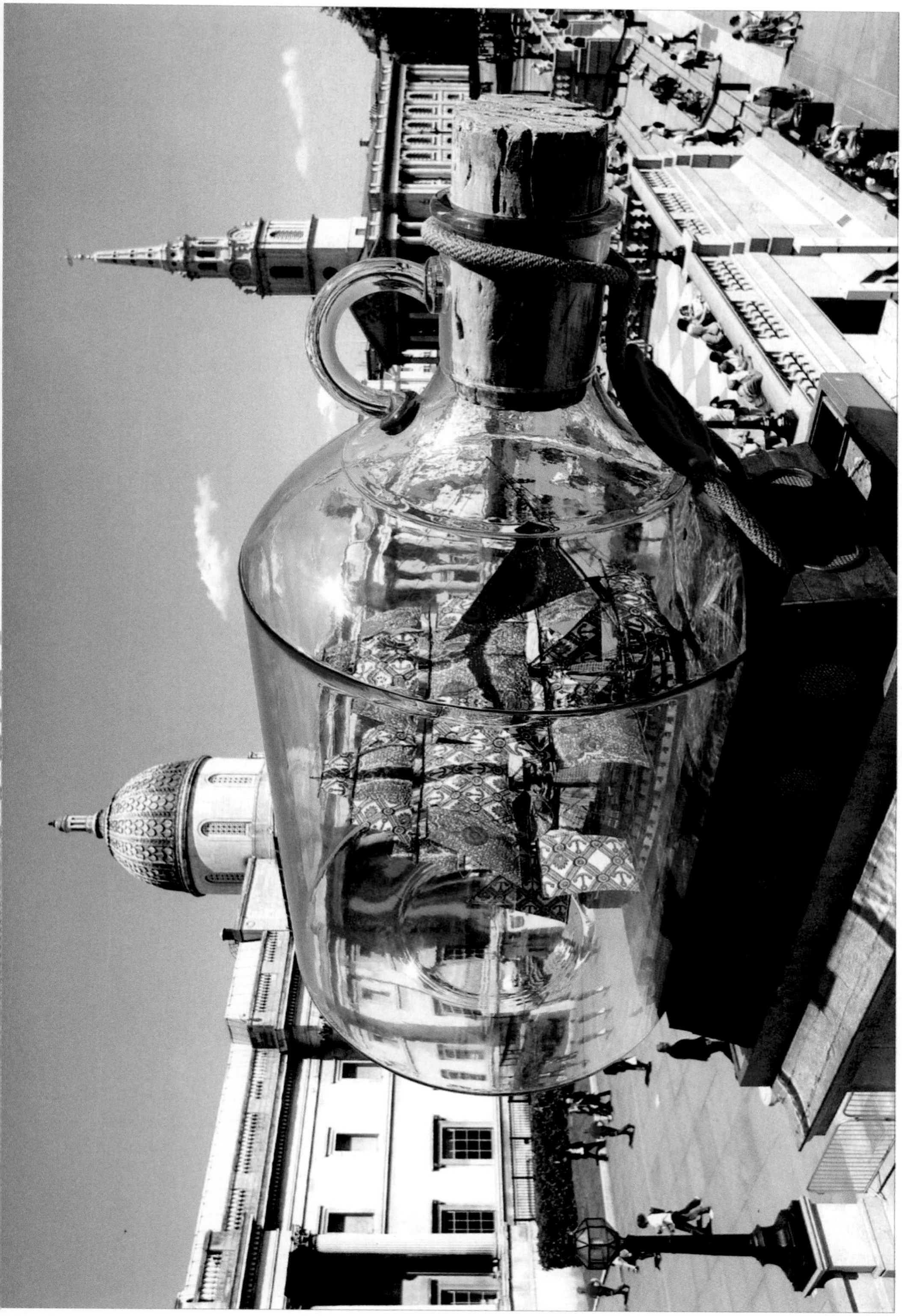

KEEP
SCORE

6min 20sec

Answers
on page 125

A

B

C

D

E

1   2   3   4   5

GENIUS

[
Finding a single difference
in these puzzles is a
challenge. Finding them all
might be impossible.
]

England's Space Program

Kate's entourage accompanies her wherever she goes

16
changes

KEEP
SCORE

5min 35sec

Answers
on page 125

A

B

C

D

E

1   2   3   4   5

A Strange Casting Call

Anyone for a nice game of checkers?

MIKE BROWN/THE COMMERCIAL APPEAL/AP

16
changes

KEEP
SCORE

⏳
6min 15sec

Answers
on page 125

Portable Amuse-a-Cat Station

This gives us paws

Answers
on page 126

19
changes

⌛

5min 55sec

KEEP SCORE ★ ❑ ❑ ❑ ❑ ❑ ❑ ❑ ❑ ❑ ❑ ❑ ❑ ❑ ❑ ❑ ❑ ❑ ❑ ❑

Under a Royal Rain

Some of the queen's youngest subjects have
waited patiently for this photo op

A
–
B
–
C
–
D
–
E

1   2   3   4   5

16 changes

⏳

5min 25sec

Answers
on page 126

KEEP SCORE ★ ☐ ☐ ☐ ☐ ☐ ☐ ☐ ☐ ☐ ☐ ☐ ☐ ☐ ☐ ☐ ☐

Tranquillity Square

Folks in New York's midtown celebrate
the summer solstice with a mass chill out

MICHEL SETBOUN/CORBIS

A

–

B

–

C

–

D

–

E

1 | 2 | 3 | 4 | 5

17
changes

⧗

5min 55sec

Answers
on page 126

KEEP SCORE ★ ❏ ❏ ❏ ❏ ❏ ❏ ❏ ❏ ❏ ❏ ❏ ❏ ❏ ❏ ❏ ❏ ❏

Pile Up

Canoe find all the changes?

A — | — B — | — C — | — D — | — E

1 — | — 2 — | — 3 — | — 4 — | — 5

15
changes

KEEP
SCORE

⌨ ⌨ ⌨ ⌨ ⌨ ⌨ ⌨ ⌨ ⌨ ⌨ ⌨ ⌨ ⌨ ⌨ ⌨

⌛

4min 55sec

Answers
on page 126

All in Good Fun

These guys are a barrel of laughs—yuck, yuck, yuck

A
–
B
–
C
–
D
–
E

1   2   3   4   5

18
changes

5min 45sec

Answers
on page 126

KEEP SCORE ★ ❑ ❑ ❑ ❑ ❑ ❑ ❑ ❑ ❑ ❑ ❑ ❑ ❑ ❑ ❑ ❑ ❑ ❑ ❑

Going Postal

Delivery around here is for the birds

20
changes

KEEP
SCORE

6min 15sec

Answers
on page 126

LIFE
CLASSICS

[
These puzzles were
specially created with
memorable photos
from the LIFE archives.
]

Driver's Ed

Where they learn the finer points of competition

LARRY BURROWS

11
changes

KEEP
SCORE

❏
❏
❏
❏
❏
❏
❏
❏
❏
❏
❏

⧗

2min 50sec

Answers
on page 126

A

—

B

—

C

—

D

—

E

1 | 2 | 3 | 4 | 5

Story Time

At least most of the children are paying attention

A

–

B

–

C

–

D

–

E

1   2   3   4   5

10
changes

KEEP
SCORE

2min 15sec

Answers
on page 126

Snip, Snip, Snip

Do you remember how a straight-edge
felt on the back of your neck?

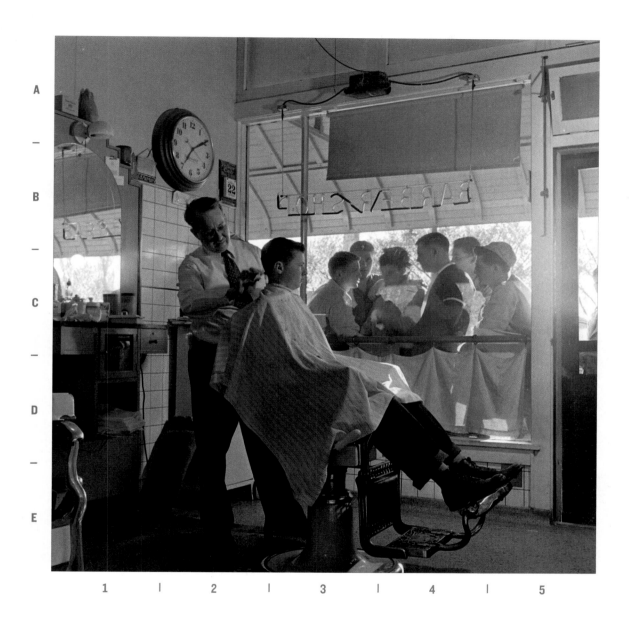

A
—
B
—
C
—
D
—
E

1 | 2 | 3 | 4 | 5

11
changes

4min 15sec

Answers
on page 127

KEEP SCORE ★ ❏ ❏ ❏ ❏ ❏ ❏ ❏ ❏ ❏ ❏ ❏

Ceremonial Sport

From little sumo wrestlers,
big sumo wrestlers grow

A
—
B
—
C
—
D
—
E

1 | 2 | 3 | 4 | 5

12
changes

4min 5sec

Answers
on page 127

KEEP SCORE ★ ❏ ❏ ❏ ❏ ❏ ❏ ❏ ❏ ❏ ❏ ❏ ❏

Fashion on Wheels

Just when was this the height of style?

NINA LEEN

A
–
B
–
C
–
D
–
E

1   2   3   4   5

9
changes

⏳
3min 50sec

Answers
on page 127

KEEP SCORE ★ ❏ ❏ ❏ ❏ ❏ ❏ ❏ ❏ ❏

Round and Round We Go

Where we stop nobody knows

CARL MYDANS

11
changes

KEEP
SCORE

❏ ❏ ❏ ❏ ❏ ❏ ❏ ❏ ❏ ❏ ❏

⏳ 4min 25sec

Answers
on page 127

[ANSWERS]

Finished already? Let's see how you did.

[INTRODUCTION]

Page 3: Cuppa Coffee? No. 1 (B1 to B2): By the size of her ear, this elephant is known as Flapper. No. 2 (C2 to D2): We always knew he was a pretty handy fellow. Nos. 3 and 4 (C4): Her cup holds more brew now, which is a good thing, considering she's going to have to share with Flapper. No. 5 (D1): The coffee pot's alteration is going to make it difficult to hobnob with fellow customers. No. 6 (D3): We're partial to unstable furniture. You'll probably see a lot more throughout the book. No. 7 (E3): It's a saucer of a different color, sort of. No. 8 (E3 to E4): Just in case she needs an extra spoon, we know where to find one.

[NOVICE]

Page 7: Cranky Kitty No. 1 (A2): Someone gave Mr. Banana a big tip. No. 2 (B2): This strawberry looks good enough to eat. No. 3 (B3): Interesting. A cat with an extensible ear. No. 4 (C2): He's keeping both his eyes on you. No. 5 (C3): It's easier to breathe with a bigger nose. No. 6 (C4): A dot is not. No. 7 (D4): This splotch is spreading out.

Page 8: High-Wire Act No. 1 (A1): Who changes the highest bulbs when they burn out? No. 2 (A5): Someone's on the job, because there's a new one in the firmament. No. 3 (B3): His hog reflects more lights. No. 4 (B4 to B5): At least one of these lights runs on a motorized track. No. 5 (C2): Red light, green light. No. 6 (C2 to C3): Don't look down, but the wire appears to have snapped. No. 7 (C4): The cycle has an extra bolt now. No. 8 (D3 to E4): She's using retractable poles. No. 9 (E2): And her leg has extensions.

Page 10: No Mere Munchkin No. 1 (B3): The shuttle's tail fin is stretching upward. No. 2 (C2): The big *D* is solid, man. No. 3 (C4): Glasses off, glasses on. No. 4 (D1): Security is really lax around here. Someone stole the parking area light. No. 5 (D4): This logo is just sliding along. No. 6 (E1): Adding insult to injury, a wheel's been jacked. No. 7 (E2): The ATM is now under new management.

Page 12: Spin Cycle No. 1 (A1): The forest has overgrown a field. No. 2 (C4): Let's take a moment to reflect on the missing *D*. No. 3 (C5): While they've been flying around, someone's been planting trees along the road. No. 4 (D1 to E1): Now this is a star of a different color. No. 5 (D3 to D4): They're spinning around so fast, even the type is turning green. No. 6 (E1): Landing is going to be a challenge with a missing strut. No. 7 (E3): He's dropped the *O* from his name. No. 8 (E4): The mike has a broken clip. No. 9 (E5): With a wing like this, he'd better say a prayer.

Page 14: Walk This Way No. 1 (A1): Who's got Vulcan ears? He's got Vulcan ears. No. 2 (A5): This character has been pumped up. No. 3 (B2): Smiles are much nicer than frowns, aren't they? No. 4 (B3): Apparently, a rising tide doesn't lift all dots. No. 5 (C1): Vulcans don't need watches; they always know the time. No. 6 (C1 to C2): His top has dropped. No. 7 (C5 to D5): Prolonged exposure to the cold has turned this sled blue. No. 8 (D3): His schnoz is shrinking. No. 9 (E1): Don't know what it means, but this is probably a typo. No. 10 (E3 to E4): His wing is wingier.

Page 16: An Electric Personality No. 1 (B3 to C3): He's had his pupil expanded. Nos. 2, 3, and 4 (C3 to D3): Not only has the nose turned purple and grown, it's also lost its shine. No. 5 (D1): It must cost a lot to keep him in lightbulbs. No. 6 (D2): We liked his ear before the plastic surgery. No. 7 (D3 to E3): A movable tongue on a neon clown is a little disturbing. No. 8 (D4): If you find a missing dimple, please return it to the Clown Signage Company. No. 9 (E5): Things are just a little brighter in this corner.

Page 18: Come Fly with Me No. 1 (A1): Either the warm sun or extra fertilizer has prompted a growth spurt. No. 2 (A2 to A3): This palm is twisting slowly in the wind. No. 3 (C1 to D1): The trunk has been relocated. No. 4 (C3): The nozzle has received an upgrade. No. 5 (D2): There's one more porthole for peeking out. Nos. 6 and 7 (D3): Did the missing strap make her leg retract in alarm? Nos. 8 and 9 (D4): As her leg has gained a few inches, a light has gone on in response. No. 10 (E1 to E2): This wave is swell.

Page 20: One Big Step for a Man A building in photo No. 6 is trying hard to scrape the sky.

Page 21: Shake, Rattle, and Roll The coaster in photo No. 3 seems a little less stable than the others.

Page 22: The House Began to Pitch No. 1 (B1 to C1): The drainpipe has drained away. No. 2 (B3): The window shade is down today. No. 3 (B4): Let the light in with Acme's supersize windows. No. 4 (C3 to D3): Is it our imagination or is this fellow a bit taller now? No. 5 (D1): This umbrella looks like it has a front awning. Nos. 6 and 7 (D3 to E4): Green umbrellas just look larger than orange ones. No. 8 (D5): The lighting has been reduced as part of an austerity measure. No. 9 (E1): A stone slab has been hauled away. No. 10 (E2): All this waiting in line has caused some foot spreading. No. 11 (E3): A lack of feet is going to cause this gent to topple.

Page 24: A Real Cowboy No. 1 (A4): Now that's a quick dye job. No. 2 (A4 to B5): This wild and crazy guy has changed his part. No. 3 (B4): The stripes are multiplying. No. 4 (C2): She's hard of hearing in one ear. No. 5 (C2 to D2): This shoe laces farther up, or is it farther down? No. 6 (C4): Does anyone have a spare muzzle strap? No. 7 (E3): She's putting her foot down.

Page 25: Hailing a Cab Nos. 1 and 2 (A3): Deflate the puff and tug out the brim and it's almost a new hat. No. 3 (B5): It's stretchy yellow tape. No. 4 (C2 to C3): Doggie wants red collar back. Now, please. No. 5 (C3): Isn't there an *l* in *taxi*? No. 6 (C4): Quick, is there a tailor in the audience? No. 7 (D3): Brake lights don't do much good in front. No. 8 (D3 to E3): Don't worry, the left leg is just behind the right one. No. 9 (D4): There's been a space-time hubcap inversion, whatever that means.

Page 26: Please Feed the Animals No. 1 (A3 to B3): These new hybrid trees grow really fast, even after being cut. No. 2 (B2): Big ear here. No. 3 (B2 to B3): Chew and swallow, then repeat. No. 4 (B5): The roof goes up and up. No. 5 (C3 to D3): The stem is a stem no more. No. 6 (C5 to D5): It's a jacket switcheroo. No. 7 (E1): Part of the pipe got swiped. Nos. 8 and 9 (E5): Take a step backward and give that dad a hand with his heavy bag.

Page 28: Bargain Bazaar No. 1 (A2 to B2): And the curtain comes down. No. 2 (A4 to A5): The design kind of grows on you. No. 3 (A4 to B4): One flap of the fringe has turned red. No. 4 (B3): This cabinet has surprising depth. No. 5 (B4): One light is better than none. Nos. 6 and 7 (C2): As the flower design has waxed, the wooden lattice has waned. No. 8 (C4): Does no price tag mean it's free? No. 9 (D1): You can pick up a replacement knob at any Bed Bath & Beyond. No. 10 (E3): It's a sad blue camel, isn't it?

Page 30: Rainy Day Games No. 1 (A3): Mr. Elastic has quite a long arm. No. 2 (A5 to B5): It's a self-inflating sphere. No. 3 (B1 to C1): We just can't resist. A sail sailed into view. No. 4 (B3): This one was trimmed. No. 5 (B4 to C4): He's no longer well-armed. No. 6 (C1): The *U* has utterly sagged. No. 7 (C2): The blue spheres are beginning to take over around here. No. 8 (E2): The red pad has spread out. No. 9 (E5): These two sections of padding are united.

Page 32: Speak of the Devil! No. 1 (A1): The manta must have been meant to lose its tail. No. 2 (B2): Is its fin extended in friendship? No. 3 (C4): Even tail fins show signs of shrinkage in cold water. No. 4 (C4 to D4): Who likes blue food? No. 5 (D2): The gourd is carved no more. No. 6 (D2 to E3): Watch out for the dread chameleon hose. No. 7 (E2): It's a high thigh bone. No. 8 (E3): And a solid pelvic girdle.

Page 34: Two Pretty Misses No. 1 (A4): Two bricks have vowed togetherness. No. 2 (B1 to B2): Beware the Red Cap. No. 3 (B1 to C1): Could this dwarf have just told a lie? No. 4 (B2): He really wants to pick his nose. No. 5 (B5): Her dainty finger is down. No. 6 (C5 to D5): Fortunately, a blue cap isn't a sign of danger, just a fashion mistake. No. 7 (D4): My, you have a bushy eyebrow. No. 8 (D5): He's noticed the girl. No. 9 (E1 to E2): Her outfit now offers better UV protection.

Page 36: Let the Games Begin

2	3
4	1

Page 37: A Purr-fect Christmas

3	1
2	4

Page 38: Striking a Pose No. 1 (B2): It's a grander doorway now. No. 2 (B3): But, alas, a shorter tree trunk. No. 3 (C2): The tall back of the gondola is made of sterner stuff. Get it, sterner stuff? Hey, at least we're not picking your pocket. No. 4 (C4): How much will the pawnbroker give us for this ring? Nos. 5 and 6 (C5): The boat speeds into view as the log floats away. No. 7 (D1 to D2): The swell boat rides the waves easily. No. 8 (D3 to E3): The piling has moved closer to shore. No. 9 (E4): Funny, earlier the heel didn't look bluish. No. 10 (E5): Rubber ducky, we love you.

Page 40: Twilight Zone No. 1 (B1): This mask sees nothing. Nos. 2 and 3 (B2): Sure, three eyes are better than two, while another mask has been hung out to dry. No. 4 (B4): Someone must have said, "Pipe down." No. 5 (C2): Amazing, a mask has been sold. No. 6 (C3): Someone (or something) has its blue eye on you. No. 7 (D4): The socket has been reamed out. Nos. 8 and 9 (E2): As a rag turns red, the table has one less leg to stand on. Nos. 10 and 11 (E3): Both the legging and the sock have claimed more territory.

[MASTER]

Page 43: Headwind No. 1 (A1 to B1): The shades are up. No. 2 (A3): A chimney is down. No. 3 (B1): The umbrella needs a good tip. Nos. 4 and 5 (B2): The window slides away in horror from the brim-deficient hat. No. 6 (B3):

The Window Protection Program has a new client. No. 7 (C4 to C5): Tall doors in the morning, umbrellas beware. No. 8 (D3 to D4): Get me a (longer) shrubbery. No. 9 (E2): If he doesn't walk faster, the grass will overgrow him.

Page 44: **Horsing Around** No. 1 (A2): The rope has failed. No. 2 (A3): He's got a bad case of swelled helmet. No. 3 (C2): Please take the time to reflect on this change. No. 4 (C5): Time to call in an electrician. No. 5 (D2 to D3): His shoe size is *H* for humongous. No. 6 (D3): The marble trim has been solidified. No. 7 (E2): The storefront has dropped an *O*. Nos. 8 and 9 (E4): The horse's tail has been cropped and, even though we don't speak the lingo, that's got to be a spelling error.

Page 46: **Lots to Juggle** No. 1 (B1): His nose is almost ready to pop. No. 2 (B2): This club has a new sure-grip handle. Nos. 3 and 4 (B3): As a club recedes into the background, the bow tie puffs up. No. 5 (B4): What makes a *HOW* great? No. 6 (B5): He's donned the nose of his profession. No. 7 (B5 to C5): The logo is taking a spin. No. 8 (C1): That's not *N* in any language we know. No. 9 (C3 to D3): He's wearing these amazing mood pants. Now you'll know exactly what he's feeling. No. 10 (C4): The handle has been absorbed into his arm. Ouch! No. 11 (D5): Having learned from all the previous Picture Puzzle button mishaps, he's got a spare one sewn on.

Page 48: **Send for Mary Poppins** No. 1 (A4 to A5): One more may just move this exhibit into a plethora of umbrellas. No. 2 (B1): There's gold in them thar reflection(s). No. 3 (B5): Green grows the umbrella. Pardon us, but how many more feeble umbrella jokes are we going to have to come up with? No. 4 (C4): One of these topiaries has high hopes. No. 5 (D2): Two ceiling lights have winked out. No. 6 (D4): But another light has been installed over here. Nos. 7 and 8 (E3): The pink umbrella is now known as Big Pink, and a gentleman has split the scene.

Page 50: **No Monkey Business** No. 1 (A2): The ball appears to have delusions of grandeur. So do the life forms. No. 2 (B1 to C2): With one fewer support this apparatus seems a bit unstable. Unstable, yeah, that's the word. Nos. 3 and 4 (C2): An extra node or nodule or nubbin, whatever you want to call it, has been extruded on the colander. And, by the way, the goggles are going strapless. Nos. 5 and 6 (D4): That's a really big thumb, and, wait for it—a missing button. No. 7 (D4 to E4): In an eco-move, the binding post has gone green. No. 8 (E1): While they were running this stupid experiment, the table quietly lengthened itself. Nos. 9 and 10 (E3): He's sporting a chimp nail and the big label is much more impressive now. Not. No. 11 (E5): The chimp's name is Frodo. Think about it.

Page 52: **A Day at the Races** No. 1 (A5 to B5): He don't need no stinking badges. No. 2 (B2): The sleeve hangs lower now. No. 3 (B3): The scarf (yeah, that tiny thing's a scarf) is following suit. No. 4 (B3 to C3): The mirror-image *9* is standing on its head. Nos. 5 and 6 (B4 to C4): *5* swapped places with *7, 7* has a new paint job. No. 7 (C3): Goodbye, Kitty. No. 8 (D2 to E2): Must be one of those new hover chairs. No. 9 (D4): This feline likes green flowers in her fur. No. 10 (E3): The seat has quite a long flap.

Page 54: **Fishing for Dummies** Nos. 1 and 2 (B4): It's a rubberized monitor, and the counter has more trim. No. 3 (B5): With all this light, no one really misses the sconce. No. 4 (C2): Without its numbers, the box feels lost. No. 5 (C4): There's a break in the fishing line, but that may not matter much. No. 6 (C5): We wouldn't drink pink water. Would you? Nos. 7 and 8 (D1): The arrows are avoiding each other, while the pot has more root space. No. 9 (D2 to E2): Two boxes have joined forces. No. 10 (D4): Please bring us the binder with the green spine. No. 11 (E3 to E5): It's a green mat now. What more can we say?

Page 56: **Street Art?** No. 1 (A4): The *BLOOM* went *BOOM*. No. 2 (A5): Based on the new sign language, the wall may be pretending to be a pub. No. 3 (B1): With its new headstock, this is now a seven-string Fender. No. 4 (B4): Wide brims are the new missing buttons. No. 5 (C1): The yellow spot has broken up with the snowboard. No. 6 (C1 to D1): Cherry-red Fenders are classics. No. 7 (C2): What good is lipstick on a fish? Nos. 8 and 9 (D1): Every good Fender deserves a whammy bar, but why is a can of paint sliding around? No. 10 (D2): A shy marker is hiding on the ground. No. 11 (D4 to D5): The painting occupies more real estate. No. 12 (E2): The strap has been separated from its bag. No. 13 (E3 to E4): The dummy is doing leg extensions. No. 14 (E5): TNT is on the rise.

Page 58: **Door-to-Door Service** The Horse Guard on the far left in photo No. 2 has let down his coat.

Page 59: **Feel the Spirit** The devil in photo No. 1 is sporting the biggest horn.

Page 60: **Dwarfed by History** No. 1 (A3): Horation Gates is looking quite lively in this painting. No. 2 (B1): The braid on the frame is rising. No. 3 (D1 to D2): He's looking like a flashback to the '60s. No. 4 (D3): Somehow this repro of the painting doesn't quite match the original. No. 5 (D4): Bigger phones used to be more important. No. 6 (D5): The backrest has an extra dimple. No. 7 (D5 to E5): The

ANSWERS

power outlet is crawling up the wall. No. 8 (E1): The bench has a leggy leg. No. 9 (E4): Power cords come in many colors, even bright purple.

Page 62: **Changing Stations** No. 1 (A5): The trees are doing their job and growing taller every season. No. 2 (B5): The number may have fallen off, but everyone knows whose bath-house this is. No. 3 (C1): The pole has been cut down to size. Nos. 4 and 5 (C2 to D2): One set of doors has gained in height, while the other has been freshened up with a new coat of paint. No. 6 (C3 to D4): Some new panel work has been done. No. 7 (C5): Just like Peter Pan, the lock has lost its shadow. No. 8 (D4 to D5): The bag holds more goodies now. No. 9 (E5): The platform has room to spare.

Page 64: **Smile for the Camera** No. 1 (A5): Where does he find shoes that fit? No. 2 (B2 to C3): He has the confidence to go with pink. No. 3 (C4): First you twist your left foot back and forth. No. 4 (C4 to C5): The red zone has doubled in size. No. 5 (D2 to E2): He seems to be falling faster than the others. Nos. 6 and 7 (D3): Is this what they mean by footloose? Nah, it's more like foot-gone. Meanwhile, this other guy has pulled in his arm. Is he waving goodbye to the foot? No. 8 (D4 to E5): Send in the clone. No. 9 (D5): The helmet design is suddenly edgier.

Page 66: **Let There Be Lights**
Photo No. 2 has a few extra lights.

Page 67: **Shuttle Diplomacy**
One of the tugs in photo No. 6 must have a zippy engine.

Page 68: **A Visit to Oz** No. 1 (B2 to C3): The HOPPERS text is a dropper. Nos. 2 and 3 (C1): If you want to give someone a hop, the big arrow points the way. No. 4 (C2 to D2): She probably bought her new top at the gift shop. Nos. 5 and 6 (C5): The tail feathers have vanished, starting a slow descent of the arrow. No. 7 (D2): She may have dropped her bracelet during the tour. Nos. 8 and 9 (D3): Someone new has crept into the poster, but some text has been lost along the way. No. 10 (D4): Hop this way! No. 11 (E2): She's wearing sole-less shoes.

Page 70: **Linemen**

6	5
1	3
2	4

Page 71: **Floral Frenzy**

3	1
6	2
4	5

Page 72: **Step Right Up!** No. 1 (A3 to B3): The fluorescent light suddenly flickered on. No. 2 (A4): The doggie has a big, aggressive nose. No. 3 (B1): The strut has ducked behind the light. No. 4 (B2 to C2): This 3 can move around on its own. Nos. 5 and 6 (B3): If they call him Mr. White Fang, do they call the clown Mr. Big Nose? No. 7 (C2): Now he really looks sur-prised. No. 8 (C4 to C5): He's donned the royal collar. No. 9 (D4): Another button hits the dust. No. 10 (E1): He thinks he looks elegant in his long-tailed T-shirt. No. 11 (E2 to E3): The light is fading as the sun sets.

Page 74: **Her Kind of Town** No. 1 (A1): Look who's dropping in for a visit. No. 2 (B3): A win-dow has been disappeared. Nos. 3 and 4 (B4): The streetlight should have turned off at day-break, but no one knows why the sculpture started growing. No. 5 (C1): Budget cutbacks have forced the removal of some outdoor lighting. No. 6 (C2): A window shade has been pulled down. No. 7 (C4): She's changed her lipstick color. No. 8 (D2): Her twin flew into town. No. 9 (D3): She's hooked her heel behind the support. No. 10 (D5 to E5): The top of the cone has been sliced off. No. 11 (E2): Her shoe snapped a strap. No. 12 (E5): Now this caution tape we can read.

[EXPERT]

Page 77: **Table Manners**

9	4	3
5	1	8
6	7	2

Page 78: **Striking Poses**
A harlequin in photo No. 5 is starting to replace his comrades—with himself.

Page 79: **Big Drummer Boys**
The second-from-the-right drummer in photo No. 6 is carrying a longer stick.

124 LIFE PICTURE PUZZLE

Page 80: **The House That Fish Built** Nos. 1, 2, and 3 (B2): As it begins a slow ascent toward the fabled celestial heaven of window-mounted heaters, in other words a wall-crawl, the Dynavent loses its . . . vent. Meanwhile, back on planet Earth, the burden of unwelcome knowledge makes this float hang low. No. 4 (B3): This represents an overabundance of ship's wheels. No. 5 (B4): This float ain't going to for long. No. 6 (B5 to C5): They're going to need a whole lot more paint than this. No. 7 (C1): My, that's a big sword you have. Nos. 8 and 9 (C2): While the vent tries to adjust to its reduced circumstances, the swordfish wonders what pollutants lead to its trinocular vision. No. 10 (C4): Don't stand below any anchor that sways in the breeze. No. 11 (C5): The flagpole seems pointless. No. 12 (D2 to D3): The eagle feathers its tail. No. 13 (D3 to E3): He looks pretty in pink. No. 14 (D4): It's suddenly a modest anchor.

Page 82 : My Precious No. 1 (B1): Gollum's named his middle finger the Poker. No. 2 (B3): This finniest fin has finished growing. No. 3 (B4 to B5): He's got green eyes models would die for. Maybe they did. No. 4 (C1): The light is at least marginally taller than before. Good enough for us. No. 5 (C4): He's finally getting dental implants. Hooray! Nos. 6 and 7 (C5): Its baleful big eye is rolling around in its socket over our puzzle changes. No. 8 (D2): In this case half a fin isn't better than no fin at all. Don't get on that plane! No. 9 (D5): Someone has a taste for cactus. No. 10 (E4): She sure has a lot of hair. No. 11 (E2): There's one more bottle of beer around here, one more bottle of beer. No. 12 (E5): Her plane must have boarded.

Page 84: Crossing Guard with Attitude No. 1 (A3): There's a copyright on spinning copyrights. No. 2 (A4): He wields a blunt weapon. Nos. 3 and 4 (B2): The traffic light offers unusual choices and the policeman has a blue light special. No. 5 (B2 to C2): There are many copies of her. No. 6 (B3 to C3): He likes big swag. No. 7 (B5): What's wrong with this traffic light? No. 8 (C2): The mirror has been mirrored. Nos. 9 and 10 (C4): One leg is gone and the other sports a reflective strip. No. 11 (C5): The base of the pole has shifted. Nos. 12 and 13 (D3): The bumbershoot has been supersized and circumcised. No. 14 (D3 to E1): The white stripe has returned to the fold.

Page 86: Handy Man Nos. 1 and 2 (A2 to B2): He's opened both eyes and is staring off to the side. Nos. 3 and 4 (A3 to B3): One nail has grown long and is such a ghastly color. No. 5 (A4 to B5): If we all work together, we can lift this wall. No. 6 (B2): He's sporting the latest in uni-nostrils. No. 7 (C1): It's got two, that's two, volume controls. No. 8 (C1 to D1): He dons his green cap when he's getting ready to leave. No. 9 (D1): His sleeve has been neatly tucked inside the overalls. No. 10 (D1 to D2): With a big enough stick, he can stir all the paint in the world. No. 11 (D3 to E4): The arm is growing back. No. 12 (E1): The bucket has a really big label. No. 13 (E2): The garbage has been around so long, it's learned to crawl. No. 14 (E5): The crack has been repaired.

Page 88: Hidden Treasures A doll in the near left of photo No. 3 has spun out of control. At least her head has.

Page 89: Clear Sailing The boat in photo No. 2 is really buff.

Page 90: All Bottled Up No. 1 (A2 to A3): The dome must be inflatable. No. 2 (B2): A water tower has been installed for the appearance of safety. No. 3 (B5): No one really minds the missing window. No. 4 (C1): It's a wide, wide window. No. 5 (C5 to D5): The cork's about to pop. No. 6 (D1): The secret police identify each other by their red shirts. Now you can, too. No. 7 (D1 to D2): Don't give away Expando Man's secret identity. Nos. 8 and 9 (D2): This reflection comes in triplicate, while a sail panel has faded away. No. 10 (E2 to E3): Four vents can suck more air. No. 11 (E5): Odd, she doesn't cast a shadow.

[GENIUS]

Page 93: England's Space Program Nos. 1 and 2 (A5): The evidence suggests that one window rubbed out the other in order to claim the entire wall for itself. Nos. 3 and 4 (B2): His hat is a little less grand than before, but she's put quite the feather in hers. No. 5 (B5 to C5): Don't worry, we took care of it and he's no longer watching you. No. 6 (C2 to D2): He's suffering from restless medal syndrome. No. 7 (C3): The budget is so tight, they can't even afford a replacement tail fin. No. 8 (C4): Call out the Royal Guard. Kate's lost an earring. Nos. 9 and 10 (C5): A short blonde woman was seen leaving the scene with a lavender tie. No. 11 (D1 to E1): She's donated her zipper to the space program. No. 12 (D3 to E3): The ubiquitous English umbrella is a little less so. No. 13 (E3): His stripes are trying to match his hood. No. 14 (E4 to E5): Doesn't she know which one is her ring finger? Nos. 15 and 16 (E5): One logo gets dyed and the other renames itself.

Page 94: A Strange Casting Call No. 1 (A1): He's been checked off. No. 2 (A2 to B2): Kick and strut your competition outta here. Nos. 3 and 4 (A3): Someone took the time to repair the wall and this face must be catching on. No. 5 (A5 to B5): A risky fashion decision? No. 6 (B1): Some people will steal anything, even a wall plate. No. 7 (B2 to C2): It's a cross of absence. Nos. 8 and 9 (B3): Her bow tie is spinning at the thought of the Case of the Missing Sewing Kit. No. 10 (B4 to E4): She no longer relies on her baton. No. 11 (B5): She's gone casual. No. 12 (C2): Here's another cross of not. No. 13 (C5): Her bracelet is seeing red. No. 14 (D2): He's got a ticket that's lost. No. 15 (D2 to E2): The angels want to wear his red shoes. No. 16 (E3 to E4): The bilious green dot is now a disgusting orange.

Page 96: **Portable Amuse-a-Cat Station** Nos. 1 and 2 (A1 to B1): The new construction is a towering addition and more than compensates for the missing piling. No. 3 (A1 to A2): The lamp is proud of its ability to swivel. No. 4 (B2 to C2): Is this the return of the prodigal pillar? Nos. 5 and 6 (B3): Anna's been replaced by Mary and they must be doing landfill for the new wing. Nos. 7 and 8 (B3 to C3): Rosy is taking a stand, and the gondola is rocking back and forth. No. 9 (B4): He's changed the color of his hair-straw and Molly has taken her seat. No. 10 (B5): These pilings make great resting spots for the birds. No. 11 (C4): The rooster has a brand-new POV. No. 12 (C4 to C5): So this is where Anna's nameplate ended up. Nos. 13 and 14 (D3): What a pretty blue butterfly and red cornflower. No. 15 (D5): We like yellow flowers, too. No. 16 (E1 to E5): The cat disdains all attempts to entertain her. No. 17 (E2): The brick removal team has struck again. Nos. 18 and 19 (E4): Magic mushrooms make his feet dance.

Page 98: **Under a Royal Rain** No. 1 (A1): Flower on. No. 2 (A4 to B4): The park staff is pruning some trees. No. 3 (A5 to B5): Everyone likes to snap a few pics. No. 4 (B1): It's not safe to steal the queen's pearls. No. 5 (B3): Security is going to yell at him for losing his ID. Oh, he's security? No. 6 (B4 to D4): His jacket is subject to color swings. Nos. 7 and 8 (B5): A pom-pom has been snatched and her jacket is deep purple. No. 9 (C1): She's all buttoned up. Nos. 10 and 11 (C2): Someone is clearly running away from the cow purse. No. 12 (C3): He hates wearing his glasses, but he needs them. No. 13 (D2): The efficient cleanup crew has removed the offending leaves. No. 14 (D5): He's got fingers aplenty. Nos. 15 and 16 (E4): His new shoes don't make up for her missing ribbons.

Page 100: **Tranquillity Square** No. 1 (A3 to B3): Acute observers will have noticed that four purple letter circles now spell out LIFE. No. 2 (A4): Stock markets remain changed. No. 3 (A5 to B5): There's not going to be any more pole-taking around here. Oops. No. 4 (B1): 4G prices are going up. Bummer. Nos. 5 and 6 (B2 to B3): A whole year has gone by, enough time for the deli to change the spelling of its name. No. 7 (B3 to B4): It's a flipping *W*. No. 8 (B4): The *M* really stands out now. No. 9 (C3 to D3): She's a very distinctive redhead. No. 10 (C4): It's the old quick-change scarf act. Nos. 11 and 12 (C5): Gee, we thought that was a FedEx truck and, hey, she looks familiar. No. 13 (D2): Please don't return the towel sweaty. No. 14 (D3 to D5): It's nice to be able to swap faces with a friend. No. 15 (D3 to E3): How did she change in public? No. 16 (D4): That water bottle looks pretty good about now. No. 17 (D5): She wearing her calmer outfit now.

Page 102: **Pile Up** No. 1 (A2 to A3): Buildings sprout up like weeds in Vegas. No. 2 (B3): Most of this canoe has gone purple. No. 3 (B3 to C3): A rib reduction is just as bad for a canoe as it is for a human. Nos. 4 and 5 (B4): One canoe gets a spray job, and the other gets out while the getting is good. Nos. 6 and 7 (C1 to C2): We're all about paint jobs and disappearing canoes. No. 8 (C2): Without some additional structural support to compensate for the loss of the crosspieces, this craft is going to crumble like a tin

can. No. 9 (C3 to C4): This time a canoe has been added to the mix. Wake me when things get good. Then again, never mind. No. 10 (D1 to E1): A streetlight has been reconfigured. No. 11 (D2): Please let this be the last paint job today. Please. No. 12 (D3): The building has been altered. We're not telling you how. Find it for yourself. No. 13 (D5 to E5): It's Arbor Day. Go plant a tree. No. 14 (E2): Minus one streetlight. No. 15 (E3): Lose the light. Oh, you did.

Page 104: **All in Good Fun** No. 1 (A1): Bet you spotted the missing spotlight. No. 2 (A3 to C3): Who told the curtain to lighten up? No. 3 (A3 to A4): Boring! It's just a blank blue circle now. No. 4 (B3): Without an official nose, she can clown no more. No. 5 (B5): His Mohawk has been hacked. No. 6 (C1): The steamer truck wants to perform so much, it's green with envy. No. 7 (C2): The logo is learning spin control. Nos. 8 and 9 (C3): His tie has taken its last bow. But at least he has this pretty flower now. No. 10 (C4): Now he can't buckle down to business. Nos. 11 and 12 (C5): Orange appears to be winning the clash of colors on his shirt and the cymbal has lost a certain pizzazz. No. 13 (D2): The circus is having a button economy drive. Nos. 14 and 15 (D2 to E3): After careful consideration the leg has been withdrawn, but where did all the black keys go? No. 16 (D4): A sock is never the same after its stripes are stripped away. No. 17 (E1 to E2): He keeps experimenting with different hems. No. 18 (E4): Now that's what we call a clown shoe.

Page 106: **Going Postal** No. 1 (A2): We likes to see them big birdies squeeze into those teeny holes. No. 2 (A3 to C3): The plane has dispensed with its training pole. Nos. 3 and 4 (A4 to B4): Where did these cacti come from? Cacti—we like to say that word. No. 5 (B1 to B2): You can too help prevent brush fires. No. 6 (B3): The slot is closed until further notice. No. 7 (C1): How are we going to tie up our ponies? No. 8 (C3): Please do not attempt to mail hirsute envelopes. Nos. 9, 10, and 11 (C4): This house is self-sealing, have they filed the appropriate address change form, and please use numbers instead of spelling everything out. Nos. 12 and 13 (C5): It's a pinkie wreath. Also, can we get a grammar ruling here? Nos. 14 and 15 (D1): It's better to read letters instead of killing them. Also this creeping corporatization has to stop. Don't destroy the public mail. No. 16 (D2): Look for your sign in the lost and found signage department. It might be there. No. 17 (D3): Box and pole are happily reunited. No. 18 (D3 to E3): The shadow shifts shape. No. 19 (D5): No stealing males around here. No. 20 (E2): Now that the rock has been kidnapped, all you can do is wait for the ransom note.

[LIFE CLASSICS]

Page 109: **Driver's Ed** No. 1 (A1 to B1): Plant a tree today and be a hero. No. 2 (A3 to C3): A telephone pole has gone the way of all flesh, or is that wood? No. 3 (B2): You see, it's like this. Stripes are easy to add or remove. And at this stage of the book, we're all pretty tired. No. 4 (C1): His smile seems a little strained now. No. 5 (C4): It's either a black cap or a very bad wig. No. 6 (D1 to D2): He must not be too overtaxed; he had the leisure to switch collars. No. 7 (D1 to E1): The license plate makes him official. No. 8 (D3): Tires belong on vehicles,

not the road. No. 9 (D4): The steering wheel now completes the circle. No. 10 (D5 to E5): He's one tire down. No. 11 (E4): At high speeds letters sometimes reverse themselves.

Page 110: **Story Time** No. 1 (A2 to A3): Where have all the sprinklers gone? No. 2 (B2): See? The painting looks good in either direction. No. 3 (B3): Fire regulations have cost them a power outlet. No. 4 (B4): They're dancing around the tower. No. 5 (C1): An extra drawer never hurt anyone. No. 6 (C3): Whoever erased the illustration had better be careful. She's the French teacher! No. 7 (C4 to D4): See what happens if she catches you not paying attention. Wham! He's outta here. No. 8 (C5): Did you ever read the story of the Velveteen Rabbit? That may explain the furry one's absence. No. 9 (D5): His suspenders have been suspended. No. 10 (E4): A nostalgic glance back at button-popping.

Page 112: **Snip, Snip, Snip** Nos. 1 and 2 (B2): Time and date are out of sync. Nos. 3 and 4 (C1): Welcome to the barbershop. Witness the odd case of a missing knob and reflection. Sinister or commonplace? You decide. Nos. 5 and 6 (C2): His sleeve has been adjusted by the Bureau, but they can't correct his tie's bad case of spots. No. 7 (C4): Just what were the headlines on that newspaper? No. 8 (D1): A power cord is missing. Alert the media. No. 9 (D2): The chair has been subtly altered by an unknown agent. No. 10 (D4 to E4): The hem has lowered itself for the occasion. No. 11 (E1): A happy spot of sunlight has been extinguished.

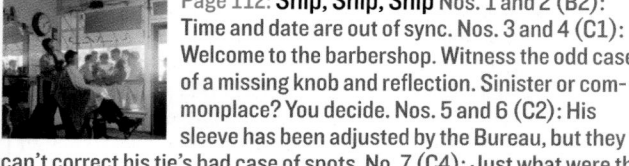

Page 114: **Ceremonial Sport** No. 1 (A2): Arm up like everyone else. No. 2 (B2): His cap has the magical zigzags. No. 3 (B3): He doesn't know which way to look. No. 4 (B4 to C4): The stripes strike again. No. 5 (B4): He still doesn't look happy. Nos. 6 and 7 (C1): One design has ousted the other, taking over the ceremonial robes. No. 8 (C2 to C3): Erasing traditional writing isn't the best way to make friends. No. 9 (C3): The splotch is getting into the rotation racket. No. 10 (C4): We hope the character flip isn't an impolite word in Japanese. No. 11 (C4 to C5): He's being careful with his arm. No. 12 (D4): He's standing on one foot.

Page 116: **Fashion on Wheels** No. 1 (A1 to B1): This is what everyone wants—less light. No. 2 (B5 to C5): One fewer streetlight will also darken things nicely. No. 3 (C1): The license plate left early. No. 4 (C2): And the shrub followed suit. No. 5 (C2 to C3): She's less of a designing woman now. No. 6 (C3): It's an off-label bike. No. 7 (C4 to D4): Without a chain, he's free to go . . . or stay. No. 8 (D5): The fence is shy a rail. No. 9 (E4): He's very polite about exposing his foot.

Page 118: **Round and Round We Go** No. 1 (A3 to B3): A floral design has been replicated. No. 2 (A5 to E5): There's a new pole in this part of the ride. No. 3 (B1): That light was too bright anyway. No. 4 (B4): The giraffe is developing its own personalized pattern. No. 5 (C2): The reins have disappeared. No. 6 (C2 to E2): So has the watchful mom. No. 7 (C3 to E3): There's never a ladder when you need one. Nos. 8 and 9 (D3): Some buttons and a pair of polar bear ears have vanished together. No. 10 (D4 to D5): The ride is down one pony. No. 11 (D5): The saddle has a little less filigree.

Solve this and become a true puppet, I mean puzzle, master.

ANSWERS Nos. 1 and 2 (B2): A new member of a certain hair club is enjoying his brand-new shades. No. 3 (B3 to C3): He's enamored of his huge badge. No. 4 (B4): We get the point. At least her point. No. 5 (B4 to C4): Her necklace has been lifted. Nos. 6 and 7 (C3): He hasn't paid careful attention to his watch, but he keeps his old badge around just in case. No. 8 (C4): He's another happy customer. No. 9 (C4 to D5): Her skirt has quite a flare. No. 10 (D1): They call him Patches.

2 min 45 sec

KEEP
SCORE

10
changes

JOE RAEDLE/GETTY

Watch them as they twirl their way into the hearts of the audience

Tripping the Light Fantastic

JUST ONE MORE